LORD JAKOBOVITS IN CONVERSATION

Lord Jakobovits in 1989.

LORD JAKOBOVITS
in Conversation

MICHAEL SHASHAR

VALLENTINE MITCHELL
LONDON • PORTLAND, OR

First published in 2000 in Great Britain by
VALLENTINE MITCHELL
Newbury House, 900 Eastern Avenue
London IG2 7HH

and in the United States of America by
VALLENTINE MITCHELL
c/o ISBS, 5804 N.E. Hassalo Street
Portland, Oregon 97213-3644

Website: www.vmbooks.com

British Library Cataloguing in Publication Data

Shashar, Michael
    Lord Jakobovits in conversation
    1. Jakobovits, Immanuel – Interviews   2. Rabbis – Great
    Britain – Interviews   3. Judaism – 20th century
    I. Title
    296'.092

ISBN 0-85303-377-3 (cloth)

Library of Congress Cataloging-in-Publication Data

Jakobovits, Immanuel, Sir, 1921–
    [Rav ha-Lord. English]
    Lord Jakobovits in conversation / [interviews with] Michael Shashar;
    translated from the Hebrew by Edward Levin.
        p.   cm.
    ISBN 0-85303-377-3 (cloth)
        1. Jakobovits, Immanuel, Sir, 1921– –Interviews. 2. Rabbis–Great
    Britain–Interviews. 3. Judaism–20th century. 4. Chief Rabbinate–Great
    Britain. I. Shashar, Michael. II. Title.

BM755.J28 A513 2000
296'.0941–dc21
                                                                00-032103

*Translated from the Hebrew
by Edward Levin.*

Typeset by Vitaset, Paddock Wood, Kent
Printed in Great Britain by
MPG Books Ltd, Bodmin, Cornwall

Contents

'Rabban Shimon ben Gamliel said … There were one thousand children in Father's house. Five hundred studied Torah, and five hundred studied Greek wisdom.' Sotah 49b

Introduction

This is a dialogue book with the former Chief Rabbi of the British Commonwealth, the late Lord Dr Immanuel Jakobovits. Lord Jakobovits was born in Germany, fled to England after Hitler's ascension to power, studied in London and filled rabbinical posts in Dublin, New York and London. The reader of this book will learn from the very beginning that Lord Jakobovits' Jewish and general education is much broader than that of the typical pulpit rabbi and encompasses both the Jewish and secular worlds. Perhaps this is why his views on Judaism, the land of Israel, Israel among the nations, Torah and science, politics and society, etc., are regarded as exceptional. Nevertheless, his background and open-mindedness made him a very successful ambassador of the rabbinical world among non-Jews, and also among those Jews who, although having abandoned the Jewish traditional way of life, are painfully aware of the profound crisis in which Jews and Judaism find themselves at the beginning of the twenty-first century.

In writing this book (the fifth in a series of dialogue books, with Yeshayahu Leibovits, philosopher; Haim H. Cohn, Israel Supreme Court Justice; Edgar Bronfman, President of the World Jewish Congress; General Rechav'am Ze'evy, Member of the Knesset), I wanted to present the reader with Lord Jakobovits' spiritual and intellectual world. His opinions as presented here raised wide and violent criticism in Israel when the Hebrew version appeared, and may do the same among the English readers of the book, be they Jewish, gentile, religious, secular, scientists or spiritual leaders. But they are being spoken in a clear and pleasant language, as 'The words of the wise are spoken softly' [Ecclesiastes 9:17], and therefore there is hope that they will be heard.

To my deep sorrow, Lord Jakobovits left this world shortly after the conclusion of our talks, held in London and Jerusalem, in English, Hebrew, German and occasionally in Yiddish. The conversations were recorded, transcribed and edited by me and approved for publication by Lord Jakobovits. Let me add that there is hardly a difference between the 'oral law' as expressed by Lord Jakobovits, and the 'written law', as published in this book.

The talks with Lord Jakobovits were held in a pleasant atmosphere and he willingly devoted to them hours of his time. I am grateful to him and to Lady Amélie for their hospitality, hoping that his words as presented in this book will be like 'Bread being sent upon the waters that will be found in the future' [Ecclesiastes 11:1], as they are dealing with topics, problems and issues of concern to every enlightened human being in our world.

I would also like to thank Edward Levin for his accurate translation from the Hebrew and, last but not least, the publisher Vallentine Mitchell, who made the English version possible.

Michael Shashar,
Jerusalem 2000

1 *Jerusalem*

'It would be possible to find within the united city areas that would also serve as the capital of Palestine like, for example, the Vatican state within the city of Rome.'

Let us assume that you, Lord Rabbi Jakobovits, were the Prime Minister of Israel and had to resolve the difficult issue of the future of Jerusalem. What would you do?

It is specifically on the issue of Jerusalem that I see a solution to the problem, even more than the question of the territories. In the territories it may be necessary to move a portion of the [Jewish] inhabitants from place to place, or at least to create new conditions to protect them in the areas of the autonomy. These are actual difficulties. In Jerusalem, on the other hand, there are Jewish residential areas and Arab residential areas, and the need to transfer inhabitants would not arise. Clearly, I oppose the redivision of Jerusalem. The city must remain united, the capital of the State of Israel, and open to all the inhabitants. I have already heard from Teddy Kollek and from others that it would be possible to find, within the united city, areas that would also serve as the capital of Palestine like, for example, the Vatican state within the city of Rome. If the Arabs were to raise their flag in their areas and even declare that this is their capital, I do not regard this as the most serious difficulty. I feel, in the light of all this, that the question of Jerusalem should not be left until the end of the negotiations; rather, they should begin with the solution of this problem, since Jerusalem symbolizes the entire agreement.

If a solution were to be found for the issue of Jerusalem, it would be much easier – mainly for psychological reasons – to also resolve the problem of the other territories. Jerusalem must be an example of co-existence between the two peoples. I am not a statesman, and I speak as a rabbi who sees the problem from the spiritual and religious aspect. According to Judaism, the raising of some Palestinian flags is not a reason to delay the peace agreement.

If tomorrow your relatives who live in the territories were to come and ask you, as a rabbi, 'What is more important: to abandon a settlement, because it is not within the boundaries of the State of Israel; or to stay, because it is part of the Land of Israel, even if not part of the State of Israel, but rather of the Palestinian state?' – what would you reply to them?

If only they had come to me before settling there. Then I would have told them to consider this more seriously, and I would confront them with the doubts and dangers which they must take into account. Since they did not come, this is a question after the fact, and not before. Nonetheless, I would tell them: If you are concerned about fulfilling the commandment of settling Eretz Israel, then it could also be fulfilled without Israeli political sovereignty in some parts. The commandment is not conditional upon Israeli sovereignty. As a rabbi, however, I must also consider the matter in accordance with the reality of the situation. Consequently, they must be told that, even according to the UN resolution, there is room for border changes, especially so that the majority of the settlements will remain within the boundaries of the State of Israel. This must be fought for, in any place where a solution can be found on the basis of new borders. On the other hand, the security of settlements such as Kiryat Arba and Elon Moreh must be assured, in negotiations of give-and-take, since it is obvious that they cannot remain where they are without Jewish defence, and there are precedents for this in the world.

Do you think that there is a chance of such a solution?

If there will be real peace here, not just on paper, then solutions will be found for all these problems. It is written in the Torah, 'Three times a year **all** your males shall appear in the place that the Lord will choose', but if everyone will come up to Jerusalem, who will ensure the defence of the borders at that time? Accordingly, the Torah promises, 'no one will covet your land'. The true solution entails that the Arabs also will recognize Israel's right to exist, and will not covet it. The main concern must be how to assuage the Arabs, so that they will not devise stratagems to decrease the dimensions of Israel and destroy it. Obviously, this will require much time and this is not a problem that can be solved from one day to the next, but this must be the goal. Unfortunately, I see that many do not hope and pray for any solution. They want everything to remain unchanged, and dream that it will thus be possible to stabilize the situation. The truth, however, is that they are dreaming and do not live in the real world. Rabbis should not say that because of religious considerations it is not possible to attain peace with the Arabs, but this is what is happening. They do not see any blessing in peace, at least not to the degree that there is blessing in other matters, as if they do not agree with the statement by *Rashi*: 'There is nothing without peace.'

You were in Hebron and in the Cave of Machpelah. If this contains the tombs of the Patriarchs, is it not against Jewish law to hold regular prayers there?

There is a problem, since we do not pray in a cemetery because this would seem to be mocking the dead. The Cave of Machpelah, however, may be an exception. When there is a fixed practice of praying there – even though it was not possible to pray there until 1967 – with an accompanying feeling of pride, then, although prayers are generally not conducted at graves, there are other considerations in this case, and I would not oppose prayer in the Cave of Machpelah. When I was there, there was a *minyan* [quorum for prayer] and I prayed with the others even though I felt somewhat strange about this. When Abraham purchased the field of Ephron, he did not purchase it merely as a burial site, but regarded this as an acquisition for the entire people of Israel, thereby indicating our possession of the site. The act of acquisition was not just as a cemetery, but symbolized our ownership of the Land. The Land was sanctified by this purchase; with Abraham's buying of the field of Ephron, he acquired a *chazakah* [possession, presumption of ownership] over Eretz Israel. Not only did he physically possess this acquisition, he thereby sanctified it, with the commandments dependent upon the Land of Israel. This is also the relationship between a man and his wife, which must be like the relationship between Israel and its land: a legal relationship [acquisition] and a spiritual relationship [sanctity].

What about the Temple Mount?

I regard as dangerous for Judaism and the Jews the attempts to hasten the building of the Temple by sewing the priestly garments, the building of an altar and even the finding of a red heifer. Our being forbidden to ascend the Temple Mount due to its holiness may not be for nothing. Because of this prohibition, we do not enter into daily conflicts with the Arabs there. It seems that the present situation is to be maintained, without change. We still have much to do, besides the Temple Mount. If only we were to accept the Torah of the Temple Mount, which is Mount Moriah, of which the rabbis said: 'Why was its name called Moriah? Because the Torah and instruction [*hora'ah*] came forth from it.' I see great danger in the attempts by certain circles to precipitate the Messianic era.

And what about sacrifices?

I wrote a comprehensive article about this in the prayerbook that I edited. Every prophet who spoke of the superiority of prayer, and possibly about the end of the age of sacrifices, promised that sacrifices would be offered in the Messianic era. Isaiah [56:7] says: 'Their burnt offerings and sacrifices shall be welcome on My altar', and so too Jeremiah and Maimonides. We must therefore understand the intention of the sacrifices. Maimonides explains in the Laws of Kings, at the end of the *Mishneh Torah*, that in the Messianic era sacrifices will be offered, and he discusses in detail the laws relating to this. And in the Laws of Embezzlement from the Temple he writes that all the sacrifices are included in the category of *chukim* [laws the rationale for which is not revealed to humans], and the world exists because of their offering. There are private sacrifices, and even communal sacrifices, which have the purpose of effecting atonement, by the slaughtering of the sacrifice and the dashing of its blood, thereby symbolizing that 'the blood is the life'. Every person has the urge to act in accordance with the heart. This urge is to be offered on the altar, thereby creating the conditions for atonement, in that the individual will recall his sin and not sin again. The offering of an animal must leave an awesome impression upon a person, so he will not forget any more and sin 'unwittingly': the individual thereby atones for his sin. Maimonides, Abrabanel, Samson Raphael Hirsch, David Zevi Hoffmann and others speak of this. I am aware of the fact that the offering of sacrifices is problematic in our times, but if this is examined in depth, we find profound thoughts concealed within the sacrificial rite.

But there are those who claim that the prohibition of sacrifices has become the outstanding symbol of Judaism.

Those who are not close to this have difficulty in understanding its basic principles. In English we say, 'Judaism has to be caught, not taught'. In other words, if a Jew has no practical experience in the observance of the commandments, it is difficult for him to accept all this. In the verse, 'The Lord called to Moses' [Leviticus 1:1], *Rashi* states that the voice was loud within the Sanctuary, but ceased outside it. If people do not enter the synagogue and do not live within Judaism, they have difficulty in comprehending and appreciating it. Outside, nothing is seen or heard – first of all, one's inner comprehension must be deepened.

2 My Father's House

'In all my years in the rabbinate, I never served in a separatist community, and this is part of my world view.'

Rabbi Jakobovits, could you tell me about your childhood and your parents' home?

I never kept a diary, neither as a child nor at the present time. I was born in Königsberg [the present-day Kaliningrad], at the time the capital of East Prussia, on 8 February 1921.

It's interesting that you give the Gregorian date for your birthday, and not the Jewish date.

The truth is that I never celebrated my birthday, but when my birthday is remembered, the Hebrew date is given – Adar 1, 5681. I was the eldest of seven sons and daughters, and I was given the Hebrew name Israel. My wife (née Munk), also is the eldest of seven sons and daughters.

The Jewish community in Königsberg numbered about 3,000 souls, and my father was the Orthodox rabbi in the city. He united the separate ultra-Orthodox community with the general Jewish community, and this influenced my positions and views regarding the rabbinate and Orthodoxy in general. In all my years in the rabbinate, I never served in a separatist community, and this is part of my world view.

Where was your father born?

My father Julius – his Hebrew name was Yoel – comes from a long line of rabbis and was born in Lackenbach, one of the 'Seven Communities' (the former Burgenland) in the Austro-Hungarian Empire. This was an ancient community, which still maintained a very Jewish life in the traditional sense of the term. There wasn't even a single Jew there who violated the Sabbath! Once my father told me that when he was bar mitzvah age, his father brought him for the first time to Vienna, the capital of the Empire. It was there, on a Sabbath walk, that my grandfather said to him: 'The person walking in front of us is a Jew, even though he's smoking.' My father stepped up the pace and passed in front of that Jew, to be certain that the cigarette was indeed lit, since he simply could not believe that a cigarette lit by a Jew on the Sabbath could burn. This was the way of life of Jews then, a complete life within the framework of Judaism. The thoughts and deeds of the majority of the Jews were entirely within Judaism. Nonetheless, my grandfather, who had nine children – of whom my father was the eldest (there was a daughter before him who had died in a tuberculosis epidemic) – saw to it that in addition to religious studies in large and renowned *yeshivot*, they would also study secular subjects. Of his six sons, three were rabbis and three became physicians. And of his daughters, one married a rabbi and the other a physician. Of my two sons as well, one is a physician and the other a rabbi; I myself am connected to both professions, and you could say that this was almost hereditary.

This was at the end of the nineteenth century?

My father was born in 1886 and studied in the *yeshivah* in Pressburg, and before that in Tzelem. This was one of the 'Seven Communities', and was named Deutschkreutz. Since the Jews didn't want to pronounce the word *kreutz* [cross], they called the place *Tzelem* [image].

When did your father come to Königsberg?

I think in 1917, when he was still single, and he married my mother there in 1919. She also comes from a family of rabbis. One of her ancestors was Rabbi Joshua Falk, the author of *Penei Yehoshua* [a collection of Talmudic novellae]. Her maiden name was Wreschner, and her father was a rabbi, first in Samter, near Posen. I will add that my grandfather wrote a biography of Rabbi Akiva Eiger, the rabbi of Posen. Afterwards my grandfather moved to Bad Homburg, close to Frankfurt-am-Main, where he served as rabbi until his death before the outbreak of the Second World War.

Königsberg was a way station for many Jews from Lithuania, Latvia and Russia, but how did your father come from Hungary to this city, of all places?

Most of the well-known rabbis in Germany came from Hungary – hence, for instance, the Hirsch, Hildesheimer, Breuer and Hoffmann families. The Jews in Lithuania still ignored secular studies, and so the

German Jews preferred to invite rabbis from Hungary, where some did engage in other studies.

On the other hand, the Hungarian rabbis were very extreme.

Later on, the circles from which my father came accepted the need to study secular subjects as well, but not in the spirit of 'Torah *im Derekh Eretz* [secular studies]', the method of Samson Raphael Hirsch. Even the Chatam Sofer, all of whom were his students, had some knowledge of secular subjects. My father studied in the University of Berlin and also in the Hildesheimer Rabbinical Seminary. He had already been ordained as a rabbi in Pressburg, but he was also ordained by Rabbi Dr David Zevi Hoffmann in Berlin. After completing his studies in Berlin and Wuerzburg, he received a rabbinical post in the small community of Randegg (near Switzerland), and after that in Königsberg.

Did he also have the title Doctor?

Yes. It is of interest that his doctoral thesis dealt with *Die Luege im Urteil der neuesten deutscher Ethiker* (The Lie in the Thought of the New Moralists in Germany), a subject which is not Jewish at all. His thesis was published as a book. He published two books in his lifetime: one on *The Lie* and the second on the Ashkenazic and Sephardic pronunciation in prayer. He was one of the first to engage in this. Later on, he was an expert *dayan* [rabbinical judge], first in Germany and afterwards in London. He specialized in personal status law, especially in *agunot* [deserted wives]. Just before he passed away, after the Second World War when he was 61, he told me that he could not sleep the last night of his life because of the suffering of the *agunot*, whom he saw in a dream pleading before him. When I later served as Chief Rabbi in England, I did not forget this. I told those women that their suffering was not due to indifference to their plight, nor was it an easy matter for the rabbis. In my role as a rabbi, I try to this very day to encourage and console people. I plant hope in their heart, even in a case in which I know the situation is almost desperate. This is a task incumbent upon every rabbi, as an integral part of his position. He must strengthen the members of his congregation with hope and faith.

My father was very strict. He worked hard and wore himself out. He wrote each and every word of his sermons in German, and memorized everything. Thus, for example, he toiled during his entire summer vacation to prepare his High Holidays sermons. Like his father, he was very ambitious and sought to push me ahead, but he often was disappointed. I wasn't an outstanding pupil. To the contrary, I did not devote any effort to subjects that did not interest me, such as history, literature and other humanistic subjects, and this displeased my father. Nonetheless, later on I did not have difficulty with my studies nor with my sermons, even though I was not ambitious like my father. All that I had to do as a rabbi, and afterwards as Chief Rabbi, was not very burdensome for me. Even today, when I have to meet a famous or distinguished personality, I don't become overly excited. My father, in contrast, required much preparation for such meetings.

Not even when you met the Pope?

No. The Pope visited England and we met. I read to him a statement, mainly on the subject of Jerusalem, which maintained that the sanctity of Jerusalem for the three monotheistic religions has its source in the sanctification of the city by the Jews 3,000 years ago. He listened, and replied that this was not the proper time to expand on this …

And the first time you met the Queen of England?

Even then I did not become overly flustered, nor when I met in Great Britain with heads and ministers of government. Most of them were also guests in our home.

Let's go back to your birthplace. Until when did you live in Königsberg?

Until 1928, when I was seven, then my family moved to Berlin. I lived in this city until I was almost 16 years old, and then, in 1936, I arrived in London, the first member of the family to do so. I was alone for a year, and then I was joined by my brother George, who now lives in Canada. After *Kristallnacht*, on 9 November 1938, my father, brothers and sisters came, and finally my mother arrived as well.

What do you remember from Königsberg?

My memories are a bit vague. I went to a *cheder* [traditional Hebrew school] and to a general school. I don't remember a single anti-Semitic incident from those years, which was not the case during my years in Berlin after Hitler took power.

Your name, as you mentioned, is Israel, but everyone who knows you calls you Immanuel. How is this so?

I may be the only rabbi in the world named after a non-Jew – Immanuel Kant, who was a native of Königsberg and never left it. The city was also known as 'Kantstadt' [the city of Kant]. My father was one of Kant's admirers, and when I was born he wanted to call me Israel, after one of his uncles, but at that time in Germany it was not acceptable to call a Jewish child Israel. Accordingly, he searched for a name beginning with I and ending with L, and so he gave me Kant's name, Immanuel.

You mentioned that your father was strict. Also in the education of his children? Did he ever beat you?

Yes. My father believed in 'spare the rod and spoil the child'. When I received a bad report card, it was hard to go home. Mother, on the other hand, was a different type of person. I learned from her to be more flexible, calm and relaxed. Both of them left their mark on me.

Was it common then for a Jewish child from an Orthodox home to go to a non-Jewish school?

There was no Jewish school in Königsberg in my time and we didn't regard this as anything out of the ordinary. On the Sabbath, of course, I did not go to school, nor on the holidays. The teachers were all non-Jews but they did not discriminate between non-Jews and Jews. Obviously, I did not have any close friends among the non-Jews who would come to my house, nor did I go to their homes. Nonetheless, there was a normal atmosphere in the school and, to the best of my recollection, I never heard an anti-Semitic remark within the school confines.

Did they teach in German in the *cheder*?

Yes. I began to go to the *cheder* at the age of five. We learned the *alef-bet* and the Pentateuch there. The studies were not intensive, as is the practice now. I did not go every day to the *cheder*, only a few times a week, in the afternoon. Even afterwards, when I studied in the Adath Israel school in Berlin, only eight hours per week were devoted to religious studies.

Was German spoken in your home?

Pure German, although my father also spoke Hungarian. They did not speak Yiddish, and I heard this language for the first time in London in the Etz Hayim *yeshivah*. Moreover, today I speak Yiddish better than German, especially in public.

It is well known that German Jews are divided into two groups. Those who lived there for generations and were firmly established and those who came from the East – the *Ostjuden*. How did you feel?

Certainly not as an *Ostjude*. The Jews who came from Burgenland did not belong to the *Ostjuden*, unlike the Jews from Poland, Galicia, Lithuania and the like. In addition, my mother, who was from Posen, was a 'pure' German and consequently I was without question a pure *Yekke*.

Was there tension between the *Yekkes* and the *Ostjuden* in Königsberg?

Most of the Jews in the city were German Jews. Many Jews, however, also came from the East but there was no tension between them. The city was renowned for its physicians, and many Jews from Eastern Europe came to the city for treatment.

Was this a mainly observant community?

There was already a Reform congregation, which was the largest congregation in the city. An organ was played in its synagogue on the Sabbath and the congregation's rabbi, Rabbi Felix Perles, was a well-known Reform rabbi.

Did your father, as the rabbi of an Orthodox congregation, have any ties with Rabbi Perles?

Yes. There were very good relations between them. Also afterwards, in Berlin, Rabbi Leo Baeck, the spiritual leader of liberal Judaism in Germany, was a friend of Father's. Both were rabbis [*Gemeinde Rabbiner*] in a single communal organization, part of which was Orthodox and part Reform.

Was your home a Zionist one or did they not talk about Eretz Israel?

As I recall, Eretz Israel was an important element in our lives, but I did not hear the term 'Zionism', nor did they speak about *aliyah* [immigration], although in the 1920s there already were Jews from Königsberg who had gone to Eretz Israel. Zionism was not a factor in my life in those years. The situation changed somewhat in Berlin, because several of my teachers and acquaintances, and several of my friends in the Jewish school, had gone to Eretz Israel.

Were there arguments in your home regarding the Mizrachi and Agudah?

Father was never a member of either of the two movements. I inherited this from him and I am not a member of any political party. I suffered as a result, because my predecessors as Chief Rabbi in England had been the Presidents of Mizrachi in Great Britain, but I refused to follow in their footsteps. I held the view that the rabbi must be connected with every Jew, regardless of party. Nonetheless, my father's views were close to Agudath Israel. He participated in the Kenessiyah ha-Gedolah in Marienbad, in which the Torah leaders of the generation took part, but he was not a member of Agudah.

Why did your family move from Königsberg to Berlin?

Father was summoned to be a *dayan* in the rabbinical court of the large Berlin community, and some time later he became the head of the court. Interestingly enough, the Reform, who also belonged to the general community in Berlin, accepted the rulings of the Orthodox court concerning personal status and conversions. Father also served as the rabbi of a small *beit midrash* [study hall-synagogue] in the city, and afterwards in a great synagogue which seated 2,000 people. The synagogue was burned on *Kristallnacht*.

Did the move from Königsberg to Berlin make an impression on you as a child?

This was a new life. Berlin was the capital of the country and the Jews were on a firmer footing there as well. It was here that I heard for the first time about the *Ostjuden*, since my father's *beit midrash* was in the heart of the area where these Jews lived, in Dragoner Strasse [the Whitechapel of Berlin].

Did you continue to attend a non-Jewish school in Berlin?

No. I studied in the Adath Israel school. The rabbi of this congregation was Rabbi Ezra (Azriel) Munk, who – years later – was to become a relative of mine, since my wife came from the Munk family. He was the rabbi of a separatist community and was regarded as the supreme authority in Jewish law. I also remember from school Meir Hildesheimer, who was one of my teachers, and also Rabbi Dr Edward Biberfeld, who was both a rabbi and a physician. When people came to his office, they were asked: 'Do you wish to see the rabbi or the doctor?' Afterwards I transferred to the gymnasium of Adath Israel, whose headmaster was Dr Nahman Schlesinger. Only graduates of the

Teacher's Seminary were accepted to work there, and I said many times that I learned more Judaism from the teachers of the general subjects in the gymnasium than from the religious studies teachers, mainly from their way of life. They weren't paid for their Judaism, but they nevertheless were Sabbath observant and God-fearing. This made a great impression on me. Among the teachers I remember Dr Nahum Wulf [later to teach in the Lipschuetz Teachers Seminary in Jerusalem] and Rabbi Dr Harry Apt [later to serve as a rabbi in South Africa]. Most of my teachers and friends perished in the Holocaust, with some finding respite in Eretz Israel, America, England and other places. I still remember that in 1934 and 1935 (until I left for England in 1936) I was once a month at the Anhalter railway station in Berlin, where the Jews would depart for Trieste, continuing by ship from this Italian port to Eretz Israel.

You mentioned that you already encountered anti-Semitism in Berlin. How so?

Hitler democratically assumed power in 1933. The Jews did not foresee what would happen but their fear kept growing. The storm troopers roamed the streets and there were Nazi demonstrations. I remember one time as I was walking in the street with my father, thugs threw potatoes at us. They also threw stones at our *sukkah*.

If Hitler had not taken power in Germany, would the course of your life have continued in Germany?

Under the conditions prevailing then, I think so. Don't forget, Jews had lived in Germany for many generations. After Hitler took power, however, Father saw the danger and in 1936 he sent me to London – like Judah who had been sent ahead by Jacob – with the entire family joining me afterwards. Father did not think then about *aliyah* to Eretz Israel. We did not even talk about such a possibility. He did not visit Eretz Israel, and I came to Eretz Israel for the first time only in 1947. I remember that in Berlin I heard a strong speech by Dr Isaac Breuer (one of the leaders of Agudath Israel) against Zionism, and especially against the Mizrachi, although he changed his opinion somewhat after his *aliyah* to Eretz Israel.

Did you see Hitler?

In 1936 I had an opportunity to see Hitler, during the Berlin Olympics. He came every day to the stadium, in the western part of the city. I was part of the crowd, even though I wasn't especially interested in sports.

I felt then to what extent a person who has actual magical power can influence the masses. When he passed on the way to the stadium, an atmosphere of hysteria was created. It was impossible not to be caught up in this. Even I, as a Jew, could not remain indifferent even though I already knew who he was. There was no television then, but it was enough to hear Hitler's voice on the radio to fall under his influence. Many years after this, when I already sat in the House of Lords, I recalled this fact in one of my speeches and warned of the possible danger of the masses blindly following a leader capable of manipulating them and inciting them to mass murder. I cautioned against the freedom given to all those who preach the use of force, to deliver their message in public, on the radio or the television. No one can know where this will end, since the masses do not have the ability or power to withstand such incitement, and they can be exploited for almost any end.

When we hear Hitler today, we gain the impression that he was a madman.

But it is a fact that a cultured people such as the Germans, including the educated, such as physicians and lawyers, became murderers! There was something captivating in his voice.

In Berlin as well, you had no ties with non-Jews?

No. I never visited the homes of non-Jews. Most of my friends were Sabbath observant, even though we did not regard people outside the [Orthodox] camp as ones throwing off all restraints. I was active in the ultra-Orthodox Ezra youth movement. My counsellor was Yoti Dunner, currently the rabbi of the Adath Israel congregation in north London. I recall that once we went to a summer camp in Blankenese, near Hamburg. I also remember that after Hitler took power, our class was invited for a visit to Lithuania, to the Jewish school in Kovno. Lithuanian Jews thought that they were secure, while we in Germany were in danger. We were greatly impressed by the visit. The rabbi there, Rabbi Abraham Dov (Duber) Schapira, addressed us very emotionally and said that we must be proud of our Jewishness. This was the first time that I had seen a Torah giant from the *yeshivah* world, and his appearance made a profound impression on me.

As a youth, didn't you ever have heretical thoughts?

My entire life has always been very natural for me. I have never had the urge to seek and find an alternative. Nonetheless, later on I was more critical of the life of the Jews as I had seen it.

Is my impression correct, that you repress to some extent the entire period you lived in Germany?

Certainly. I also opposed visits to Germany.

And even in recent years you haven't changed your opinion?

In general, I have resolved not to visit Germany, even though I was born there. To this day I find it difficult to speak in German in public (even when I was in Switzerland, I lectured in English and not in German). After the war there were many Jews who would not travel to Germany or purchase German goods, but the situation changed as time passed. To some extent, Nahum Goldmann was responsible for this. Goldmann was active in obtaining reparations from Germany, and I also regarded the acceptance of reparations money from Germany as a positive action. I once said at a meeting of the Claims Conference, in Goldmann's presence, that we Jews did more for Germany than Adenhauer did for the Jews, since the reparations agreement returned it to the family of nations. It seems to me that he also shared this view.

Later, in the early 1960s, I came across the *Jahrbuch der Juedisch Literarischen Gesellschaft* [Yearbook of the Jewish Literary Society] that had appeared in Germany in the 1920s. I read an article in it, that had been translated into German, from a protocol of the Portuguese Jewish community in Hamburg, from 300 years ago. The Jews in Hamburg had some degree of internal autonomy. Someone told the community council about a Jew who had visited Spain, and he asked how to respond to this. It transpires that apparently there had never been an official ban against returning to Spain (according to my teacher, the historian Cecil Roth); nonetheless they deliberated over this visit 150 years after the Expulsion [from Spain]! There still existed the consciousness of the disaster in Spain, to the extent that the community discussed the imposition of a punishment on anyone visiting there. I think the punishment consisted of suspension from the synagogue for three months. I said to myself that if this is how they related to the expulsion of about 200,000 Jews, 150 years later, then certainly after the Holocaust we should not visit Germany. I accepted this upon myself, even though I did not speak of it in public, and I did not make it the rule for the members of my congregation, but my position was known.

And you haven't visited Spain either?

The founding meeting of the Conference of European Rabbis was held in Amsterdam in 1957. The first President was Rabbi Israel Brodie, the Chief Rabbi of the British Commonwealth. The host was Rabbi Aaron Schuster from the Netherlands. I was Chief Rabbi of Ireland at the time and I remember that we were received by the Queen of The Netherlands, Wilhelmina, who revealed great interest in Jewish topics. We blessed her with the 'Who gives of His honour to flesh and blood' benediction; we explained the content of the blessing to her and this made an impression upon her.

Another time we gathered for a conference in Brussels and we were received by King Baudouin, who also expressed an interest in Jewish life and spoke with many of us. The third time, in 1992, the conference was held in Spain and we met with King Juan Carlos in Madrid. The Spaniards commemorated then the 500th anniversary of the Expulsion. Before that I had not visited Spain. We were in Toledo, in the Del Terenzito synagogue, which had been a church for centuries, and which was returned to the Jews in a formal ceremony. We prayed there for the first time since the Expulsion. The King received us in his palace in Madrid and he as well took great interest in Jewish subjects. He told us then that he intended to visit Israel. I responded that if he were to do so, he would be the first monarch to visit Israel since the establishment of the State. He did indeed do so in 1993. He also was the one who cancelled the Expulsion decree that had been issued half a millennium earlier by Ferdinand and Isabella, King and Queen of Spain.

When I served as Chairman of the Association of European Rabbis, the German rabbis asked me to hold a conference in Germany as well, but I did not agree to this. Nonetheless, when there was a possibility of receiving money for the Memorial Foundation from the German government, directly, for Jewish cultural purposes, I wrote, as head of the Memorial Foundation, to Chancellor Kohl, requesting additional financial assistance for activity in Eastern Europe, and I offered to give him a report on the expenditure of the money. He invited me to come to him in Bonn, together with the Director of the Foundation, Dr Jerry Hochbaum, and we were received quite cordially. We spoke in English (with a translation into German), and he asked a great many questions about the condition of the Jews. We had been preceded by a Jewish delegation that had presented him with many demands in an unpleasant manner. He was angry about this, but he told us that if the Jews were interested in cultural objectives, he would support the request and speak 'with his people'. He mentioned a sum of 10,000,000 marks for two years, which was a considerable contribution for us. This was my only visit to Germany, for communal affairs.

And you never felt the need to visit Königsberg, the city of your birth?

No. Neither Berlin nor Königsberg. To the contrary, if I were to visit, I would feel very bad, because of the Jewish blood that had been shed.

Nonetheless, even though I do not advocate permanent Jewish life in Germany today, we are obligated to care for the Jews who live there now.

And therefore it is difficult for you to reconstruct the Berlin period?

I have memories, but upon my arrival in England, life began new for me, also in terms of language, and it may be said that my adult life started there, especially since my higher education was conducted in English. What happened in Germany is vague in my memory even though these were not unpleasant memories, at least not until Hitler took power.

Were your world view and way of life influenced mainly by home or by school?

Until today, my father is my most influential teacher and master, even though he died in 1947. I remember him, quote him and often ask myself: what would he have said? My mother also greatly influenced me. I also received much from the schools I attended, especially the Adath Israel school in Berlin and afterwards the educational institutions in London. I studied one year in the school of Rabbi Dr Solomon Schonfeld, who was one of the founders of the religious schools in England. My close friends also influenced me. They were followers of the 'Torah *im Derech Eretz*' school, but not necessarily the Frankfurt version. They possessed wider horizons and sought values also in the general culture and its literature, and, of course, in the world of science. At any rate, I was raised from an early age in an atmosphere that the world around was not to be ignored, but was to be related to, albeit critically, and at times with reservations. My world view was therefore already fashioned in my youth. My views and attitude toward Eretz Israel (and afterwards to the State of Israel) also were already formulated then.

Did this world view contain an important element of Torah study or more of piety?

Berlin was primarily the practical world, one of the observance of the commandments. Studies were not so intensive. We learned some Talmud, but not in an insightful manner. My knowledge then of the 'sea of Talmud' undoubtedly did not match that of my son at the same age, and certainly not that of my grandson. I will quote the commentary of the *Malbim* [Meir Loeb ben Jehiel Michael] on the verse 'One generation shall laud [*yeshabach*] Your acts to another' in Psalms [145:4]. He interprets *yeshabach* as if it were *yashbi'ach* – to improve. In other words, the knowledge of the Torah improves from one generation to the next, and this is happening before our very eyes. My children unquestionably have received a much more intensive Jewish education than I did, and my grandchildren even more so.

Have all your brothers and sisters remained observant Jews?

All of them with no exceptions, and also my wife's brother. This is nothing out of the ordinary today, but this was not a common phenomenon then.

3 Youth in London

'We live in the Western world and within its culture, and we cannot ignore our surroundings. The young generation among the yeshivah *population, which has no general education, is liable to face many dangers.'*

When you left Berlin, did you know that this would be a final parting?

Yes. Even though I returned once, for my brother's bar mitzvah celebration, I knew that my future would not be in Germany. When I left, my father came with me to London and arranged everything. I was accepted into a boarding school, where there were four of us young people from Germany – Loewe, Loeb, Lowenthal and myself. I said then that I was in the lion's den [*Loewe* is lion in German]. I had studied English in Germany but I spoke the language quite poorly. Before much time had passed, however, I spoke English fluently, and after nine months in England I passed the matriculation examinations.

When you compare the Jewish schools that you attended in Berlin and those in London, do you find noticeable differences?

The direction was similar, but in London intensive Jewish education was more prominent. We learned more Gemara and we lived in the world of the Talmud. Piety, on the other hand, was emphasized to a greater extent in Berlin. It was assumed that one could be a pious Jew without being a Torah scholar. After a few months in London I also began studying in the Etz Chaim *yeshivah*, and I thereby adopted the *yeshivah* outlook. At the same time I also attended University College and Jews' College, and already then I learned to integrate the two worlds.

Can you compare the Etz Chaim *yeshivah* in London then with today's *yeshivah* world?

In this *yeshivah*, as in others, emphasis was placed on the study of Gemara. The studies were conducted in Yiddish. I was profoundly influenced by the head of the *yeshivah*, Rabbi Elijah Lopian [who later came to Eretz Israel and was a *mashgiach* (spiritual supervisor) in the *yeshivah* in Kefar Hasidim] who was a master of *Mussar* [ethical teachings] – perhaps the greatest in the world in his time. The world of *Mussar* was new to me and I was attracted to it, unlike some of my fellow students. I was very close to him and was a guest in his house every Sabbath. I also was personally close with his sons, and this tie was maintained after he came to Eretz Israel. I still remember some of his talks and quote from them. I found in this world values that I had not known beforehand.

An additional outstanding teacher of mine in the *yeshivah* was Rabbi Nachman Greenspan, a very modest individual even though he may have been the greatest Torah scholar in England. He also was very knowledgeable in non-Jewish disciplines, and I became close to him as well. I will also mention Rabbi Leib Gurewitz, who would later become *yeshivah* head in Gateshead. He prepared me for my rabbinical studies and for ordination [*heter hora'ah*]. In 1946 I was ordained by the three of them, after having studied eight years to this end.

Can you describe your daily routine?

Every day I went to study for half a day in the *yeshivah*, and afterwards to Jews' College to receive the degree of Minister, and also to university. Jews' College required its students to learn Greek and Latin, and to pass the examinations in these subjects. I had already studied Latin for a number of years in Germany, but this language did not interest me. On the other hand, I studied Greek for the first time now, and it attracted me much more strongly. I also studied Syriac, in order to read the *Peshita*, the Syriac translation of the Torah.

The *yeshivah* did not oppose your university studies?

My studies in the university were received tolerantly, nor did Rabbi Lopian oppose them. To the contrary, they talked to me about this and they appreciated such studies.

How many students were in the *yeshivah* then?

Some studied the entire day, while others came to learn only in the evening. There were a total of about 50 students.

Can you describe the studies in Jews' College?

When I entered this institution, I was not yet cognizant of the tensions between it and the world of the *yeshivot*. This I would learn later. I was the last student to enter Jews' College on the basis of an examination by Dr Buechler, who was a noted scholar, and it was not easy to be accepted by him. I was tested on the *Chumash*, *Rashi* on Deuteronomy, several tractates of the Talmud and sections of the *Shulhan Aruch*, and on matters relating to prayer – On what day is *Lamnatzeach* recited? – and I passed the test. My teachers were Professor Isidore Epstein, who would later become the director of the institution and who also edited the translation of the Talmud into English. He was full of knowledge in all areas of Jewish studies. An additional teacher was Professor Arthur Marmorstein, an outstanding academician, and Dr Cecil Roth, the well-known historian. He was very close to me and we became friends. He and his wife visited us on occasion when we already lived in New York. I studied a bit of Gemara there (I studied Talmud mainly in the Etz Chaim *yeshivah*, where I was also ordained as a rabbi) and, more importantly, interpretive methods, the art of speaking and how to get along with laymen. The role of a rabbi is not only knowing how to give a lesson, but how to lead his community and function as a spiritual leader. To this end he must sense the ways of thought of the laymen. This training is frequently lacking in those who did not study in a similar institution, but only in a *yeshivah*. In Jews' College we studied Judaism – Bible, history, Jewish bibliography, etc. – on an academic basis, so that those laymen who are college educated can receive something from the rabbi. Today I have come to learn that any rabbi whose education comes solely from the *yeshivah* encounters difficulties in this realm.

When you studied at the university, did you participate in student life?

No. Nonetheless, I recall that at the time of the Munich agreement in 1938, there were debates among the students, and one of the heads of the British government, Rab Butler, an under-secretary in the Foreign Office, spoke against the Munich agreement. I listened to him, and I was surprised to see that even within the government there were those who opposed this agreement. I also read at the time the infamous article in the *London Times* in which it was reported that the agreement with Hitler would be at Czechoslovakia's expense, and this greatly worried me.

Can you make a comparison between the Hildesheimer Rabbinical Seminary in Berlin and Jews' College?

The Hildesheimer Seminary had a philosophy based on the teachings of its founder [Hildesheimer]. Consequently, its graduates can be identified by what they studied in the Seminary. Jews' College did not have a special and unifying world view. No movement was characteristic of this institution. This was a school for Judaism, without any specific and defined orientation, although everything was done with fidelity to Jewish tradition.

Why? Because there weren't any suitable people?

The teachers in the college did not have a viewpoint as did Rabbi David Zevi Hoffmann and Joseph Wohlgemuth, who were among the outstanding teachers in the seminary in Berlin. There were great scholars at the college, but they did not look for a way to educate rabbis in accordance with a specific philosophy. The institution was and is a place of study and research, but not a source of inspiration for and influence upon the community at large. In Germany Judaism was a matter of philosophy, of a direction in life. In London, and in England generally, in contrast, there was much less interest in a philosophy of Judaism. The entire approach of the rabbi to the members of his congregation is different. He is not perceived as one who directs the intellectual world and outlook of his congregants. He gives classes, but he does not especially engage in their spiritual world. The Orthodox rabbinate in Germany, in contrast, was the heir of the teachings of Rabbi Samson Raphael Hirsch, who was concerned that every rabbi who came out of his seminary would have a distinctive character. In London no one pays attention to which seminary this or that rabbi came from. It makes no difference if he was ordained at Yeshivah University in New York or at another institution. It therefore seems to me that even Rabbi Joseph Baer Soloveitchik did not have students in the full sense of the word. If the goal is that the pupil will be in his teacher's image, with his ways of thought, then American rabbis are not the pupils of Rabbi Soloveitchik. I said once to my brother-in-law, Rabbi Fabian Schonfeld, who regards himself as an outstanding pupil of Rabbi Soloveitchik: 'How is it that you, who asks his advice on every halachic subject, do not accept his opinion regarding matters of Judaism and Zionism?' (Because regarding the State of Israel the Rav, as he was called by his pupils, was extremely moderate, in contrast to his pupils, the overwhelming majority of whom are extremists!) 'For such matters', he answered me, 'he is not my rabbi.'

Was there no cohesive position regarding Eretz Israel in the Hildesheimer Seminary as well?

There was a position. My father, of saintly memory, acted in accordance with his rabbis, who possessed love of Eretz Israel, although not a special attitude toward Zionism.

To which of these two institutions, in your opinion, should one aspire?

Certainly to Hildesheimer! I was too young to study there, but this institution is much closer to my heart. If I had the opportunity, I would establish a similar institution. In the early 1930s, when Rabbi Jehiel Weinberg headed the institution, the attempt was made to transfer the rabbinical seminary to Jerusalem, but this was opposed by Rabbi Hayyim Ozer Grodzinski and the rabbis of Eretz Israel. A few years ago people sought to establish a rabbinical seminary in Eretz Israel, as part of Bar-Ilan University, but the rabbinical establishment opposed this, and it did not come about. Then as well they relied upon the prohibition of Rabbi Hayyim Ozer.

Is Jews' College an important institution for British Jewry?

Undoubtedly. Most of the rabbis in England who have been successful in their position are graduates of this institution. Today the majority, after studying in the institution, are ordained in Israel and return to England as rabbis. They are more successful in their role as spiritual leaders than those who studied only in *yeshivot*, who have no knowledge of Jewish philosophy and certainly not of general knowledge.

How many students were there in your time?

Not more than 20. Today there are more. I will mention that Ruth Sarna, as the only woman in the institution, studied together with me. She was an excellent student and extremely religious. After I received a rabbinical post in London, we worked together to establish a committee for premarital education in accordance with Judaism, mainly for young couples. This institution, known as the Jewish Marriage Council, still exists to the present. I also engage in this subject a great deal, for example, by encouraging the formation in schools of a programme for studying personal relations in accordance with Jewish marital law, especially now when this subject is so essential. At the time she gave a new interpretation of the blessing 'who has not made me a woman', which is engraved in my memory to this day. According to her, the blessing does not express contempt for the woman, but rather the contrary, great esteem for her. According to her, this blessing is to be recited with great intent, since men do not know from what difficulties and suffering they have been rescued each and every month, and they therefore must recite a blessing. She married Dr Chaim Royde, who combined Torah and greatness in worldly matters, and founded the Beis Yaakov school in Manchester. To our sorrow, she passed away at an early age.

Implicit in your words is criticism of the *yeshivah* world.

I am highly supportive of the *yeshivah* world. My sons and my grandsons studied and study in *yeshivot* for many years. Nonetheless, I have several comments to make. I said once that in Jewish history there were two approaches. The first was positive towards general education, and was found in Spain, Italy and Germany until the Holocaust. Maimonides was the guide in this direction, and he also regarded this as of value for Judaism too. This approach gave birth to physicians, poets and philosophers and, even if they had limits, they accepted general education as a part of their Judaism. The opposing approach, which found expression in the school of *Rashi* and of the Tosafists in Germany and France in the Middle Ages, and in Eastern Europe until the Holocaust, did not engage at all in general education and had no interest in it. Its leaders viewed such study as a waste of time. Both approaches are dependent upon the general atmosphere of the environment. In medieval France, Provence and Italy, the cultural level – of non-Jews as well – was very high and it was not possible to exist happily without relating to the world of general culture. The Torah giants there accordingly saw the need to study the surrounding world, from the Jewish aspect. In other lands, such as France in the time of *Rashi* and the Tosafists, and afterwards in Eastern Europe, in which the general cultural level was not high, there was no need for such an encounter, and the Jews could concentrate on the limited world of Judaism.

At present, we live in the Western world and within its culture, and we cannot ignore our surroundings. The young generation among the *yeshivah* population, which has no general education, is liable to face many dangers, which I lament. Furthermore, today, when it is the fashion to study in a *yeshivah* without the goal of 'to observe and to do' for the general welfare, without caring for the material future, we are in fact creating many loafers who are supported by a father or father-in-law, or merely rely upon the public to support them. According to the Gemara, only one of 1,000 who enter the study hall comes forth to engage in instruction, while today, of all the masses who study, hardly any go forth, neither as rabbi-leaders nor as rabbinical judges, and not even as accredited teachers. And what will be the end from the economic aspect, in terms of the Diaspora communities and also in terms of the State of Israel? Since the ultra-Orthodox world increases demographically much greater than the secular world, especially in Israel, and will become the majority in the not-distant future, we must ask: who will run the State, the universities, the army and commerce in the modern world? I am very concerned about this, although a positive response will eventually come, and necessity will also bring in its wake the correct solutions, as in the words of the English proverb, 'Necessity is the mother of invention.' Along the way, however, there will be extremely difficult problems.

On the other hand, I also find in the *yeshivah* world vital and positive force. I was recently in Kiev, the capital of the Ukraine. The community there was destroyed in the Holocaust and during the time of the Communist regime, leaving desolation and ruin. And now new life is coming into existence there, due to people from the *yeshivot*, who manifest creative power. And this is the situation here as well. At present in Israel there are more *yeshivah* students than university students! It should not be forgotten that this world was destroyed in the Holocaust, and out of the ruins its leaders succeeded in building a new world. This is an unprecedented achievement, even if it entails dangers if we will not take care to steer its future development in the correct direction.

But your view is in the minority on this subject!

I took matters up on this subject with the heads of the *yeshivot*, including with Rabbi Eliezer Shach. My son Shmuel is close to him and he brought me to him. I talked with him about this, and he said: 'There already are physicians who are meticulous in their observance of the commandments, and there will be more.' He also added that in the future, when the demand will be different from what it is today, it will be possible to overcome the difficulties. He has faith and trust in God, but in my view he does not see the situation as it actually is. He is already over 90, and the concern for this situation will fall on the shoulders of the next generation.

How do you explain what he said?

This is a response to the Holocaust. The ultra-Orthodox circles, whose world was destroyed in the Holocaust, felt after this that they must concentrate on rebuilding their world, with everything else becoming secondary. And indeed, they succeeded in this mission, combined with their disappointment with the surrounding world. Today's world, that is hedonistic, materialistic and lacking in values, stands in such striking contrast to Judaism and repels the ultra-Orthodox world. They consequently have reached the conclusion that if they will not build an all-encompassing wall, they will not be able to continue to exist. This situation, however, can continue for only one or two generations.

At present, the *yeshivah* world has become firmly based once again, and my concern is that it will be capable of relating to this new situation. I once heard from Rabbi Pinhas Teitz of Elizabeth, New Jersey, who delivered a speech in London, that when he came to his community more than 30 years ago and entered the home of one of his congregants and saw [Jewish] books there, he knew that this was an inheritance from the person's grandfather. The father may possibly still have been able to read them a bit. The son, however, certainly could not. While today, when he enters a house in which three generations live and in which there are books, he knows that these are the books of the grandson – and he studies them daily – and the grandfather knows nothing! This is a blessed revolution that has occurred in our lives.

If so, then is everything fine?

I understand the position of the ultra-Orthodox, but I am especially distressed by their not attempting to see the complexity of the situation. Many of them are not willing to accept someone else's opinion, even though Judaism is built on reciprocal influence – hence the School of Shammai and the School of Hillel, the Sadducees and the Pharisees, the Hasidim and the *Mitnagdim* [opponents of Hasidism] and others. Our entire lives were constructed on such tensions, and from within them sprang the dynamics of Jewish life. Today, once again, there is no inclination for this reciprocal fructification; each one says, 'Accept my view', and makes no attempt also to understand the other.

Did you ever think about an academic career?

For some time I wanted to be a scientist, and I even enrolled at Queen's College in London to this end. But my father guided me in another path, and wanted me to continue the tradition of my forefathers in the rabbinate, and this I did. And then, a few years ago I was sent an invitation to receive an honorary degree from this same college, even though, according to the regulations of this college, only someone who was enrolled there as a student is entitled to receive an honorary degree from the institution. They burrowed about in the archives and discovered that I had indeed been enrolled for a single day, and I therefore was entitled to receive an honorary degree from them!

My father insisted that I become a rabbi, and it seems that he – and Divine Providence – knew better than I what I should do. I would later find proofs that they were right. I have had six appointments as a rabbi in my lifetime: three in London before I was married, followed by ten years as Chief Rabbi of Ireland and eight years in New York, and finally 25 years as Chief Rabbi of the United Hebrew Congregations of the British Commonwealth. All of these positions came to me by chance, and I did not have to compete for them.

How so?

The first instance occurred in 1941, when I was still a student in Jews' College and in the *yeshivah*, before I had even thought about becoming a rabbi. During the war the Jews of London were scattered throughout the countryside, and I volunteered to lead the prayers and deliver sermons during the High Holiday season in a small community near London. Among the worshippers there was the head of a large synagogue in Brondesbury, London, where *dayan* Harry Lazarus served as rabbi. He was already elderly, and the members of the congregation were looking for a temporary successor. The head of the congregation suggested that I become the rabbi of his community, but I answered that I was not interested (because I still was a student). He replied to this: 'We will find a way for you to be a rabbi and a student at the same time.' He added that even if I did not think to accept the position, it would be good if I were at least to come for Sukkot, which I did. The synagogue board was amenable to all my demands, and so I responded affirmatively to them, for 200 pounds sterling per year. In the following years I received two additional appointments in London, the last in the Great Synagogue in the East End where I was the last rabbi of this venerable congregation.

Then in 1948, also by chance, the members of the Dublin community heard about me. They also sought a replacement for a position that had remained vacant since 1936, upon the *aliyah* to Eretz Israel of Rabbi Herzog, to serve as Chief Rabbi of Eretz Israel. They turned to me, but I was not enthusiastic about this because Dublin was a city quite remote from the Jewish centres even though it contained a community that was very active Jewishly. Nonetheless, I said to myself that I would accept the position, at most for ten years. I was still single, but

I promised the members of the community that I would marry (I had already heard something about a woman from the Munk family, the daughter of Rabbi Eliyahu Munk of Paris, but I had not yet met her) and I functioned as the rabbi in Dublin for exactly ten years. The community comprised more than 5,000 souls at the time and was at the height of its strength (today it has shrunk to about a quarter of this).

Afterwards, also by chance, a new synagogue was built on Fifth Avenue in mid-town Manhattan and the members, observant Jews, were searching for a rabbi, not necessarily an American. They heard about me, as the Chief Rabbi in Dublin (Jews in America usually only hear about non-Jews who come from Ireland ...) and they offered me the post, even before the synagogue had been dedicated. This time as well I was not certain if I wanted to be the rabbi of a congregation that had not yet been born, but its heads implored me and I finally accepted the position which I filled for eight years.

Was the same the case for your term in office as Chief Rabbi of the British Commonwealth?

Similar things can be said about the position of Chief Rabbi in England. They appealed to me two years before I accepted the post, when Rabbi Israel Brodie, my predecessor in the post, ended his term in office. I refused, saying that if I were to leave my position in New York I would go to Eretz Israel (not as a rabbi), and not to London. My children were studying properly in America, I was satisfied and I had no reason to leave. Besides which, the Jacobs affair raged at the time in London, with many opposing his appointment as Chief Rabbi. The atmosphere was extremely unpleasant, and I therefore turned down the offer. In the end, the late Dr Yaakov Herzog [who had been the Director-General of the Israeli Prime Minister's Office] was appointed to the position. At the time the *Jewish Chronicle*, the weekly newspaper of British Jewry, waged a campaign against the institution of the Chief Rabbinate in England, and I feared that the struggle would continue. I therefore was pleased by the appointment of Dr Herzog, hoping that he would restore the institution to its former glory. I was very close to him. We had studied together in the Etz Chaim *yeshivah*, and had become friends. Due to his illness, however, he was not installed, and he passed away at an early age. Once again a vacuum was created and I was approached by Sir Isaac Wolfson, the president of the United Synagogue and the chairman of the committee for the selection of the Chief Rabbi, who offered me the post. The electoral body was composed of 200 representatives of congregations in England, as well as in Australia and New Zealand, but in practice Wolfson decided. He visited us on occasion in New York, and he always prayed in my synagogue on Fifth

Avenue. I was quite close to him and he urged me to accept the position, promising to meet all my demands. Accordingly, I had a private agreement with him.

Meaning what?

For example, I did not want to be overly involved in the collection of funds whenever the need arose, and I asked that he place at my disposal a fund from which donations would be made to institutions. He also sought to build in London an institution similar to Heikhal Shlomo [the seat of the Israeli Chief Rabbinate] in Jerusalem, in order to raise the standing of the Chief Rabbinate in England, which was supposed to be the seat of the Rabbinate. He even asked me to search for a suitable site, but this plan did not come to fruition. Afterwards, when I had assumed the post, I quickly learned that the question of location was not at the centre of things. My goals were completely different, and I won his support, albeit not to the degree for which I had hoped. At any rate, the appointment as Chief Rabbi also came in opposition to my aspirations. I did not think or dream about this. I was raised in London and I knew Chief Rabbi Hertz quite well but I did not imagine that the day would come when I would fill his shoes. I remember that when I assumed my first rabbinical position in London and I encountered difficulties, I turned to him. Hertz was a dignified individual and one who radiated authority. I addressed his secretary, Mrs Benjamin, and requested a meeting. The date was set and I came to the meeting. I entered his office. Hertz was sitting and occupied with his writings on the prayerbook. When he saw me he said: 'What do you want, young man?' I laid my troubles before him and I poured out my heart. He listened and said: 'Look, if you were to multiply your troubles a hundredfold, you would know what mine are ...' It was as if he said that the Chief Rabbi's more serious troubles should greatly console me. Years later, when I served as Chief Rabbi, I found that he had been right.

More than once I said to my rabbinical colleagues who were just assuming their posts not to hasten the Messiah or the will of the Creator. If Divine Providence directs you in a certain way, do not reject this out of hand. There are many instances in which Divine Providence well knows what is good for a person, and in my life this is a fact.

What part did your wife play in your decisions?

I always consulted with her and with the children. Before I accepted the post of Chief Rabbi in England, I feared that my fate would be similar to that of my predecessors. Rabbi Hertz had six sons and none of them followed in his path, and I was very apprehensive about this.

What profit is there in an exalted position if one loses the children? My wife told the members of the community that I would accept the position only on condition that our family would have first priority. When we received an invitation to visit the outlying cities for the Sabbath, I insisted that the invitation would include at least some of the children, and so they too became part of the establishment.

Did it happen at any time that you accepted a post against your wife's wishes?

We always came to an understanding between ourselves. Obviously, we did not always share the same opinion initially, but in the end, I did nothing against my wife's wishes. I would say that on the eve of Aaron the priest's death, Moses ascended with Eleazar to Mount Hor. It is said there, 'Moses divested Aaron of his garments and put them on his son Eleazar, and Aaron died there on the summit of the mountain' [Numbers 20:28]. *Rashi* says on this verse: 'Say to him [Aaron]: Happy are you that you will see your crown being given to your son, for which I am not so privileged.' Every time I received any honour, I thought that all this is worth nothing if my sons would not follow in my footsteps. May the Lord be blessed, my sons and my grandsons are continuing in the path of the Lord, thanks mainly to my wife. Furthermore, since I was the firstborn, as was my wife, I learned that someone who grows up in a large family is less egotistical than an only child. Thus, for example, when we received any sweets, I always knew that I first had to give six parts to my brothers and my sisters, and to keep for myself only the seventh part, and this happens in my children's homes as well.

Were the relations between the children good?

Of course we also fought but in general we are close to each other, to this day. We are scattered over three continents: America, Europe and Asia. My younger brother was one of the founders of Kibbutz Lavi in Lower Galilee. Two of my brothers live in Canada, one in Toronto and the other in Montreal, and I also have a brother in London and a sister in Switzerland. I had another sister in New York, the first wife of Rabbi Fabian Schonfeld, who passed away. Three of her daughters live in Israel. We are very close to the present, even though my brother-in-law is very extreme in his political views and his way was never mine.

4 *Home and Family*

'I can say wholeheartedly that if it had not been for my wife, I would not have succeeded – not in Dublin, not in New York and not in my position as Chief Rabbi of the British Commonwealth, which sits in London.'

When did you begin to establish a family?

I was 27 and still a bachelor. According to the Gemara, one of the criteria for the selection of a rabbi is that he be married. The reason for this is that a leader who is not married and is not responsible for his family cannot also be a leader and a total advocate for the people of his community. I already was the rabbi in Dublin, and I promised the members of the community that I would soon marry. Relatives and friends arranged for me to meet the daughter of Rabbi Munk in Paris. I had heard about this distinguished family and in late 1948, towards Hannukah and on the way to Switzerland, I passed through Paris and prayed in Rabbi Munk's synagogue. When he saw me he invited me to his house. During the meal he proposed that Amélie, his daughter, would show me Paris … And so it happened that we actually decided to wed when the two of us were at the top of the Eiffel Tower.

What was Rabbi Munk's world view?

He was active in Agudath Israel, but with criticism. In practice he had no choice because the Mizrachi was weak in Paris. He succeeded the rabbi who had filled this position for about 60 years. Rabbi Munk died in New York in 1983 in his late seventies. He was renowned for his book *The World of Prayer* and his commentary on the Pentateuch in French. He also wrote on the Kabbalah.

How did you – you and your future wife – speak to each other?

In German; although her mother tongue was French and my regular language was English, both of us knew German. Her father was born in Paris and was known as the 'French Munk'. During the war her family fled, going from one place to another in France until they crossed the border into Switzerland and were saved. After the meeting in Paris, I returned to Dublin and we continued to correspond. The idea that she eventually would have to come to Dublin never crossed her mind; this was so to such an extent that she had to find the city in an atlas. Nonetheless, we decided to meet a second time in Manchester, in the house of Rabbi Felix Carlebach, and it was there that I said to Amélie: 'Perhaps we should say *"Mazel tov"*.' Afterwards my future wife travelled to Gateshead for several months of study, because the founder of the girls' school there, Adolph Cohen, was her uncle (he was married to her mother's sister). In the meantime I was installed by Rabbi Israel Brodie, the Chief Rabbi of England, as Chief Rabbi of Ireland (he had previously been my teacher in the art of giving sermons at Jews' College). At that time, however, it still was not known that we were engaged and so she did not come to Dublin for the installation. The wedding was held in Tammuz 5709 [July 1949] in Paris. The custom there was for the groom and the bride – as well as the parents – to sit under the bridal canopy like king and queen (I wanted to initiate this in London as well, but without success). I also wore a *talit* [prayer shawl] under the bridal canopy. Rabbi and Mrs Herzog arrived for the *Sheva Berakhot* [the seven blessings recited at the conclusion of the festive meals held during the wedding week]. (My wife says to this day that Mrs Herzog was **the** ultimate rabbi's wife in the whole world.) After-wards we returned to Dublin to my house, which belonged to the com-munity and which had also been the home of Rabbi Herzog. Several years later Yaakov Herzog came to our house. My wife showed him the apartment and pointed to one of the rooms, saying that this was her daughters' room. Yaakov said: '*Rebbetzin*, can it be? This is the boys' room. I and my brother Chaim lived in this room ...'

I can say wholeheartedly that if it had not been for my wife, I would not have succeeded – not in Dublin, not in New York and not in my position as Chief Rabbi of the British Commonwealth, which sits in London. Not only did she greatly influence me, she herself participated fully in the work of the community and was active in three spheres: first, as the wife of the rabbi and his helpmate; the second sphere – the family, especially the children (she devoted a great deal of time to them, so that they would not be victims of the office) and the third sphere – the community. She was very active and made many friends whom she brought close to us.

Did she always travel with you?

On the major trips. We were in Australia seven times and every year in America. We generally saw things eye to eye, even if these were controversial subjects. Thus, in relation to Israel, Zionism, the peace process and so forth we were as one. So too our sons and daughters. One of my sons, who lives today in Jerusalem, in a neighbourhood in which religious fanaticism is pronounced, may have distanced himself somewhat from my views, possibly also under his wife's influence. Nevertheless, he understands me. The rest of my children, the oldest son in America and my daughters in London, are far from being extremists.

Did your wife take part in the decision to move to New York?

The decision to move from Ireland to America was not difficult for the both of us, which was not the case regarding the decision to move from New York to London. In America we enjoyed everything good and I was not overly occupied, and the move to London, to assume the post of Chief Rabbi – when England was in the throes of a major crisis regarding the very necessity of this institution – was hard. All our friends asked us: 'Why should you jump into the fire?' But after consulting with rabbis, relatives and friends, and especially with my father-in-law Rabbi Munk in Paris, I decided to respond in the affirmative. He told me that, from the moral aspect, I could not refuse the position because it was liable to fall into the hands of someone not worthy of it, or that it would be abolished due to the crisis regarding the Rabbinate.

What do your children do?

At present, all our children are married and we have more than 30 grandchildren, may they increase. One of our two sons studied in the Kerem be-Yavneh *yeshivah* and afterwards in Ponivezh, and he feels an affinity to Rabbi Schach. Now he works in the Harry Fischel Institute in Jerusalem, as the deputy editor of the *Rashi Hashalem* project.

Was this his decision to come and live in Israel?

We were in New York on the eve of the move to London, where there was no suitable school, and so he went to Israel. The second son remained in the Ner Israel *yeshivah* in Baltimore and afterwards studied medicine in London. He wanted to be in his parents' house while a medical student, and after receiving his degree he returned to America to be the doctor of the Ner Israel *yeshivah*, in addition to his permanent position in Sinai Hospital, as an expert in gastro-histology and as a lecturer at John Hopkins University.

Did you agree that he would study medicine?

Yes, there were many physicians in my family, and I too am close to the medical profession.

Did your daughters also engage in academic studies?

They all studied in women's seminaries: in Gateshead in England or in Israel. The elder one studied in Jerusalem in the *Michlalah* [women's college] of Rabbi Yehudah Kuperman, who was one of my students in Dublin.

What about university studies?

I would agree to this but religious girls do not seek this today, and they are content with Jewish studies. This, at any rate, is the situation with my daughters. But if, for example, they wanted to study medicine, I would agree to this.

Do any of your daughters work outside the house?

All are engaged in educational matters within the community. My eldest daughter, Esther, was the first to found in London the Binah Institute, for children with learning difficulties, with the aim of incorporating them within the general Jewish educational system. Another daughter, who is married to the physician Dr Adler, is his medical assistant.

Nonetheless did you direct your sons more to higher education, or did you make no distinction in this matter between sons and daughters?

There was no difference on my part. There was no need to urge my children; however, we always saw the woman's primary role as being a 'woman of valour' [i.e. a proper wife] and a mother of children. We suffer greatly today from the fact that emphasis in the Jewish society is not placed upon woman's self-expression within the walls of her home. Her natural role is not located at the centre of her life but only at the fringes. In this manner the Jewish home loses its worth, with very great losses. We stressed that the Jewish home will be faithful to the

Lord, and children engaged in Torah study and observance would be raised in it. And indeed, all my children grew up in this way, and the members of the third generation are growing up in this manner as well. I think that one of the tragedies of our generation is that many families no longer view the home as a source of pride.

When did you visit Israel for the first time?

In 1947. I came from London, on the maiden voyage of the ship *Kedmah*, and I find it difficult to reconstruct my emotions. I came together with a group of teachers from England, and we sailed for ten days, via Gibraltar and Marseilles. The reception for the *Kedmah* was held in the Tel Aviv harbour. The ship dropped anchor at a distance of a kilometre from the shore and we reached land in small boats. I had many relatives in Eretz Israel, including Dr Falk Schlesinger [the director of the Shaarei Tzedek Hospital in Jerusalem], who was my mother's cousin, and Dr Tobias Jakobovits, my father's brother who lived in Tel Aviv. I saw the land 'through its length and its breadth'. I visited the *Kotel* [Western Wall], where I prayed and recited *Kaddish*, because I was in the year of mourning. Even then, however, I found it difficult to have the proper intent for prayer at the *Kotel*. In my opinion, this is more of a venue for the recitation of Psalms than for public prayer. I was also in Hebron, and already then they threw stones at us. I also visited Rachel's Tomb and the Dead Sea, and we went as far as Metullah and Tel Hai. The visit made a profound impression on me, and it was then that I formulated my view regarding Eretz Israel, and afterwards regarding Zionism and the State of Israel. With my relatives I saw what was happening in the land, not just the view from a hotel. I heard two things that worried me then. First, the position against the British. They hanged the two British sergeants then, and the situation was very tense. It was difficult to accept that the *Yishuv* [the Jewish community in Eretz Israel] regarded the British, and not the Arabs, as the chief enemy. As regards the Arabs they said: 'You will not be a problem, after the departure of the British we will easily overcome you.' Second, no mention was made of the rights of the Arabs, and this disdain bothered me very much, even then.

I had a cousin, Moshe Jakobovits in Kibbutz Masuot Yitzhak in Gush Etzion (who was later in captivity in Jordan). He was the local Haganah commander and he invited me for the Sabbath. Chief Rabbi Herzog was also there for that Sabbath, and following the prayers he was requested to say something. As is well known, he was a strong Anglophile, from the time he had been Chief Rabbi in Dublin. I remember his saying that a midrash states that the Messiah will come riding on a white donkey, and he added: 'And I think that Britain is the white donkey ...' He apparently sensed the excessive hatred towards the British and sought in this manner to moderate it. In this same direction I would cite, years later, the midrash that states that the 100 notes of the *shofar* [ram's horn] on Rosh Hashanah correspond to the 100 wailings by Sisera's mother. Rabbi Weinberg, the author of *Seridei Esh*, commented on this:

> Sisera was wicked and an enemy, but he too had a mother who lost her son and we as Jews must identify with her pain.

I certainly see no justification for what the Arabs did to the Jews, and they themselves are responsible for their bitter fate. Nonetheless, as Jews we must relate to them differently than non-Jews would. Many do not agree with me on this issue. I regret that no one sees the current situation through Jewish eyes, and certainly not the religious and the ultra-Orthodox. To the contrary! They, more than others, rely upon 'my own power and the might of my own hand' (Deuteronomy 8:17), on material and strategic means for the defence of the state, without taking into consideration world opinion. In my view, this is an approach that is contrary to the spirit of Judaism. I am very concerned that we are losing the Jewish feeling of compassion. On the other hand, I always opposed negotiations with terrorists and also with the PLO. Obviously, we are not to rely upon miracles, but we must not forget that 'for not by strength shall man prevail' (I Samuel 2:9), and that the victory over the enemy is also dependent upon the merits of the Jewish people.

And the thought to stay didn't cross your mind then?

Already then I had longings to live in Eretz Israel. I was still single, and when I was in Eretz Israel I opened my eyes in this direction as well and met a number of girls. I was still in London then, and if I had found a proper wife in Eretz Israel it is very possible that I would have stayed, but that is not how things turned out.

5 *The State of Israel and the Holocaust*

'I consider myself a religious Zionist and accept that upon the establishment of the State of Israel something great occurred in the annals of the Jewish people.'

Do you remember the establishment of the State of Israel?

Yes. I was in London then, and we felt that a great event in the annals of our people was taking place. Nonetheless, it was not yet sensed within the community that from then on the lives of the Jews would be completely different. There was very great excitement and also very great worry. Afterwards I heard that Nahum Goldmann said that he was in contact with the leaders of the Arab states and that matters would be straightened out very soon. He maintained that if his advice had been taken, the War of Independence (and also the following wars) would have been prevented. Just, however, as the consciousness of the Holocaust was not felt immediately after the war, because what was told was beyond the comprehension of the intellect, and decades would have to pass until we would comprehend the full significance of the Holocaust, a similar situation prevailed regarding the establishment of the State. It still was not sensed that this was a revolutionary event that would change the history of the Jewish people, from then on.

When I came to Dublin the State of Israel was already one year old. It was the practice to sing *Hatikvah* in the synagogue after the Sabbath prayers. I told the members of the community that it was not the custom to add to the prayerbook a song that had not been composed as a synagogue prayer, and I put an end to this practice. Some people were very angry at this and accused me of being an anti-Zionist, even though this charge was baseless. I thought that *Hatikvah* does not belong to the prayerbook. Something similar happened when I came to America in 1958. The practice in many synagogues there is that two flags flank the Ark: the American and Israeli flags – and this was the case in my synagogue on Fifth Avenue. I expressed my opinion that the flags should be displayed on Israeli Independence Day but this should not be the practice on every Sabbath. I reasoned that the flag was not part of the prayers, and I cancelled this practice. There as well some opposed me but in the end my opinion was accepted.

You said that the establishment of the State of Israel opened a new page in the annals of our people, in what sense?

One thing is clear: there is a vision and there is the reality. After the Second World War Israel is at the centre of the life of the Jewish people. We live in a period in which people want everything to happen **immediately**, but we still do not possess the necessary perspective. More than 400 years passed between the conquest of the Land by Joshua and the conquest of Jerusalem and the building of the Temple, as a historical process requires, but today we insist that everything must occur at once. We do not have the patience to see the growth of the plant. But just as there are laws in Nature bound up with time, so too in history. The fact that we have not obtained ownership of all of Eretz Israel at one time is understandable to me and does not arouse difficulties for me. This is a law of history and I therefore am not disappointed. For me as well, my belief is that Eretz Israel belongs to us and was promised to us by the Creator of the Universe, as an eternal assurance to our forefathers. I am not certain, however, that we are already worthy to realize this promise. This takes time.

What, in your view, is Zionism?

For many years I have already yearned to immigrate to Israel. I used to think and say that if I would leave America, I would come to Israel – until I was offered the post of Chief Rabbi in England. In my opinion, the renewal of the State is an event of religious significance, and I consider myself to be a religious Zionist. Every Sabbath I recite the prayer for the welfare of the State of Israel, and not only for the well-being of its inhabitants as many ultra-Orthodox rabbis do. I regard myself as at least a potential *oleh* [immigrant]. I similarly feel very close to everything that happens in Israel, although I am not a member of any party. I also see the great damage caused by the connection between religion and political parties in Israel. As a rabbi I do not wish to receive orders from anyone, but rather to be independent.

Does present-day Zionism have spiritual content?

We must remember that we are only at the beginning of the process. We are the eternal people, developments take time and everything cannot be completed quickly and in an artificial fashion. I am not surprised that we have not yet reached the fulfilment of our aspirations. It is in my power to hope and to wait patiently. It is clear today that there are still great flaws in the State. It is difficult to say that this is a country with spiritual content, and it is certainly not a Torah state. We must not forget, however, that to this day Israel finds itself in a state of war, and the cardinal need is for defence. This certainly was not the goal of the return to Zion. It is my hope that from now on we will not have to devote all our efforts in this direction. When the State stabilizes, we will live in peace and the people will develop. Who knows what creative forces our people will possess? The greatest failing in Jewish history is liable to come to pass, if the majority of the inhabitants will not care if we will be an exemplary state or a country like all others.

Ben-Gurion said at the time that a Jew from the Neturei Karta [the most extreme anti-Zionist ultra-Orthodox faction] who dwells in Eretz Israel is, in his eyes, a bigger Zionist than someone who lives on the banks of the Hudson River and claims that he is a Zionist.

I agree with this statement by Ben-Gurion but I do not know whether Diaspora Jews insist that they be given the right to be called Zionists. Moreover, most of the current-day *aliyah* comes from the circles that do not even politically recognize the State. They come because Torah study flourishes there, and they are unquestionably more Zionist than those who speak a great deal about Zionism but do not themselves immigrate to Israel. On the other hand, I did not concur with other things that Ben-Gurion said. His views were strange. For instance, he was opposed to the opinion that the State arose from amidst the suffering of the Holocaust and as a consequence of the sympathy towards us that the nations of the world revealed after it. In my opinion, the supernatural energy of the Jewish people then had its source in the Holocaust. I similarly do not agree with his vision that the State will be a model, but not in the spirit of the prophets of Israel. Thus, for example, I found his relations with the Burmese Prime Minister U Nu to be foreign and strange. He had views that can hardly be accepted today but, nevertheless, we cannot make little of his merit as the founder of the State and as one of the greatest leaders in the history of the Jewish people.

What about the Zionist vision?

From the outset, there were two visions in Zionism: the vision of the secular, who built the country, being the majority; and the religious vision. The secularists thought that the problem of the Jews would be solved by the establishment of the Jewish State. Not only Herzl, Leon Pinsker and Moses Hess already were of the opinion that the problem of anti-Semitism would be solved in this fashion. It is clear at present, however, that we still have not attained this. The world relates to the State of Israel, today as well, differently than it does to any other country; nor has anti-Semitism come to an end. It would appear that it is our fate to be 'a people that dwells apart' [Numbers 23:9]. Religious Jews accept this, while the secular Zionists did not and do not want to countenance it. It is plainly visible today that secular Zionism is bankrupt and is undergoing a crisis. Its vision is not being fulfilled, with the consequent creation of a vacuum. The ultra-Orthodox, in contrast, have another vision: that of a Torah state and religious values. Nevertheless, they do not regard the State as a means to realize the vision of the Torah and the prophets, and for this I weep even more than for the bankruptcy of the secular. The ultra-Orthodox do not devote any thought to the establishment of an exemplary state that will radiate moral influence upon the entire world and manifest a special attitude towards all its inhabitants, an attitude built on the ideals of righteousness and justice. I do not see any efforts being taken to ensure that the country will be a place without murder and crime, and that it will truly be 'a light unto the peoples'. Both the religious and the secular no longer have such a vision, and so we have lost the most important thing of all. When the Prophets spoke of the Return to Zion, they certainly did not conceive that Eretz Israel would become a refuge for the persecuted and nothing more, but this is what is happening now. Everyone, including the ultra-Orthodox, regard the State solely as a city of refuge. Some of the guilt for this rests with the appeals, that paint Eretz Israel in pitiful colours, as if the State of Israel is a refuge for the downtrodden. Ordinary Jews in the United States, however, find it difficult to identify with a state of the miserable! In my opinion, this has caused grave damage also to *aliyah*, especially from the Western countries. At present, neither the secular nor the religious think seriously about *aliyah*, since they regard Israel to be a sort of city of refuge, but not as a place worthwhile and fit in which to live under optimal conditions. This is a distortion of the Jewish vision, and this was not the goal of Zionism and the establishment of the State in accordance with the vision of the prophets and the aspirations of the Sages, when they said 'May our eyes behold **Your return** to Zion in mercy' [from the *Amidah* prayer].

I am not certain that this is the image of the State. Many American Jews come to visit, nonetheless. Isn't the fleshpot the deciding factor?

Perhaps this is not the only reason, but one of them. Many Jews from the West regard Israel as a place of refuge in time of trouble, and some of them – including some among the Orthodox – think of immigration to Israel only in an emergency. Donations are therefore a sort of insurance policy for times of trouble but, as far as I am concerned, this is a corruption of our concept and goal. The establishment distorts the Zionist idea.

And what is your attitude towards and interpretation of the [midrashic] three vows that presumably forbid the return to Zion?

Most of the ultra-Orthodox rely upon this to the present day. But this is not my philosophy. I consider myself a religious Zionist and accept that upon the establishment of the State something great occurred in the annals of the Jewish people, and that this is part of Divine Providence and of the Jewish aspiration to draw near to the period in which we, as a people and a society, and not just as individuals, will be able to create Jewish values, even if this cannot be attained from one day to the next. Those who do not accept this can also rely upon historical proofs that we should not think of independence for the Jewish people prior to the advent of the Messiah. According to Nachmanides, a positive commandment of the conquest of Eretz Israel is incumbent upon us, which is not so according to Maimonides and *Rashi*. There were and are disagreements on this important issue, and we cannot say with certainty who is right and who is in error. Besides this, the ultra-Orthodox world has difficulty in accepting a state whose entire orientation is secular and they have a hard time in ascribing to the Holocaust religious and spiritual significance.

And not even the Holocaust changed anything regarding this subject?

No. The State was founded out of the distress of the Holocaust, and I do not accept Ben-Gurion's view that even without the Holocaust the State would have been established immediately following it. There is a connection between the two.

Could we not say today that opposing immigration to Eretz Israel, as was done by most of the leaders of ultra-Orthodox Jewry, was a mistake?

At present, most of the *aliyah* come from ultra-Orthodox circles. It seems to me that before the Holocaust, on the other hand, the leaders of ultra-Orthodox Jewry erred greatly. At the time, however, they regarded Eretz Israel as a place for those who had thrown off the restraints of religion; they therefore were apprehensive and did not encourage their youth to immigrate. They also opposed immigration to America, which appeared to them to be a *'treife* [non-kosher] country'. Recent decades have witnessed disagreements regarding those bearing responsibility for the Holocaust. The Zionists argued that if the heads of the ultra-Orthodox had told their people to immigrate to Eretz Israel, millions of Jews would possibly have been saved, and there is something in this argument. The ultra-Orthodox, on the other hand, claim that the Holocaust came as punishment for the throwing off of the yoke of Torah. In my opinion, it is a tragedy that we disagree among ourselves regarding guilt for the Holocaust – are the ultra-Orthodox or the Zionists to blame? – and thus the Nazis emerge blameless.

And there are some among the ultra-Orthodox who say that Hitler was the punishment for Zionism!

I totally reject this! I am afraid of these mutual accusations between the ultra-Orthodox and the secular. A disaster for Judaism will emerge from this, and those who are truly guilty are liable to come out of this blameless. The first in the ultra-Orthodox camp who wrote about this publicly was Rabbi Yitzhak Hutner. He argued that the blame for the dimensions of the disaster does not rest with the ultra-Orthodox for having prevented their people from immigrating to Eretz Israel, but rather with the Zionists, since they were concerned only with *aliyah* to Eretz Israel and were not interested that others would be saved by immigrating to other places. According to him, Hitler's decision to destroy the Jews had its origins in the meeting between the Mufti and Hitler (after the outbreak of the war), in which the Mufti convinced Hitler of the 'Final Solution'. The Mufti, so writes Hutner, was an extreme Jew-hater, 'which was the fault of Zionism', that sought to establish a Jewish state in the Middle East. I corresponded then with Rabbi Sherer, the President of Agudath Israel, and told him that it would be terrible if the Jews were to accuse each other for the disaster of the Holocaust, and the indictment of the Zionists by the ultra-Orthodox subsided.

Should not the rabbis and Hasidic rabbis be blamed, even indirectly, for not foreseeing what was about to happen?

I do not regard the great Torah scholars as prophets, but other leaders also did not see what would happen, and I do not fault them. The great Torah scholars argued against the immigration of East European Jews into America and into Eretz Israel, since they feared that they would thereby become alienated from religion. This is indeed what happened, and we must understand this.

Doesn't the Holocaust undermine faith?

The Holocaust obviously aroused difficult questions regarding faith, and this cannot be disregarded. Thus, for example: Why did so many righteous and pious people, specifically, die? We must raise the questions, even if we have no answers. A similar problem, with the same degree of severity, exists when a small child dies suddenly. In this case as well we may ask: Where was the Holy One, blessed be He? If the tragedy is infinite, it cannot be multiplied. The problem resulting from the fact that millions of Jews were killed, is the same issue that arises when a single child dies. This is the content of the Book of Job. Our understanding of the Holy One, blessed be He, has not changed as a result of the Holocaust, as is argued by a number of post-Holocaust theologians.

I heard once from my father that man's great hopes are to live for ever and to know what the future holds in store. But, he said, if this hope were to be realized, this would constitute a disaster for humankind. A man who lives for ever will do nothing, but say: Why today or tomorrow? I shall wait another year, or even hundreds of years. And if he sees into the future, what will be his end? If the Jews of Europe had known what their fate would be, they could not have lived even the years that preceded the Holocaust. The same holds true for a person with a terminal disease. If he could foresee this, he could not live until he fell ill.

This is like a person who goes past an unfinished building and sees only total disorder. The architect, in contrast, knows what the eventual plan of the building will be. We still live within history, and as ones who are not experts, it appears to us that this was a period of chaos. But, when all is said and done, perhaps we too shall know what was the purpose of everything, even concerning the Holocaust. When the pogroms took place in Russia at the end of the nineteenth century, this was a terrible tragedy. The entire world was aroused, even though the number of victims did not exceed several thousand, but the pogroms led to the migration of millions to other lands. If they had remained, they too would have perished in the Holocaust. In other words, it became clear after the fact that the pogroms also contained a blessing; and who knows if the State of Israel would have been established in 1948, if it had not been for the Holocaust. In a historical perspective, when 'the deeds of the Rock are perfect' [Deuteronomy 32:4], when history will be fully revealed to the naked eye, then we will see that 'all His ways are just' [*ibid.*] and that whatever we do not comprehend today nevertheless is of significance.

Isn't it too dangerous to articulate what you just said now?

I want to be precise in my words: I did not say that the price was justified. We must not weigh one against the other: the victims on one side and the establishment of the State on the other. I said that we must wait, and then there may possibly be revealed to us explanations that we do not see and are incapable of understanding at present.

It may be that in the future it will be revealed that great deeds come from great tribulations. As a rational human being and as a Jew, I do not accept the argument that we must not think about this and that we should not seek to see the ray of light in everything. We must examine these matters, and we cannot escape by saying that we do not think about this. Jews were created so that every day they would search and examine the secrets of the universe. There is a lesson for the future in this, and we cannot disregard this issue. Clearly, there are many question marks, but in the distant future logic in the annals of our people may very well be found. We see that even the destruction of the Temple led to the creation of great forces within the Jewish people, by Yavneh and its sages, and all that consequently came into existence. Then too people were incapable of assessing these events at the time of their occurrence.

But it is a fact that the Holocaust remains on our current agenda.

I am greatly apprehensive regarding the cult of the Holocaust and the Holocaust industry. Museums that are being established throughout the world, writers and film-makers who make money from the Holocaust, and so on and so forth. I was in Hollywood when it was made public that the founder and director of the Wiesenthal Center in Los Angeles, Rabbi Hier, would receive an Oscar for a documentary movie on the Holocaust. He undoubtedly had good intentions, but I have my doubts about all this. It is questionable whether the trend to look back and not ahead, and the view that only in this way will the Jewish people be renewed, are in accordance with the spirit of Judaism.

Looking forward is the main thing. In his book *Introduction to the Talmud*, Rabbi Zevi Hirsch Chajes explains the Talmudic dictum: 'Every place in which it is written "*va-yehi* [and it was]" is an expression of suffering, and every place in which it is written "*ve-hayah* [and it will be]" is an expression of joy.' According to him, when we look forward, we are full of joy and we realize the optimism within the Jew. When, in contrast, we gaze towards the past, the suffering is even greater. It is true that the Holocaust contains a lesson for the future, but it is not correct that it directs Judaism. All of Jewish theology has changed after the Holocaust, in comparison with what preceded it, and I cannot accept this!

Chairs in Holocaust studies have been established in many universities, thus increasing the danger that the content of Judaism will be changed, and that they will not leave it as it has been from ancient times. There were many disasters in the course of our history, but none of them changed the direction of Judaism and its philosophy of life. To the contrary, they strengthened belief. The current claim that the history of the Jewish people cannot be understood without the Holocaust occupying a central position is dangerous. Obviously there is an obligation of *Zakhor*, remembrance, but this cannot become the main component of our faith and of Jewish studies. Can we imagine that the Rabbis would have included in the Talmud a 'Tractate of Destruction', or the 'Book of the Holocaust', the reading and study of which would be obligatory, within the context of Torah study and observance?

Perhaps the reason is that these Jews have difficulty in identifying with living Judaism, with the observance of the commandments, and the Holocaust fills this void for them.

It is this that I fear. The Holocaust is not a substitute for Judaism! It is a fact that there are those who regard the study of the Holocaust as more important than the study of Judaism, and I have publicly opposed this trend more than once.

Nonetheless, what do you say to someone who maintains that he has lost his faith after the Holocaust?

It is difficult to answer him, just as it is difficult to answer anyone who claims that he does not believe in God. We say, 'we will do and we will obey' [Exodus 24:7], and faith comes from the doing. Observance not for the Torah's sake will lead to observance for its own sake. I can be sympathetic to those who say that as a result of what they experienced they lost their faith, and I do not consider them to be wicked. I must be considerate of them, but I do not think that they have a more convincing reason not to believe than there is at the sight of other disasters in the world, both for the individual and for the collective. It is the same problem, and it does not intensify as a result of the dimensions of the Holocaust. The great challenge facing believing Jews is to view Judaism as something exalted that the world needs, but not enough is being done in this direction.

Nor can I accept the argument that the entire purpose of the fact of the Jewish people's survival is to prevent a similar destruction in the future. A people cannot exist solely in order to exist and not be destroyed, even though there are many Jews who think so at the present time. They even see in the existence of the State a similar limited purpose, but this too is a distortion of Judaism. After the Holocaust we must find ways so that we shall continue to be the eternal people, which has a purpose and mission in the world. The Holocaust is not only the suffering and the killing, but also what was built in it and after it. The ultra-Orthodox camp, the majority of which was destroyed in the Holocaust, built following it a new and vibrant world, and if we will not educate the next generation on this basis, we will be untrue to the history of the Holocaust.

In your opinion, is it appropriate to mention the Holocaust in the prayers?

I insist upon this. In England we formulated a *kinah* [lament] for the Ninth of Av that memorializes the Holocaust, and it is printed in our book of *kinot*. We also recite a special *selihah* [penitential prayer] in memory of the Holocaust on the Tenth of Tevet [fast day].

But the ultra-Orthodox oppose this.

This is based on the view of Rabbi Velvel Soloveitchik. He found that after the Chmielnicki pogroms [in Poland, 1648] there was a request to introduce a special *kinah* in memory of the martyrs, but the leading Torah scholars of the time ruled that we may not add to the existing prayers. As it is written in the 'O That My Head Were Water' *kinah*, which is recited on the Ninth of Av: 'Take this to your hearts, prepare a bitter eulogy. For their slaughter is no less weighty than the burning of the House of our God ... And we may not add a[nother] season [of mourning] for the destruction and the conflagration.' Rabbi Soloveitchik maintained from this that such a proposal is to be opposed. I think that the opposition stems mainly from the fact that the secular assumed the task of commemorating the Holocaust beginning with the Warsaw Ghetto revolt, and he did not want faithful Jewry to participate in this, because the ceremonies of the secular are not conducted in accordance with Jewish tradition.

6 The Rabbinate in Ireland

'My children learned Gaelic, and when they wanted to hide things from us, they spoke among themselves in this language.'

Let's turn to your first rabbinical post.

I was appointed Chief Rabbi in Ireland in 1949, to succeed Rabbi Isaac Halevi Herzog. The post had been vacant since 1936, when Rabbi Herzog immigrated to Eretz Israel as Chief Rabbi, succeeding Rabbi Avraham Isaac Hakohen Kook. When I came to Dublin, I still heard a great deal about Rabbi Herzog. Thus it was said that in 1922, when Ireland became an independent republic and issued its own currency, the image of an animal appeared on every coin, in place of the likeness of the King of England. On the shilling was the likeness of a bull, on the penny the image of a chicken and on the half-penny there was a pig. One of the congregants came to Rabbi Herzog and asked him: 'Is it permitted to give a half-penny, with the likeness of a pig, to charity?' Rabbi Herzog responded: 'Don't be a pig, give a whole penny to charity.'

During the first wedding I conducted in the Great Synagogue, I saw that the congregation – men and women – was mixed, even during the *Minhah* service. When I expressed my surprise at this, they told me that this had been the practice during Rabbi Herzog's time, 'and why should you introduce something new'. I received this reply every time I didn't like something. I doubted the veracity of the answer so I went to one of the veteran congregants, to hear reliable testimony. 'It is true,' he said, 'that this was the way it was during Rabbi Herzog's time as well, but he never saw this, because he didn't pay attention to it …'

Although this was a community in the provinces, the position in Dublin nevertheless gave me experience in the rabbinate on the national level. I had to have ties with members of the government and bureaucrats, with members of the clergy and with the press, which would later prove to be helpful to me as Chief Rabbi of the United Hebrew Congregations of the British Commonwealth.

In this post I also visited the Vatican, representing the rabbis of Europe. The issue at the time was that pressure had been generated in the 1920s to change the world calendar, in order to establish a fixed calendar for every year, so that every 1 January would always fall on Sunday. This proposal was raised for commercial and economic reasons, in order to impose a 'world order' on countries such as India, in which life is conducted in accordance with different calendars. Since there are 365 days in the year, not evenly divisible by seven, one day has to be taken away from every year, and only then will every year begin on the same day. According to this proposal, the superfluous day would be called 'empty day'. This proposal would result in the Sabbath falling on 31 December, followed by the empty day, with the 1 January falling on the succeeding day. Clearly, we as Jews have no possibility of changing and moving the Sabbath day. Rabbi Hertz, who had been the Chief Rabbi in England, had already fought on behalf of the Sabbath in the League of Nations in Geneva. He appeared there, delivered an impressive speech and the proposal fell. After the war the proposal was raised once again and we knew that if the Catholic Church would be opposed, the scheme would be rejected this time as well. The truth, however, was that the Vatican had not shown a great deal of opposition because the day of rest had already been changed once, from Saturday to Sunday. Nonetheless, I made contact with Vatican officials and also with the Papal astronomer, a man from Ireland named MacDonald who had the deciding voice in the matter. As we were both 'from Ireland', he received me and, after a wide-ranging conversation, he agreed to oppose the plan, and it was indeed abandoned afterwards.

Did you devote your time exclusively to the rabbinate?

My work in Ireland also enabled me to allocate time to academic studies, and I wrote my doctoral thesis there. I selected a topic pertaining to the reasons for the commandments, which greatly interested me. When I discovered, however, that someone had already written about this, I changed the subject. I was in Ireland, and I saw that the Catholics had much to say about medical ethics (because of this it is forbidden to perform abortions in Ireland and even birth control means were confiscated by the customs), and I asked myself: What do we as Jews have to say about medical ethics? I delved into the subject, and I discovered that nothing had been written about this, apart from the Talmudic and halachic literature, which was accessible only to halachic experts. For example, if a student, scientist or physician wants to know Judaism's position regarding abortions, transplants, euthanasia, etc., he cannot find any material – in Hebrew or in any other language – even though our sources contain a wealth of material on these topics.

Then I said to myself: If the Catholics have much material concerning this, Judaism – the mother of religious ethics in the world – must certainly have no fewer sources, and we should search for them, and adapt and publish them. I said this and I took action, calling this 'Jewish medical ethics' (a term which I coined).

The burden of the rabbinate was still not overly oppressive, and I worked on the subject for a number of years. Every day I would spend several hours in the library, with no one bothering me. When I finished writing the work, I submitted it to the University of London. They then told me that they had no readers possessing expertise in this new field who were capable of evaluating the thesis. They eventually found three professors: the first was Isidore Epstein, who specialized in Talmud and responsa at Jews' College; the second was Professor Zigfried Stein, a scholar of medieval literature; and the third, Professor Charles Singer, the son of the author of the prayerbook in England and a world-renowned authority on the history of medicine. He in effect was my chief tutor and referred me to sources from the distant and recent past dealing with this subject and their influence upon medicine, to the present day. When I finished the writing of my thesis, I was told that if I wanted to publish it I would have to shorten it, which I did.

When I lecture on this topic now, I relate that I came to it under the influence of the country in which I served as rabbi, since the Catholic background in Ireland is 'responsible' for my having chosen this subject. At any rate, I found that Judaism has much to contribute to humankind in this realm. In the House of Lords as well I often touched upon this subject concerning, for example, artificial insemination in accordance with Judaism. This is already taught now in institutions for higher learning, and in Ben-Gurion University in the Negev a centre for the study of Jewish medical ethics has been established (with a donation from Mendel Kaplan), bearing my name. At the time, however, I was ploughing virgin soil. This was a new topic, and the *Jewish Encyclopedia*, which had been published at the beginning of last century, does not even have an entry on the subject. The *Encyclopedia Judaica*, which was published in Jerusalem in 1970, on the other hand, already devotes six entries to these issues, most of which I wrote.

Is there any similarity between the Catholic and Jewish approaches in this sphere?

There is similarity and there are significant differences; for example, on the issue of abortions. We do not say, as they do, that in a time of danger the foetus cannot be touched, not even in order to save the mother. Moreover, the Catholics are of the opinion that even if the mother and the foetus were to die as a result of non-intervention, an abortion must not be carried out, and it is preferable that both die rather than one be killed. According to their teachings, the foetus has full rights as a human being from the inception of the pregnancy, which is not our position. If we regarded this as murder, we too would say so. Judaism, however, maintains that the foetus is not an independent person until it is born. Consequently, in an instance of danger to the mother, even if not actually life-threatening, or even if there is a fear that the foetus will be born with a serious defect, there are reasons to be lenient and permit an abortion. The Catholics, in contrast, oppose abortions in every case. Many mothers have died as a result of this. They inject baptismal water into the mother's womb, so that the foetuses will die as Christians.

And they actually act in this manner in Ireland?

Officially, yes. In practice, however, from time to time permission is granted to cause an abortion indirectly. Nonetheless, there are fundamental differences between Judaism and Catholic Christianity on this issue and on several other subjects, such as the determination of death and also regarding the physician–patient relationship. We give preference to the good of the patient over everything else. Thus, for example, if the giving of information to a patient with an incurable disease is liable to cause him harm, the physician will not tell him this. The Catholics, in contrast, insist that everything must be told to the patient, so that he will prepare himself for the next world and recite confession. There are, however, also points of similarity. I was interested not only in opening a new chapter in Judaism, I also sought to show that in this sphere as well Judaism has something to contribute to the moral life of humankind. This is *Kiddush Hashem* [the sanctification of the Name of God] before the non-Jewish peoples, as it is said: 'And all the peoples of the earth shall see that the Lord's name is proclaimed over you, and they shall stand in fear of you' [Deuteronomy 28:10]. This is not only a religious ideal but also something with tangible benefits that will raise the standing of the Jewish people in the eyes of the non-Jews. For the religious, and especially for the ultra-Orthodox, this is not a worthy sphere of endeavour, and for this as well I weep, in the words of the prophet.

Can you mention additional subjects?

I will also mention the subject of *shechitah* [ritual slaughtering]. In London I had no connection, nor did I engage in this subject, except in defence of *shechitah*, an issue in which I was greatly involved. In Dublin, however, there were problems of ritual slaughtering and *kashrut* which came to my desk, and this aided me afterwards in my future positions.

Who were the Jews in Dublin?

Almost all were Lithuanian Jews. As a *Yekke* from Germany, I lived almost as a stranger, but my wife and I nevertheless felt at home among them. Five of our six children were born in Dublin. When, years later, I met in London with the Irish ambassador in Britain, I told him that I was more Irish than he, because five of my children had been born in Dublin. When I accepted the post, I thought that I would remain there for ten years at the most, which was the case, and those were very happy years.

In my time there were 5,400 Jews in the city, and most of the members of the community were Sabbath observant. Today the community has shrunk to about one-quarter of this. There was a Jewish elementary school in Dublin then, and I added to it a secondary school, which is active to this day. My children attended this school. They also learned Gaelic, and when they wanted to hide things from us, they spoke among themselves in this language. The elementary school maintained a high level of education, as did the secondary school. Most of the pupils were Jewish, but there also were some non-Jewish children in the classes, who did not participate in prayer and religious studies. I had seen this only in Auckland, New Zealand, and I even started a quarrel with the members of the community there. They had the non-Jewish children participate in religious studies, required them to wear *kippot* [head coverings] and even had them participate in the prayers, to which I was opposed. I told them that they must see to it that these children would engage in Christian religious studies and they were not to be included in Jewish religious classes. In the end they accepted my proposal.

At the time were there still many in Dublin who spoke Yiddish?

Yes, this was still a very traditional community, and classes were held there every day. The community was also very active and very Zionist. Thanks to Rabbi Herzog, there were no anti-Zionists in the community and the *aliyah* from there – which, relatively speaking, was the largest from the Western countries – was on a high level both quantitatively and qualitatively.

What issues faced the rabbi of a community such as Dublin?

As the Chief Rabbi in Ireland, seven rabbis served under me. In addition to Dublin, there also was a quite large community in Cork, about 160 miles from Dublin, which had a magnificent synagogue. I visited it a number of times. Several months after assuming this position, I was summoned to this city, because an instance of apostasy had occurred in it. One of the students, from a respectable family, had converted to Christianity. I met with this apostate and asked him why he had done this. He replied that he had searched and had found the light in Christianity. During my stay in the city I received a message from the local bishop, who took pains to bring to my attention that if I would interfere in this matter, he could not guarantee the safety of the city's Jews. I considered this to be a serious threat, because this was a small community surrounded by a sea of non-Jews. With a torn heart I came to London, to Dayan Yehezkel Abramsky and told him about this. He listened and calmly told me: 'What have you lost? An apostate!' It was as if he wanted to say that, all in all, this concerned an apostate. This axiom was engraved in my memory, especially when I encounter those who collect money for the war against the mission, with emphasis placed solely on the missionaries. In my opinion, the main challenge facing faithful Judaism is not to concentrate on the war against conversion to Christianity, but in the struggle against assimilation and casting off the yoke of Judaism; against those who have no religion, especially since the number of Jewish converts to Christianity is minuscule. A well-known journalist in London, who had researched this subject, once told me that the missionaries expend much more on the baptism of a single Jew than we spend on Jewish education in the country! Matters should be viewed in the proper perspective. The missionaries undoubtedly employ improper and even abhorrent means, but our primary task must be to return the losses due to intermarriage and the lack of belief in and knowledge of Judaism.

Do you recall any other anti-Semitic incident?

I once had a run-in with the Archbishop of Dublin, in relation to Israel. This was in 1949, a year after the establishment of the State. Demonstrations were held then in Dublin to guarantee the safety of the Christian holy places in Israel. Until then the Jews of Dublin had never experienced anti-Semitism, and suddenly they were faced with a new reality. The heads of the community came to me and suggested that I meet with the head of the Catholic Church, who had a great deal of influence, and I met with him in his residence. He apparently was interested in ascending in the Church hierarchy and being appointed

Cardinal of all Ireland, and he sought a way to find favour with the heads of the Church in Rome. He may possibly have thought that through me he would attain something in regard to the status of the holy places in Israel, and that this would be of help to him. During our talk, he expressed his opinion that the Christian holy places were in danger, and he demanded to receive from me written assurances from the government of Israel regarding their status and safety, and regarding freedom of religion for Catholics. I replied that the Israeli government would undoubtedly take measures to ensure complete religious freedom and the rights of every religion. Notwithstanding this, I suggested that he write to the Israeli authorities. Upon hearing my suggestion, he seemingly threatened me, and said that if he would not receive such assurances, he could not guarantee the safety of the Jews of Dublin, and he even put this in writing.

There was still no Israeli embassy in Dublin, and so I travelled to London, for a meeting with the Minister Mordecai Eliash. He, however, did not reveal much interest in this matter, which was forgotten after a while. Here I saw for the first time to what degree Jews living outside Israel are dependent upon what happens in Israel. I was a young rabbi at the time, only 28 years old, and I learned a lifelong lesson from this.

Were there instances of intermarriage in Dublin?

Not in my time, due to the vibrant Jewish life and also because of the Catholic nature of Ireland. Today there already are problems in this area as well.

Can you describe your daily schedule?

My daily schedule included consultations with members of the community, not only on matters of Jewish law, *kashrut*, and personal status matters [i.e. marriage, divorce], but also general issues, such as the question of immigrating to Israel. I naturally encouraged this. Besides this, the entire educational system in Ireland was under my supervision and I devoted a great deal of time to this. There were seven synagogues in the city, and each Sabbath I prayed and delivered a sermon in a different one, as I did on the holidays as well. I took care in the preparation of my sermons, and I still have the texts of what I said.

Was there a problem with those who did not observe the Sabbath? Were you strict or lenient with such individuals?

Those who opened their businesses on the Sabbath did not ask my opinion. When they came to the synagogue and the question arose of whether to call them up for the reading of the Torah, I relied upon the responsum of Rabbi David Zevi Hoffmann in his book *Melamed le-Ho'il*, who discusses this question and rules leniently. He does so for two reasons: first, he writes that what is stated in the *halachah*, that one who desecrates the Sabbath is like a non-Jew in all respects, was stated in the instance in which the Sabbath violation was not only done publicly, but also deliberately and as a demonstration that this person does not want to live like all the Jews; consequently, he is like a non-Jew in all respects. At present, however, when Jews open their shops on the Sabbath and are not precise in their observance, they do not do so in order to anger the members of their community but rather because of problems of livelihood, or out of 'natural desire'. Second, when they are in the synagogue, they are observing the Sabbath and may possibly repent; therefore, being called up to the Torah is not to be withheld from them, and this is how I acted. The question is more complicated if Jews are married to non-Jewish women. I opposed the giving of public honours in the synagogue to such people, and I acted accordingly. When I was later Chief Rabbi In England, I issued directives in this spirit to all my congregations. I was of the opinion that anyone who is not concerned for the honour of Israel should not seek honour in Israel.

But weren't there Jewish public figures in England who were married to non-Jewish wives?

As a general rule, no. The situation is more difficult in America, but there is no umbrella organization of synagogues there, and every rabbi is master of his own house and does as he pleases. In my synagogue on Fifth Avenue in New York I took care that such individuals would not be honoured. Obviously, I took pains that anyone wishing to be married in the synagogue, even if not a member of my congregation, would produce a document attesting to his Jewishness and his unmarried status, and if he was a convert, that he had been converted in accordance with the *halachah*. Both in Dublin and in New York, all those at whose weddings I officiated were invited to us for a Sabbath meal before the wedding, so that they would see a Jewish home and the Jewish way of life, and to this day some of them still speak of that Sabbath with us.

When I was in Dublin, I also came into contact with Lubavitch for the first time. There were ritual slaughterers of theirs from Paris in the city, who were under my supervision as Chief Rabbi. They slaughtered meat for Israel, and the question arose of freezing the meat. Rabbi Herzog permitted koshering meat if it was completely frozen, but not all the rabbis agreed with his ruling. This was during the time of the previous Lubavitcher Rebbe, and they displayed dual loyalty. Their Rebbe had the first and last word, although they accepted me as the rabbi of the country.

Lubavitch Hasidism has great strength in the world. I supported their education councils on five continents and I regard their educational activity as outstanding in all the history of our people, especially in remote locations where only they are active. I was in several small communities in western California, where only the emissaries of the Rebbe are active, and they do great work, and also in Scandinavia and south-west Asia. If it were not for Bnei Akiva and Lubavitch, there would be no Jewish life of any sort in many places. They are also strong in South Africa and in Australia, but, unfortunately, they act alone and are unwilling to cooperate. Nonetheless, they deserve to be congratulated for their pioneering work in attracting people to Judaism at universities and in remote locations where no other rabbis or emissaries had been active. This is the exclusive and unique merit of the last Rebbe, and this must be acknowledged. He was a personality for whom anything that happened in the world was not new to him. This was noticeable when people visited him and spoke with him about the Jewish world. I came to him a number of times, and we spoke in Yiddish about many matters. On the other hand, I discovered that not only was he not a Zionist, he was an anti-Zionist. Not only did he not accept the Zionist idea and the religious significance of the State, but he stated outright that the Jewish society in the State of Israel was like a Jewish community anywhere in the world, and that the Israeli government is no more than Jewish leadership in any other location. Lubavitch rabbis also refused to recite the prayer for the welfare of the State [of Israel]. When I told them that this was our version of the prayers in England, they agreed only half-heartedly. In the prayer for the welfare of the State they do not say 'Bless **the State of Israel**', but '**the inhabitants of Eretz Israel**'. Nor did the Rebbe encourage *aliyah* to Eretz Israel, and many times he advised those who asked his opinion not to immigrate to Israel. Notwithstanding this, he was one of the [political] extremists, and every time he intervened in political affairs he caused much harm, in my opinion. For example, in the Yom Kippur War and in the Lebanon War, he incited the IDF to conquer Damascus and Cairo. General Arik Sharon was one of those closest to him. I don't understand how, as a religious Jew, he could have supported such extremism. Also regarding the territories he was an extremist. I corresponded with him on this subject and I asked him how, on the one hand, he absolutely opposed the return of territories 'even less than a single step', while on the other hand, he did not recognize the State? His response was that this did not pertain to the sanctity of Eretz Israel, but rather to the security of the State. I, however, am of the opinion that in matters of security we must rely upon the security experts. In my opinion, this is a much more profound matter. The Rebbe represented thought in terms of kingship and viewed matters in a different light.

Also concerning the 'who is a Jew' issue, he put pressure on his people in Israel and throughout the world, and it seems to me that there has never been such propaganda in all our history but to no avail. I wrote once to the Rebbe of Gur – the predecessor of the current Rebbe – that this was very harmful, because this activity would lead to our being compelled to approve Reform conversions. Dr Yosef Burg, who had been Interior Minister, told me that there was a delegation of Reform rabbis in Israel who met with Rabbi Ovadiah Yosef and asked that he recognize their conversions. I feared increasing pressure on us, as rabbis outside Israel, to accept such converts. My position was supported by the European rabbis, and we did not pass a resolution in the spirit of Lubavitch. It is a fact that the entire issue suddenly dropped from the agenda, as if it had never been. This was despite it having been a central issue in the Jewish world, under Lubavitch influence, for years. In the opinion of the Rebbe, the Reform and the Conservatives are beyond the pale because of their conversions, and he accordingly waged his war. The truth be told, we too reject their conversions, but this is no reason to create such a major controversy throughout the entire Jewish world. I was almost the only one to oppose this entire campaign. I argued that it was not within the province of the Knesset to determine 'who is a Jew', because many of its members do not accept the Torah of Israel. Furthermore, will the Arab Members of Knesset decide by vote who is a Jew and who not? I thought that this was not a matter for a secular authority, and I could not acquiesce with his view.

What about the messianic tendencies within Lubavitch?

I see this to be a very great danger, because it is known what happened to false prophets and false messiahs during the course of our history. They caused harm that is not easily remedied. I do not know to what extent the Rebbe himself was the motivating force and initiator of this movement, but he undoubtedly could have stopped the messianic campaign, even with only a hint, but he did not do so, not even when he still possessed all his powers. I expressed my negative opinion of this phenomenon in many places, and I still consider it to be a great danger. To say that, according to Maimonides, the Messiah is already on the way and that all that remains is to press a bit and he will reveal himself – where is this to be found in Maimonides? To the contrary! Maimonides says that we are not to delve into this. This is opposed to every Jewish outlook! I wonder how a great person such as the Rebbe could have permitted such things. Nonetheless, his good influence on our generation is unsurpassed, and no one can match him in this realm.

And what will be the fate of Lubavitch, after his death?

He apparently did not prepare a successor (because no successor is prepared for the Messiah), and this is very dangerous, especially in the case of someone possessing such power and influence as the Rebbe, and who knows what will be in the End of Days? There is talk about several candidates, including Adin Steinzaltz (I heard that there was a great deal of tension between him and the Rebbe, because Steinzaltz possesses dovish views), but this is just talk. I have grave doubts whether Lubavitch Chasidism will be able to continue its activity as it has to the present.

7 The Rabbinate in New York

'I found it challenging to build an Orthodox centre in the heart of Manhattan, not far from the Reform Temple Emanuel.'

Your next stop was New York.

When I came to New York for Rosh Hashanah 5719 [1958] for the dedication of the synagogue, it had only 20 families, and when I left after eight years, the membership of the congregation numbered more than 200 families. I knew almost all of them personally; all were in our house on occasion. Most of them were of Eastern European extraction and some had come to America from London. The head of the congregation, Herman Merkin, who hailed from Leipzig, came to New York via England, as had both the cantor and myself, which influenced the version of the prayers. Thus, for example, every Sabbath we recited the prayer for the welfare of the President of the United States, like the prayer for the welfare of the monarchy that is the practice in England, which was not customary in American synagogues. The President at the time was Eisenhower, with Kennedy elected after him. Until his election, I blessed 'the President of the United States', without stating his name. After Kennedy's election, Herman Merkin came to me and said: 'In England you state the name of the monarch, so why don't you state the name of the President here as well?' I agreed to his request and did so in the future, but not without stirring up a controversy. The Vice-President of the synagogue, Max Cantor, was a die-hard Republican, and he complained: 'You didn't call Eisenhower by name, but this nothing you do call by name?' I said to him: 'If this is your opinion about the President, then he really is in need of prayer.' Another vice-president was Herman Wouk (the author of *The Caine Mutiny*), who was very active.

Were most of the congregants Sabbath observant?

Yes, to a certain degree. They organized after a dispute erupted in the Zichron Ephraim Synagogue on 67th Street, where the rabbi was

Arthur Shneyer. The reason for the argument was the women's section. It had been situated on the second floor in the Zichron Ephraim Synagogue, and they moved it to the men's level, with the erection of a *mechitzah* [partition]. This, however, was not kosher enough for some of the worshippers, who broke away and founded the Fifth Avenue Synagogue. I was chosen to be the founding rabbi and within a short time the synagogue, which is situated in mid-town Manhattan near the big hotels, was well known. We had distinguished guests from abroad. Every Sabbath after the prayers we held a large Kiddush and made people feel at home. When I travelled throughout the world afterwards, I always met Jews who knew me from the synagogue, to which they had come to pray when they were in New York.

I found it challenging to build an Orthodox centre in the heart of Manhattan, not far from the Reform Temple Emanuel. I said jokingly that from now on there would not only be a Temple Emanuel, but also a Synagogue Immanuel (named after me ...). The synagogue was renowned, and people came to visit it from all over the world.

This was a synagogue in which the men prayed on the second floor, and the women on the third floor. When I came, I found that there was an elevator there that was operated on the Sabbath by a non-Jew. I was not very pleased by this practice, because of the problem of telling a non-Jew [to perform an action on the Sabbath that is forbidden to a Jew]. I summoned the designer of the elevator and asked him to solve the problem by installing an automatic elevator, which he did. This was the first 'Sabbath elevator' in the world. Following this, a similar elevator was installed in the Deborah Hotel in Tel Aviv and in other places, and now there are hundreds of places in which a Sabbath elevator is in operation.

Did you have time left for academic work and writing?

During my entire term in office there, about eight years, I was the editor of the congregation's newsletter, in which I published studies on the weekly Torah portion. One year I wrote every Sabbath an essay in which I explained the connection between the Torah portion and the qualities of Eretz Israel (later published as a booklet by the Rev. Reuben Turner, Director of the JNF Education Department, London). Another year the central topic was the Sabbath, to which I found an allusion in each Torah portion. I published this in printed form as well. Another series was devoted to the moral to be learned from each Torah portion. I found a great deal of satisfaction in such activity. I delivered sermons every Sabbath: on Sabbath eve a short talk, about five minutes long, and on Sabbath morning an actual sermon. Every Sabbath I also delivered an introduction to the Torah portion and the *haftarah*, which took up a great deal of my time. In England I also requested every rabbi to deliver a sermon on the Torah portion before the Torah reading, which had not been the practice previously.

Did you also relate to current affairs?

Yes, but not to politics. I was very careful about that. It is accepted in America that before elections the rabbi advises the members of his congregation for whom they should vote. Most rabbis acted in this manner and did not conceal their position, taking into account the good of Israel and American Jewry. I never took advantage of the pulpit for mundane matters. I limited myself to matter of Torah and Jewish law, or Judaism's viewpoint on contemporary issues. I never mentioned a single name not within the context of sacred matters. I also acted in this manner afterwards in London.

Were there tense relations with members of the congregation on occasion?

This happened. For example, when I wanted the members of the congregation, which included many wealthy individuals, to contribute to Jewish life in America and also outside the country, by establishing an institute for the study of Jewish medical ethics. I also tried to involve them in other matters, but this was very difficult. They thought that the synagogue was supposed to be a sort of club, in which everything would be conducted with great pomp and ceremony and membership in which would be a great honour, but not beyond this, even though, personally, some of them were engaged in public affairs and some were even among the leadership of American Jewry. My relations with the members of the congregation were generally quite good. The synagogue board was active in organizing lectures, and activities for women and youth. Besides this, as I had suggested, the rabbis in mid-town Manhattan – Rabbi Joseph Lookstein, Rabbi Leo Jung, Rabbi Herbert Goldstein, myself and others – would meet on occasion but, after some time, due mainly to the lack of support by our congregants, these meetings did not lead to an ongoing relationship.

What was the criterion for membership in the congregation? Was it necessary to be Sabbath observant?

We did not insist on this. The majority of those interested in being members were Sabbath observant, or at least were sympathetic to and appreciated the values of faithful Judaism. They had some access to Orthodoxy, otherwise they would have joined the Reform Temple

Emanuel, which was nearby and much bigger. They were even proud to be members in our congregation, and sought to show in public that it is possible even in this part of Manhattan to be an observant Jew, thus contributing something to the honour of faithful Judaism. As a general rule, people were accepted on the basis of a recommendation by veteran members. A question arose once regarding someone who was a *cohen* and was married to a non-Jew or to a divorcée, and then I intervened, but I generally did not step in and I was happy at the rise in the number of members.

Could you develop the congregation as you wished?

All the arrangements within the synagogue, as well as the version of the prayers and practices, were in accordance with my views. And all the rabbis who succeeded me told me that they follow in my footsteps to this day. Of greater importance was the fact that I had time to be involved in matters outside the congregation. I delivered many lectures, in almost all the important congregations in America and Canada, and this activity also contributed to the good name of the congregation.

Did you accept invitations only from Orthodox synagogues?

No. Also from Conservative and even Reform congregations, but on condition that I would not speak within their synagogues. When I was invited to a lecture series, I always said that the Torah was not given only to Orthodox Jews, and I am obligated to teach those who do not accept upon themselves the yoke of the commandments. There were rabbis who opposed my position, but the congregants generally did not oppose such a stance. Nonetheless, in most instances, most of the congregations that I visited naturally were Orthodox. To the present, however, at times I also accept invitations from Reform congregations. Once I even spoke at the Leo Baeck College in London, the centre of Progressive Judaism in England and their rabbinical seminary.

Did you also have ties with non-Orthodox rabbis?

I had personal relationships with several of them, even with the rabbi of the Reform Temple Emanuel. Our relationship was that between two colleagues. A Conservative rabbi, the editor of their prayerbook, was also a guest in our synagogue on occasion. One time he brought me a new Passover Haggadah. There were no changes in the Hebrew text, because they assumed that most of the readers would not understand, but the English text was somewhat distorted, to conform to America. I found there, for example, that in Grace after Meals, in which the

Hebrew reads '*Ha-Rachaman Hu **yolicheinu** komamiyut le-artzeinu* [May the Merciful One lead us erect to our land]', the translation changed 'lead **us**' to 'lead the homeless of our people'. I did not oppose such meetings, and at times I even initiated them.

There were a number of rabbinical and communal organizations in New York that were not purely Orthodox, such as the New York Board of Rabbis. Pressure was put on me to join this organization. I was told that halachic matters were not discussed there, and I therefore said that if this was the case, what use did I have of a rabbinical board? And I did not join (although there were Orthodox rabbis affiliated with the Board, especially since not even Rabbi Soloveitchik had a clear position on this question). The Synagogue Council also had representatives from non-Orthodox synagogues, whose activity was important. I did not become a member of this body, because this constituted a sort of recognition of there being different streams in Judaism, all of which are authentic, to which I was opposed. Nor were my congregants interested in this. On the other hand, I was very active in the Federation of Jewish Philanthropies of New York. The Federation had a Synagogue Division which dealt with charitable activities in hospitals, and other such work, and there were non-Orthodox rabbis in this department. What connected us was charitable activities and the guidance of physicians. Since I was very interested in medical matters, we published a guide on matters of Jewish law for hospitals, doctors, nurses and patients. I was the first editor of this manual, which appears to the present in thousands of copies.

A few years later, a similar *Guide for Physicians* was published in Israel as well, and I participated in this activity. There is a Jewish hospital in Philadelphia, Einstein Hospital, which is the largest in the state of Pennsylvania. Its director invited me to lecture on Jewish medical ethics, and he told me that there was great interest in this topic. When I asked why, he explained to me that when the Jewish hospitals were founded, there was a need for them, because in many instances the patients did not speak English, and Jewish doctors could not find places of employment. Today, in contrast, there is no need for such institutions, because kosher food can be had in any hospital, even the non-Jewish ones. Nonetheless, he said, because the Federation supports us, we have to find a subject that will justify Jewish support, and Jewish medical ethics is such a topic. In this way people will know that Jews have something to contribute in this realm, even if it is not studied in depth or applied.

Did you have ties with Jewish organizations such as the American Jewish Committee or the American Jewish Congress?

Not in America. But afterwards, especially in my role as President of the Memorial Foundation for Jewish Culture, I had such ties.

Were you also in contact with non-Jewish clergymen?

Yes. My approach to this subject was positive, albeit with certain limitations. I lectured on occasion on Judaism in non-Jewish and Catholic universities. It also happened that students or women's organizations came to our synagogues and asked for explanations about Judaism. I should note here that in America the rabbi is not only the spiritual leader but also the chief executive officer. He is the one at the wheel, who has to decide on various issues. In England, on the other hand, this is not the case. Communal decisions are in the hands of the synagogue presidents and boards. In America, the rabbi takes part in every meeting of the synagogue board, in contrast with practice in England. Consequently, the standing of the rabbi is stronger in America, on condition, of course, that he succeeds in his position. Nonetheless, the rabbi's place is not assured indefinitely. When he is appointed, he generally receives a contract for a year or two, with the contract then being extended, but much time passes before he is appointed rabbi for life. Many rabbis never attain this status. After two years in my post I was invited by my congregation to be its permanent rabbi, but I turned down the offer. I did not see myself remaining there for the rest of my life, since I thought that there were limits to what I could do, and I even thought about an academic appointment after ending my function as rabbi. I built the congregation, and I found satisfaction in this, but I did not think that I would stay there for ever. I had already noted that I also had the possibility to engage in writing. I was the editor of the halachic literature section in *Tradition* magazine, in which I collated whatever I found in this realm in halakhic journals (*Ha-Maor, Ha-Pardes, Or ha-Mizrah* and others). I collected this material in a book entitled *Jewish Law Faces Modern Problems* that was published by Yeshiva University.

Did matters concerning conversion also come before you?

I did not have any direct involvement with conversions, divorces or *kashrut*. On the other hand, I was very exacting in matters pertaining to weddings, for anyone not among the members of our congregation who was married in our synagogue. My *posek* [adjudicator of Jewish law] was Rabbi Joseph Elijah Henkin, a pleasant person with broad horizons. It happened that Jews who were members in a Conservative synagogue and had received a writ of divorce from the Jewish Theological Seminary came to me and asked to be wed in our synagogue. I asked Rabbi Henkin's advice, and he always told me that if the witnesses who had signed the writ of divorce could be found and if they were observant, the writ of divorce could be relied upon and a second wedding could be held; especially since there were Orthodox rabbis and teachers who took positions in non-Orthodox synagogues, or in synagogues without a proper *mechitzah*, and even received rabbinic permission, at least temporarily, for this. It is of interest, regarding a Conservative synagogue, Rabbi Moses Feinstein wrote in *Igrot Moshe* to Rabbi Eichenstein in St Louis (who functioned as Chief Rabbi of the city), who wanted to find a large hall for his son's wedding, and all he could find was the hall of the Conservative synagogue: 'I generally oppose this, for appearances' sake, but since you are known as the Orthodox rabbi of the community, they will not err regarding you, thinking that you prayed with them.' He therefore permitted him to rent their hall. He added that weddings within a synagogue should generally be opposed, but in this case he granted permission, because there is no sanctity in a Conservative synagogue … As is well known, following the death of Rabbi Aaron Kotler, Rabbi Feinstein became the leading *posek* in America, also with the approval of the Council of Torah Sages in Eretz Israel.

Did people also come to you seeking advice on personal matters?

Certainly. At times my intervention helped, even in instances of intermarriage, but it usually is too late when people come to the rabbi.

What about the relations between rabbis and the *yeshivah* heads?

Once I published an article in *Tradition* entitled 'Rabbis and Deans'. I wrote that after the war there was a trend to transfer the centre of the Torah world from the rabbis to the *yeshivah* heads, so much so that today the latter are much more influential in the ultra-Orthodox community than pulpit rabbis. This trend, however, was responsible for the destruction of congregations. The *yeshivot* became the source and centre of ultra-Orthodox life, and when people speak of the renewal of faithful Jewry, they think first of all about the *yeshivah* world. The *yeshivah* heads are the chief spokesmen, and their view, '*da'at Torah*', often prevails. This, however, is a strange concept. This is not *din Torah* [Torah law], but *da'at Torah* [literally, the view of the Torah], which is not explicitly written in Jewish jurisprudence and law. Although I too regard them as the leading Torah authorities of our time, we must not forget that this is only one aspect of Judaism. It is one thing to be a great Torah scholar and another to be an adjudicator of Jewish law and a spiritual leader who is capable of guiding and influencing all Israel. The *yeshivah* heads represent the force of Torah, and they have done wonders in increasing the number of students and improving Torah study. But they are not pulpit rabbis, and they do not decide the *halachah* in the accepted sense. Rabbi Moses Feinstein, for example, was a *yeshivah* head, but he had previously been a pulpit rabbi, and he therefore had a sense of what this was all about when queries were advanced for his decision. Being a congregational rabbi is part of the preparation to be a great *posek*, but those who dwell in the 'four cubits of the Torah' and engage solely in it are often responsible for their rulings being representative only of the halachah, and not of the way of life. It is true that the rabbinical judge 'can rely only on what his eyes see', but if they do not see the current situation, as relates to the Jewish people as a whole and even in relation to the non-Jews, because he has no experience in these realms, then his rulings concerning the world at large will be lacking.

Does this explain the stringency that dominates the ultra-Orthodox world?

Without question! There is a new stringency every day in Bnei Brak, and this is also the source of their fanaticism. In order to deliver a ruling for the public and not for an individual (and if he is a *yeshivah* student, why shouldn't he go to his teacher, the *yeshivah* head?), in matters of running the country and policy, 'a ruling that is strange in the eyes of the world should not be issued'. The *yeshivah* heads are, in great degree, detached from the people, and neither see nor take into account the public's reaction. I view this as a danger to the development of the *halachah*. It would be preferable for Jewish law to be in the hands of rabbis (on condition that they possess the required expertise) and not in those of the *yeshivah* heads. In addition, as a result of this the communities, which should function as the centre of spiritual life, have almost been destroyed. This is especially pronounced in Israel. In the past the rabbis had a great deal of influence, even over those who were not members of their congregations. The Chatam Sofer, for example, was not only a great *posek*, he was also the rabbi of his congregation, as were his successors. This is emphasized on their tombstones, as I saw during my recent visit to Pressburg. They issued rulings as rabbis, because they lived among their people. This is not so today.

8 The Rabbinate in England

'There is no rabbinical position without problems and without disputes. On the whole, however, I do not regret having accepted the post.'

We are moving to England.

I came to England at the beginning of 1967, and I was installed as Chief Rabbi in the Hebrew month of Nisan 5727 [1967]. In the installation speech I noted that three institutions – the monarchy, the priesthood and prophecy – began in the month of Nisan: first it is the New Year for kings; second the beginning of prophecy as it was said to Moses, the father of the prophets: 'This month shall mark for you the beginning of the months' [Exodus 12:2]; and third, the establishment of the Sanctuary and the priesthood in it. I stressed that the priesthood, prophecy and kingship are intertwined and that at present this is the role of the rabbi. He must be a priest, teacher and halachic expert, in the spirit of the verse, 'They shall teach your norms to Jacob and Your instructions to Israel' [Deuteronomy 33:10]. A king – as it is said: 'Who is a king? The rabbis', meaning the rabbis must also function as members of the communal administration, who are influential not only in ritual subjects, but also in matters of general interest. And a prophet, that is to say rabbis, must look at life not necessarily from the current viewpoint, but with a long-range view. In the past, the major task of the prophet did not consist of foretelling the future, but rather of translating the events happening in the world, which is also one of the duties of the rabbi at present, even though most rabbis do not think about this. Already then I wanted to tell my new congregation that I was willing to work with all the Jews affiliated with my congregations, but I must also stress the limits. As regards everything that is acceptable to all of us, such as the defence of Eretz Israel and the Jewish people, Zionism, anti-Semitism and relations with non-Jews, we would work together, but as for the matters regarding which some of the Jews (the Reform) chose to separate themselves from the community, I would not be able to cooperate, and so I conducted myself in almost all my years in the rabbinate.

Did they agree with you?

The Six Day War broke out a few months after my arrival, and it could be said that this marked my actual entry into my post. In other words, my real installation was upon the outbreak of the war. This had already been preceded by a severe crisis, and the Jewish world was gravely apprehensive regarding the fate of the State of Israel. I called my congregations to mobilize for the defence of the Jewish people and the State, and the community was roused to action. Large sums were contributed and there were also volunteers who went to Israel, and I felt obligated to strengthen this trend. Nonetheless, there were those who attacked me for calling for a 'mobilization' on behalf of the State of Israel. The best-known journalist in England, Bernard Levin, a columnist in the *London Times*, assailed me and said that the Chief Rabbi should not speak of mobilization on behalf of a foreign country, since this constituted 'double loyalty'.

How did you respond?

On the first day of the war, the Zionist Federation called for a mass gathering in the Royal Albert Hall, the largest hall in London, which was completely packed, with many people crowded together outside as well. I spoke at the gathering, and replied to Bernard Levin that this was 'dangerous nonsense'. We must know that Britain is our country and land, and our obligations as citizens are to it. My people, however, is the Jewish people; they are my brethren. And if my people is endangered, I am obligated to aid it. I quoted the words of Moses: 'Are your brothers to go to war while you stay here?' [Numbers 32:6]. Thus, we too cannot allow ourselves to sit without taking action in this hour. The speech created a stir even years afterwards. When I left the hall, a young woman who spoke Hebrew came up to me and cried bitterly. I had difficulty in calming her down. 'My country is in danger and I don't know how to pray,' she said, and asked me to pray in her name. Of course I fulfilled her request. And then, in the Yom Kippur War in 1973, we organized blood donations in two synagogues in London, and many answered the call. From time to time I went there, and then a young woman came over to me and said: 'Do you remember that someone came up to you and asked you to pray in her name in the Six Day War? I was that person. This time as well Israel is in danger, and once again I ask you to pray in my name.' I replied, 'During all these years you didn't learn to pray yourself? Nevertheless, I will pray in your name, and with even greater intent.'

After the gathering in the Albert Hall I convened an assembly of all the rabbis of England, including the Reform, and about 140 people came. We discussed the actions that we should undertake, and I established an Israel Division headed by Rabbi Maurice Unterman (the son of the Israeli Chief Rabbi at the time). In actuality, I established then the Chief Rabbi's Cabinet, to strengthen relations with the community, so that the Chief Rabbinate would exert influence on different activities, and so that I would receive precise information about what was happening in the communities and the important organizations. Departments were established for education, students and Christian–Jewish relations, and there was a department for the appointment of special rabbis among the student population; we also gathered information about events in Israel. All this came into being in the wake of the war.

When you assumed the rabbinate, didn't you have a plan of action?

Even before my arrival, the subject of education in the schools was first on my agenda, but I didn't know, for example, if I would be active among students as well. I planned to concentrate on the educational sphere, both qualitatively and quantitatively. I devoted efforts to the construction of new schools, the intensification of Jewish studies and raising the educational level. This was the reward for all my labours. As a result, however, of the establishment of the Student Department, this subject also occupied a central place in my activity. We established a new organization (Jewish Education Development) and a fund for the development of Jewish education.

At the beginning of my term of office I was a guest of the synagogue in Marble Arch, where several important members of the community pray. I delivered a speech in order to win their support for the new fund, and I asked why education was of such prime importance for me, more than for my predecessor. My answer was based on the verse, 'This is my God and I will enshrine Him; the God of my father, and I will exalt Him' [Exodus 15:2]. There is a difference between an inherited attitude towards the Creator and an attitude towards Him that is born of self-persuasion. There was a time when Jewish life was stable, when it was sufficient to believe in the God of our fathers; today, however, the youth does not accept the way of God as an inheritance and out of respect for one's parents, until the son will continue by naturally following in his father's footsteps after him. Rather, there is a need for self-persuasion, which will come primarily through suitable Jewish education, because if he has no 'This is my God', he will have no God. When I came to England, only 16 per cent of school-age children studied in Jewish day schools. By the time I left, the percentage had more than doubled, and the quality of studies had also risen. This trend is continuing, and education is at the centre of communal interest. Before I came, emphasis was placed on the building of magnificent synagogues, and in my time I dedicated the last synagogue of this type. Rather, I told the Jews there that now is the time to emphasize education in schools, and therefore synagogues are constructed today so that they may fill many functions.

Isn't it true that Jews build large and lavish synagogues so that they won't lag behind the churches where they live?

This may be true in America, where churches and synagogues are mentioned in the same breath, but this is not so in London. Schools are the key.

Immanuel College in London, which is named after me, is today a very well-known school. Its pupils were even invited to meet the Queen. This was my crowning achievement in the realm of education and I am happy that the institution keeps growing. The budget for construction and the 14-acre campus in the green belt around London is based on contributions from the fund for the development of Jewish education, and until now ten million pounds sterling have been donated to the school! The current budget comes from the tuition paid by the parents. If this school did not exist, its pupils would go to a non-Jewish school. The school is mixed, but there are separate religious studies classes for boys and girls. The College is somewhat similar to Carmel College (which has a dormitory), but more parents who send their children to Immanuel come from Sabbath- and *kashrut*-observant circles.

The Jewish schools are already bearing fruit, and the new communities cannot be compared with the old ones. There is much more observance and sympathy for Zionism in the new ones, and this is clearly a result of the intensification of Jewish education. Until my arrival, the Jews only contributed pennies to education, therefore I turned to the leaders of the United Israel Appeal and said that I was dependent upon them, that only they were capable of organizing large contributions. On the other hand, if they would not support me in my efforts to strengthen Jewish education, a situation was liable to be created that in a generation or two there would no longer be Jews, and there would no longer be contributors to any Jewish matter, including Israel and its needs. In order for the Appeal to be successful, Jewish education would therefore have to be strengthened. My view was gradually accepted by the Appeal leaders, with large sums allocated for education, for the strengthening and expansion of the existing schools, and for the construction of new schools. We spent more than two million pounds on the establishment of the first new school during my term, a sum which would have been unthinkable previously.

Are most of the teachers from England?

There are also emissaries from Israel, but fewer than in the past. There were times when we were totally dependent upon teachers from Israel, to teach Hebrew and so forth. At present, people are sent from England to Israel for pedagogic training and then they return to England to teach.

Who is in charge of Jewish education in England?

The Jewish Board of Education is responsible for the schools of the United Synagogue, and there are also other bodies. I should mention that in recent years the salaries of the teachers and the rabbis have risen considerably.

Are the schools supported by the government?

Most of the Jewish primary schools receive government financial aid, according to the number of pupils but the ultra-Orthodox schools, which are private, do not receive any government support. They do not want any interference in their educational affairs, and therefore Jewish education constitutes a considerable burden on the shoulders of the parents. My daughters, for example, pay up to £20,000 a year for their children's education! Families of limited means obviously receive assistance, and almost every child whose parents desire a Jewish education for him or her will receive it.

In my role as Chief Rabbi in England, I had the opportunity to influence the education of a new Jewish generation of more than 10,000 pupils, who currently receive extensive Jewish education, which their parents and their parents' parents lacked. When you start with youth at an early age, you can attain a great deal; not by indoctrination, but by providing an example and presenting the beauty and rationality of Jewish life. I am certain that Jewish life contains much logic, and that great values are to be found in it. If we strive to educate a new generation on this basis, there is hope.

What about other charitable institutions?

There are no Jewish hospitals in England. On the other hand, there are large old-age homes, which receive government aid. The average age in the largest old-age home is 88! The problem today is that there often are parents and children who no longer work. The burden still resting on the shoulders of the working population is therefore quite great. It seems to me that in a number of years the few wage earners will no longer be able to care for the majority who no longer work. In my opinion, the working years must be extended, and people should not be obligated to retire at the age of 60 or 65.

Is all the money collected from donations spent on local needs?

Of the contributions by English Jews, which total about 40 million pounds per year, more than half is sent to Israel. This is more than in America or in Australia. Besides this, every university in Israel and many other organizations have Friends organizations in England, all of which collect money. The community donates about five million pounds for education, about ten million for social welfare and the synagogues tax their members for dues on a progressive basis. The total annual budget of the community comes to about 70 million pounds (including government allocations).

Is the community well organized?

Yes. The organization is strong and very centralized.

What is the role of the Board of Deputies?

The Board represents the Jews *vis-à-vis* the government, the public and the press. According to its constitution, I and the Sephardic *Hacham*, Rabbi Dr Solomon Gaon [who resigned] constituted the religious authority; everything pertaining to religious and halachic matters was to be brought before us, and our ruling was binding. Although non-Orthodox congregations, and even secular organizations, are represented in this body, it is accepted that the community is essentially Orthodox. A few years ago the Reform and the Liberals – who constitute about 20 per cent of English Jewry – exerted pressure to make them too among those deciding on religious affairs. I agreed to a compromise on this issue, and established that they would have to right to consultation and expression, but the power to decide would be in the hands of the Chief Rabbi and the Sephardic *Hacham*. This arrangement functioned properly. It happened that the Board issued statements concerning Israel that were not in accordance with my views, but, generally speaking, conflicts did not arise. Until now this body has numbered 600 members, but there is a recent trend to reduce the number. The Board convenes up to six times per year, and its members primarily discuss topics pertaining to Jewish affairs in the world at large: subjects relating to Israel, CIS Jewry, anti-Semitism and so forth. The government and the parliament view this body as the Jewish representation. I hoped that this institution would gain the power in England that similar institutions have in Australia, South Africa and New Zealand. In these countries, the domain of the Board also extends to fund-raising appeals and other matters which, unfortunately, is not so in England. The current President of the Board is Justice Samuel Feinstein, a traditional Jew who attends synagogue every Sabbath.

What were your relations like with the Reform?

In my relations with the Reform community, I sought to find a way which would not lead to a permanent split, especially in matters of personal status and conversion. In my first years as Chief Rabbi, in conjunction with the *Hacham* Gaon (but not always with the approval of the Beth Din), I almost reached an agreed-upon formulation, relying on what I remembered from Berlin, that within the general community there would be only one organizational framework. Thus, for example, Dr Leo Baeck, the leader of German Jewry in the time of the Nazis, was a member of the rabbinical body of the general community, as was my father. In other words, within the community there were different branches under a single roof, and even the Reform accepted all the rabbinical court rulings, which were in accordance with the *halachah*. On the other hand, the Reform ran their synagogues by themselves. I once said that each country has its own special 'plague', on a different background. In Hungary, the controversy centred around the location of the *bimah* [Reader's' platform] in the synagogue; in Germany, the organ; in America, men and women praying together; and in London, a mixed choir. My proposal was close to the situation that had existed in Berlin. We almost came to an agreement but, since the Reform were a small minority in the community and in practice received instructions from the Reform movement in America, in the end they did not agree to an arrangement in this spirit, according to which they would be accepted as a recognized part of the general community as long as they would accept instructions from our Beth Din regarding personal status, particularly divorces and conversions, while their leadership would act on matters pertaining to the synagogue and prayer.

But the ultra-Orthodox also did not accept you as Chief Rabbi.

They belong to their own communities, and they have separate slaughtering and rabbinical courts. At present they constitute about ten per cent of English Jewry, and their numbers are growing. Furthermore, currently half of the Jewish day schools in England belong to the ultra-Orthodox.

Were there also disputes between you and the ultra-Orthodox?

Yes, at times. For example, I came from America and there all the religious schools are called '*yeshivot*'. In these institutions, half the day is devoted to religious studies and half to general subjects. Upon my arrival, I proposed establishing such '*yeshivot*', but then I received a letter from the heads of the *yeshivot*, warning me not to use this holy name for schools in which secular subjects were also taught. Things reached such a state that I was even threatened with excommunication. Also when I ruled in the Board of Deputies that I could live with the compromise to consult (not to decide!) with the Reform leaders, I was met by fierce opposition from the ultra-Orthodox, who even left the Board. Since, however, unlike my predecessors who did not come from the ultra-Orthodox camp, I had grown up among them and had received similar education, they had difficulty in dealing with me. On the personal level I was accepted by them, even though I was attacked in their newspapers and charged with having too 'liberal' tendencies. Actually they had to justify their leaving the general community, and I served as a sort of scapegoat. But in matters concerning education and financial aid, as well as issues that required contact with the authorities, they also requested my help.

The years in the rabbinate in England were therefore not very peaceful ones?

It is impossible to be a rabbi who is accepted by all one's brethren but rather like Mordecai, in the Book of Esther, a rabbi may seek to be 'popular with the majority of his brethren'. There is no rabbinical post without problems and conflicts. All in all, however, I have no regrets about accepting the position or about the decisions I took, although at times I would have formulated them differently.

What about the man who succeeded you as Chief Rabbi, Jonathan Sacks?

He is in his early fifties and, to some extent, he is my pupil. He was born in England and he too studied at Jews' College. Sacks was a leading student of Rabbi Nachum Rabinowitz (currently the head of the *yeshivah* in Maale Edumim, in Israel). He is extremely talented, a brilliant speaker and quick with a pen. He is very successful and represents the community both within and *vis-à-vis* the outside world. His approach and relations with the community are good. On the other hand, he sometimes encounters difficulties in his relations with other rabbis. This is because he never was a pulpit rabbi with responsibility over a congregation and its members, nor did he rise up from the ranks of the rabbinate. Before he was chosen, a search was conducted for a rabbi from America or Israel who would accept the post. In the end, however, preference was given to a rabbi born and raised in England, and I think the choice was successful. He emphasizes attracting those who are distant from Judaism, while I concentrated on strengthening those close to Judaism, by means of intensive Jewish education.

Would it be correct to state that the position of Chief Rabbi of the British Commonwealth is especially prestigious?

After my arrival in London as Chief Rabbi, I was asked to be on the Board of Trustees of four Israeli universities: the Hebrew University, Bar-Ilan, Beersheva and Haifa, and I undertook to attend the board meetings once a year. I was also on the Board of Trustees of Shaarei Zedek Hospital, until differences of opinion arose on religious matters. I visited Israel more than 160 times and was involved in various matters, and I also attempted to increase the Judaic spirit of the universities. Thus, for example, a rabbi was appointed for the students at the Hebrew University and classes in Judaism were initiated. Bar-Ilan, in contrast, was not as successful in integrating general and Jewish studies as was Yeshiva University. It apparently is difficult in Israel to bridge the gap between such conflicting factors. It is a fact that many Orthodox parents preferred to send their children to other universities, and not to Bar-Ilan, since they did not want to connect the holy and the secular. I was critical of Bar-Ilan University, although I supported it to the best of my ability, and I am currently a member of its Board of Trustees.

To what degree does the Chief Rabbi have connections with the authorities?

The post of Chief Rabbi is not officially recognized by the government, and the latter plays no part in his selection. Nonetheless, the authorities recognize the Chief Rabbi as the spokesman of the Jews and Judaism. This entails many invitations to various ceremonies and, to the present day, I have also received six honorary degrees from different universities in England.

Is there a rule that the Chief Rabbi must retire at the age of 70?

Rabbi Hertz once said that Chief Rabbis never retire, and they die only infrequently. After Rabbi Hertz's term, due to tension between him and the President of the community, Sir Robert Waley Cohen, it was decided to limit the appointment to the age of 70. Rabbi Hertz had called for rabbis to deliver sermons against the 'White Book' of the British government, and Sir Robert Cohen opposed this, arguing that one should not speak on 'politics' from the synagogue pulpit! He sent telegrams to all the community leaders and demanded that they should not permit the rabbis to deliver anti-government sermons in the synagogues. Eventually, however, a majority of the rabbis supported the Chief Rabbi. Rabbi Brodie was the first to retire and not die while in office. As for myself, I can say that, like the High Priest on Yom Kippur, I entered safely and after 25 years emerged unscathed from this position.

Was this also the case in regard to your personal security?

Absolutely. I could not leave my house without personal guards. In Jerusalem I feel much safer than in London, where I could not travel on the underground, but only by private car.

If so, then 'the entire world is one' [Babylonian Talmud, Kiddushin 27a]!

This is exactly what I wanted to say. In Israel at times I declare that I have the right to intervene and express my opinion on different matters. When people come and say to me, 'What right do you have to do this, as long as you live in London?' I reply, 'My – and not only my – personal security is dependent upon what happens in Israel. Events in Israel influence my fate in London. There have already been attacks against Jews in Paris, Brussels and in other places, which have even ended with the loss of life, not because they are citizens of those countries but because they are identified as Jews who are connected to the Jewish State. This is a shared fate, that gives us the right to express our opinion concerning what happens in the State of Israel.'

9 *Interrelligious Dialogue*

'Just as I do not wish to examine or discuss any religion other than my own, I have no desire for others to examine or discuss my religion.'

Do you support dialogue with Christian clergymen?

I have accepted the instruction of Rabbi Joseph Dov Soloveitchik, who maintained that a distinction is to be drawn between social and ethical relations pertaining to interests shared by Jews and Christians – which are to be strengthened – and a theological debate. In London I was always a member of the Council of Christians and Jews. The Presidium of this organization is composed of the heads of the Anglican, Catholic and independent churches and the Chief Rabbi, in the name of Judaism. There were five Presidents in the Council and we discussed subjects concerning the members of all religions, which was highly beneficial to the community. I view this as a means of gaining esteem for Judaism and I believe that as Jews we are obligated to sanctify God's name publicly. When I hear in Israel, especially from rabbis, statements such as, 'What do we care what the *goyim* say', I reply that the simple meaning of sanctifying God's name in public means to sanctify His name **among the non-Jews**. The Redemption will not come because we are worthy of it, but rather so that the non-Jews will not say 'Why has the Lord acted thusly with this people.' Consequently these ties are of importance and they should not be neglected. It was said to Abraham, even before his entry to the Land, 'And all the families of the earth shall bless themselves by you' [Genesis 12:3]. We must ensure that we will be a blessing and contribute to humanity as a whole.

On the other hand, I took no part in any religious debate or theological dialogue. I am not willing to deliberate with non-Jews concerning my relationship with the Creator, how I conduct myself in my prayer or why I act in accordance with the commandments of Judaism. These are intimate matters. Just as I do not discuss with others my relationship with my wife, I similarly refrain from talking with them about these subjects which are personal and individual. This was my guiding line and I enunciated it many times in public. As regards theology, I said many times: Just as I do not wish to examine or discuss any religion other than my own, I have no desire for others to examine or discuss my religion.

Did you encourage interreligious groups?

Yes. Obviously, there were limits, but in my opinion it is important to find common topics for discussion, since we all live under the shadow of materialism. If the religious groups will diminish, we too will weaken. I found that in Catholic countries the Jews are more pious than elsewhere. It was already stated in medieval Jewish literature: 'As they become Christian, so they become Jewish.' It is in our interest that the non-Jews will live in accordance with their religion.

Does this also pertain to the question of religious education in schools?

I publicly expressed my opinion in America when the United States Supreme Court, based on the separation of church and state in the Constitution, forbade the reading of the Bible and prayers in schools. Jewish organizations financed and supported this ruling, which is still in effect. In England no Jew would think to tell the non-Jews that they cannot teach religion or pray in their school, but the Jews in America have their own ideas. Even the Orthodox did not fight against this ruling. Only the Lubavitcher Rebbe and I openly opposed it. In a letter which appeared in the *New York Times*, I asked how could Jews, who had given monotheism to the entire world, oppose religious influence in the school? I added that it was in the Jewish interest for non-Jews to be Christian and live in accordance with the ethical principles based on religion. Many people attacked me for this and charged me with violating the wall of separation between state and church that is so sacred to the American Jews.

How do you explain the difference between the position of the Jews in England and those in the United States?

In England, equal rights were granted to Jews as individuals, and at present there is no discrimination between Jew and Christian. Consequently, the Jews never even thought to demand equal rights as a community and to insist that their religion have the same status as the state religion. The Jews in England do not think that they suffer as a result of their being a minority or because the Queen is the head of the Anglican Church. In America, by contrast, whoever came to the continent enjoyed equal rights, and therefore the Jews insisted upon their right to equality, not only as individuals but also as members of a special group. They speak there in one breath about churches and synagogues, and about priests and rabbis. Thus it happened that when the President of the United States lit a Christmas tree on the White House lawn, the Jews protested against this practice, claiming that it violated the separation of church and state in the Constitution. The Jews also objected when the Postal Service issued a Christmas stamp bearing a religious symbol. In my opinion, the American Constitution speaks only of the prohibition of making any one religion the state religion. It does not state that religion may not be taught in the school, but the reality is that this view was accepted, as a result of Jewish pressure.

Something similar could not happen in England. In this country and in Europe in general, the Jews already were victorious in the struggle for emancipation because they demanded equal rights as individuals, which is not the case for American Jews, who demand such rights collectively, even though Christians constitute the overwhelming majority of the population. The Jews in America feel as if there is still anti-Jewish discrimination and that the struggle is not yet finished. In England Jews feel that the struggle for emancipation was over long ago.

Doesn't this lead to anti-Semitism?

Absolutely! The Christians want to be Christians and want their children to be able to pray, therefore I strongly opposed the position of the Jewish organizations and I wrote about this. This reveals that the life of the Jews is extremely dependent upon the environment in which they live. The majority of English Jews and American Jews arrived in the same wave of immigration, after the pogroms in Eastern Europe of the 1880s. Almost all of them wanted to go to America but some disembarked and remained in England, thinking that this was America. Nonetheless, English Jews are very different from American Jews, even though both groups share the same origins. In America, the Jews still struggle for their social rights, with the perception that they have not yet attained their goal. They still do not feel at home, and the fight goes on. American Jews are much more self-conscious than the Jews of Europe. When elections are held in the United States, everyone knows if any of the candidates are Jewish or Catholic. This is not so in England. Most of the candidates – including the Jews – are not known because of their religion, because they do not wear their faith on their sleeve. The Jews in America, even if they do not admit this, feel less secure than European Jews, who have already reached their goal.

Is there any difference between anti-Semitism in England and in America?

England is a flexible country, one that is usually very tolerant. It is inconceivable that an organization such as the American Ku Klux Klan could operate openly in England. Obviously, there are anti-Semites, but not public ones as in the United States. Relatively speaking, there are many more Jewish Members of Parliament than their equivalents in America, even though the percentage of Jews in England is much smaller than that in the United States. The Jewish immigrants in England at the end of the nineteenth century found an organized community in the country, along Orthodox lines, and they found their place within this framework. In America, in contrast, the new immigrants found almost nothing; furthermore, the Orthodox were the last to come to the country. In consequence, English Jews are usually more religious than American Jews. The Liberals and Reform still do not feel that they are as accepted in England as they are in the United States.

Then are you more optimistic regarding the future of English Jewry than that of the Jews in the United States?

Yes. Undoubtedly, from the qualitative aspect. More than 30 per cent of the children in England attend Jewish day schools, in comparison with less than ten per cent in America. But specifically in America, and in Israel, the ultra-Orthodox are increasing and strengthening, while this is not so pronounced in England.

Let us return to the relations between Jews and non-Jews.

I have lectured in prominent public venues, such as the Institute of Directors, the most important business body in England, which convenes every year in the Royal Albert Hall (the largest hall in London). I spoke there before 5,000 people, each of whom is a director of importance in his field. I was the main speaker, on the topic of obligations and rights. I said that we are living in a period in which everybody talks about the rights – of minorities, women, human beings and so on – and demands what others owe them, while Judaism does not have a 'Bill of Rights', but rather the Ten Commandments; that is to say, orders, demands. As Jews, we do not think that we have the right to demand anything; rather we have obligations towards our fellow men imposed upon us: such as, the giving of charity (it is written: 'Open your hand to the poor and needy' [Deuteronomy 15:11]). The commandment of opening one's hand is not imposed on the poor, but on the rich man. The obligation is on the giver, and not the recipient. I stressed this, because there was tension between workers and employers in England at the time.

Why were you invited to this forum?

It is possible that they heard about me. I was already known, especially since my installation ceremony was carried by all the media. It was attended by a government representative and a representative of one of the churches, and even by the representatives of Reform Judaism. When I was asked whether to invite them, I answered in the affirmative, and added that I regarded myself as the Chief Rabbi of all English Jews, and not only of those who accept my authority.

Were you also invited to conferences outside England?

I was the first Chief Rabbi to receive an invitation from the World Economic Forum, which convenes in Davos, Switzerland, in which experts and statesmen from many countries participate. The participants also included Bishop Botoluzi from South Africa (who also visited Israel), who came over to me and took an interest in my lecture. I spoke there about the state of religion in our time, and I was the first to raise this subject in the Forum. I also made connections with different people. I was also the first Jewish lecturer at the annual Lambeth lecture series, in which the Archbishop of Canterbury invites a well-known figure to speak. The lecture is generally held in a church, but I asked to transfer it to a hall, and my request was naturally honoured. A kosher reception was held afterwards, and this was a special event. I spoke about the relations between Judaism and Christianity, particularly, and about interreligious relations in general.

On such occasions, do you spread before them all the views of Judaism?

One must use one's intelligence. Obviously, I would never present a challenge to their faith. I speak to them about anti-Semitism and about Israel, but not about the tenets of their faith. I had no qualms about this, because the education I received enabled me to maintain good relations with Christian clergymen, and several of them were even guests in our home.

And when they ask about Judaism's attitude towards Christianity?

About a week after my first visit to Australia, the Pope also went there, and in interviews in the press and on television, I was asked if there was any connection between his visit and mine. I replied that I did not know of any such connection, but he may have come to indicate that the Old Testament preceded the New. That is to say, Christianity has a position towards Judaism, that Judaism preceded Christianity. Judaism, in contrast, does not have such a problem, since it was formulated before the emergence of Christianity, and therefore one cannot demand that Judaism has a formal attitude towards Christianity. In short: I do not interfere with their beliefs and rites, just as I do not want them to intervene in matters of our faith and ritual.

Not even if the question arises: Is Christianity, and its belief in the Trinity, a monotheistic religion? – a subject that is discussed, for example, by Maimonides?

No, I am interested in dealing with points common to the three religions – Judaism, Christianity and Islam – such as the question of morality in society. We have common interests in this, and we must consult with each other regarding our responses, especially when this relates to legislation in Parliament. We must emphasize the shared and not what sets us apart. This is my world view on this subject. The non-Jews accepted this, as well as the fact that I do not participate in joint prayers. Everyone must pray 'each in the name of his God', as the prophet Micah spoke [4:5].

This was the verse that President Shazar quoted to the Pope when he visited Israel in 1964. In these meetings with Christian clergy, was there at times a feeling of an anti-Semitic undertone?

I did not sense this, certainly not in my function as Chief Rabbi. But it is patently difficult for them to accept the return of the Jewish people to its land. Their claim for 2,000 years that the dispersion of Israel among the nations is proof of the veracity of Christianity is no longer valid. They are not prepared to accept this fact.

And therefore they have not recognized Israel until recently?

Now, when even the Arabs accept the fact of Israel's existence, they cannot maintain this stance. They have no choice. Nonetheless, they are unwilling officially to acknowledge their theological difficulties. I spoke with the Pope about this during his visit to Manchester, and my statements were published in my book in English (*If Only My People – Zionism in my Life*, Weidenfeld and Nicolson, 1984).

Did you visit the Vatican, in your role as Chief Rabbi of the British Commonwealth?

I was once in the Vatican, in the 1950s, in order to discuss the proposed calendar change and the danger it posed to Sabbath observance, as I have already mentioned. But I have no special interest to visit there, even though it was the fashion in America that every rabbi who sought recognition for his rabbinical standing had to visit the Pope. This was true even for Orthodox rabbis, such as Rabbi Arthur Shneyer and others.

If you were to receive an invitation, would you accept?

It would depend upon the subjects to be discussed. There are some common topics in which we are interested, such as anti-Semitism, the attitude towards the State of Israel, cooperation on ethical matters and other such subjects. In such instances I would accept, on condition that we would be equals, but I would not initiate such a visit. All the Anglican archbishops, on the other hand, were guests in our home, and I participated in receptions they held. The first Catholic cardinal during my term of office in England, Archbishop Hinnen, was one of those active (in the time of John XXIII) to change the attitude of the Catholic Church towards the Jews, to such an extent that when he passed away, the newspapers reported that he had been close to the Chief Rabbi. I also went past his coffin at the lying-in-state, and this was accepted favourably.

Will you go into a church?

Perhaps for a visit, but not during prayers or a religious ceremony. The second cardinal, Basil Hume, and I also enjoyed close relations, and we called each other by our first names, Basil and Immanuel. He was a modest and wise man, he had pious tendencies and a sense of humility. He influenced public opinion in England, since he was a true man of the spirit.

Do they know anything about Judaism?

There once was a head of the Anglican Church who not only knew Hebrew but taught it as well. When he visited Israel, a speech in his honour was prepared in Latin, and he responded in biblical Hebrew. Generally speaking, however, they do not have a serious knowledge of Judaism.

You mentioned that in your youth you never had any non-Jewish friends. Is this so to the present?

Later on, the situation changed. I should mention, for instance, James Parkes, a scholar and expert on anti-Semitism in England who once invited me to spend the night as his guest at his home in Cambridge (of course, I brought kosher food). He was an Anglican clergyman with liberal views, and he possessed an extremely large library on the subject of anti-Semitism. Parkes presented me with questions regarding the observance of the 613 commandments in the modern world, since he had difficulty in understanding this. Besides this, my wife would invite women from different circles, including Church circles, to our home, since we were of the opinion that it is impossible to form a close relationship with someone without meeting with him on a social basis. The Archbishops of Canterbury, six I believe, visited our house. The relations with them, and also with representatives of the Catholic Church, were good. Thus, for example, during the Leningrad trial, when Yosef Mendelevich was sentenced to death, I received a request at Christmas to call the Cardinal, to intervene on his behalf. I did so immediately, and the Cardinal promised me that he would do whatever he could, and that same day he was in contact with the representative of the Russian Orthodox Church in London. If I had not known these people on a personal basis, it is doubtful whether I could have acted in this manner. Prime ministers, foreign ministers and university heads also were guests in our house, since it is impossible to be an influential rabbi without such ties.

What about the royal family?

Before my retirement, I thought of inviting the Prince of Wales to my home. I put out feelers and received the reply that he wanted to invite me to his palace, and even requested of me a list of up to 18 people whom I would want to be invited as his guests. He received the list from me, which included the heads of the community and several personal friends, and he invited them. The Prince was the host, and he delivered a speech very friendly to Jews and Judaism. (Princess Diana was not present, since she was attending another event.) I, for my part, spoke about the first Jews in England, who apparently had arrived here during the Roman period. There is evidence that they had been brought to England as slaves, and therefore came to the British Isles even before the Anglo-Saxons. Later, at the time of the battle of Hastings in 1066, Jews came from Europe and founded a number of communities in London, Norwich, York and other locations. They included a number of Torah scholars, one of whom was Rabbi Yom Tov, who came from Joigny in France to York, where he died a martyr's death in 1190. He composed a *selichah* [penitential prayer] that is recited to the present on Yom Kippur night. This is the only Anglo-Jewish contribution to be included in all Jewish prayerbooks. In 1290 the Jews were expelled by Edward I and then there were no Jews in England until the time of Oliver Cromwell, who defended them. Manasseh Ben Israel, a rabbi from Amsterdam, sought permission for the Jews to live in England. He argued that until there were Jews dispersed from one end of the earth to the other (which is the meaning of the name Angleterre – the end of the earth), the final Redemption would not come. Cromwell granted this request and since then Jews have lived in England. The first came from Holland, and were mainly those who had been expelled from Spain, and founded the first Sephardic community. They were joined by German and Eastern European Jews, who came in the great wave of immigration in 1880. I related this in short to the Prince, and I also spoke of the attitude of the Jewish community to Israel, and explained that the majority of Jews are Zionists. I spoke for about a quarter of an hour. The Prince was quite interested in my speech and in his response, which also lasted about a quarter of an hour, he spoke of the extent to which the English appreciate the contribution of the Jews to English economic and cultural life.

Did you also engage in dialogue with Christians?

In the mid-1980s I received from the Academy of Catholic Bishops in Germany an invitation for a dialogue with Jews in Aachen. A delegation from Israel, including Dr Geoffrey Wigoder, Professor Zeev Falk and others also participated in this dialogue. I was asked to speak there about medical ethics in Judaism. I wrote to them that in principle I was willing to participate in the conference but that I would not set foot on German soil, and I hoped that they would understand my reasons. The reply I received was that not only did they understand but for this reason they had decided to move the venue of the session in which I was to speak from Germany to a nearby city in The Netherlands. All the participants came to a monastery in Holland and then returned to Germany after the end of the session. I remained, almost alone, in the ancient building. This was a very strange sensation for me.

Were some of them interesting individuals?

Among the bishops, I met Professor Henriks, who appeared to me to be a true friend of the Jews and Israel. In the course of our conversations, especially when we talked about recognition of Israel by the Vatican, I said that it was difficult for us as Jews to understand why the Vatican does not maintain diplomatic relations with Israel, since it maintains such relations with almost every other country in the world. I expressed my view, that the reason for this is religious-theological: for thousands of years the Christians declared that the Jews were punished for not having accepted their Messiah. They are dispersed among the nations and they will find no rest until they accept the New Testament. This, so they believe, is proof of the truth of Christianity over Judaism. I continued with a question: If this is indeed the reason, it would be understandable; but why do they not explicitly state this? The pretexts, as if the reason is due to the lack of final borders between Israel and the neighbouring Arab countries, as in Eastern Europe, are not valid, because the Vatican has recognized those countries. He replied that he feared that there was indeed a theological reason for this, and he assured me that he would act to the best of his abilities to change the situation. Henriks spoke of a public statement they had planned to issue, but they had run into a stumbling block. The representatives of the Vatican informed the representatives of Jewry that they hoped there would be a declaration based on a draft which stated that not only does the Vatican recognize Israel, but that the Church was involved in anti-Semitism, with the consequent increased hatred that culminated in the Holocaust, in which the Church also had a part. Afterwards, they apparently thought that it was premature to publish such a declaration. They deal with eternity, and they have time for this.

And us?

I will relate the following about this: in the late 1960s we were on a mission to Israel. I was already the Chief Rabbi in England. We visited Qumran and Masada, after which we met with Professor Yigal Yadin, who was Deputy Prime Minister at the time. He spoke of the war against the Romans and the Bar Kokhba rebellion. After he finished speaking, I asked him: How, in your opinion, should we teach the Masada episode to the youth? From the viewpoint of great heroism or as a major catastrophe? (At the time, I had read the book by Yehoshafat Harkavi, in which he argued that the Bar Kokhba rebellion had been disastrous for the Jewish people.) His reply was: of course, we want to emphasize the great heroism! I said that I had difficulty in accepting this approach, which was in opposition to the spirit of Judaism. We are commanded and permitted to sacrifice our lives if a foreign government seeks to have us renounce our religion. In such a case, the rule of 'One should allow oneself to be killed rather than transgress' is in force, but this was not the situation of the warriors of Masada. I further stated: Perhaps you don't know what your father had told us in the past.

What had you heard from his father?

When I came to Ireland in 1949, the community celebrated Israel Independence Day with a lecture or speech by someone from Israel. That year I invited the famous archaeologist Professor Eliezer Sukenik, Yigael Yadin's father, who was the first Jewish scholar to examine the Qumran scrolls, which had recently been discovered. In his lecture, Sukenik noted that at the same time that excavations were conducted in Qumran, excavations were also conducted in London and the boot of a Roman legionnaire had been uncovered. He added: How significant is this contradiction! In the Land of Israel they found a 2,000-year-old parchment, a parchment with sacred writings on it, while Roman leather was used by soldiers from far off who came to crush the freedom of another people! Yigael Yadin, who had not heard this from his father, thanked me for telling him this. I responded: 'They [call] on chariots, they [call] on horses, but we call on the name of the Lord' [Psalms 20:8].

10 *The Royal Feast*

'The Queen sat next to me and patiently waited until I had finished eating the kosher meal.'

Did you know the Prime Ministers in Britain?

I knew all the Prime Ministers starting in 1967. The first was Edward Heath, who was no great friend of the Jews nor of Israel. It happened that we – my wife and I – were his private guests in his home in Salisbury, and of course we saw that there would be kosher food for us. We spoke of the place of religion in England. Although I knew that he was not a friend of Israel, I raised this subject and also corresponded with him about this. He was followed by Harold Wilson, a great friend of Israel. We met at several functions. James Callaghan and his wife were invited to our house a few days after our granddaughter was born. Our daughter was living in our home at the time, and we were happy to inform the Callaghans of this. Lady Callaghan asked to see her, and whenever we met afterwards, she mentioned my grand-daughter Avigail.

Did you meet the Queen?

Yes, at least once a year, on the memorial day for the war dead in Whitehall. Among the other religious leaders, I represented the Jewish community. I also received an invitation to be her personal guest. Such an invitation also honoured the Jewish community. When my pre-decessor, Rabbi Brodie, accepted such an invitation, he ate only fruit and suffered from a stomach-ache afterwards. We decided to request kosher food, and this became the standard practice: in the royal palace, in Parliament and in other places, we were served kosher food, and even the regular menu was changed to match ours. The only difference was that we received a double portion (since the food was ordered from a kosher restaurant), and it would take a long time for us to finish what was on the plate. The Queen sat next to me and patiently waited until

I had finished eating the kosher meal. On this occasion she told me that she had recently visited Germany for the first time. She expressed interest in Jewish communal life, and even invited us to Windsor. We were four couples, and I wondered what I could bring her as a memento that she did not already have. I thought to bring her the prayer in honour of the coronations of Queen Victoria and King Edward VII, and after them George VI and the Queen Mother. I explained to her that the prayer is recited in Hebrew and English, and that her name was given in Hebrew: Elisheva. She paid special attention to the prayer in honour of her father and she called the Queen Mother to see it. Immediately afterwards she ordered this memento to be kept in her library.

We spent the night in the palace. We were given a suite, with separate rooms for me and my wife, with a common room in the middle – all according to the demands of protocol. At the entrance a sign had been posted with my name. I must say that the regal splendour is indeed felt there, and especially during the banquet.

Can you describe the course of the meal?

First, people meet in the reception that precedes the banquet, in order to become acquainted. The Queen Mother, the Duke of Edinburgh and some of their children were present, along with the four invited couples. Afterwards, a break of about half an hour is announced, in order to change clothes for the banquet. When we entered our rooms, the bath was ready, but there was not enough time to bathe, lest we be late for the meal. So that no one would suspect that we hadn't bathed before the banquet with the Queen, we splashed some water on the floor … It is interesting that when we were at the reception, the servants took the coins out of the pockets of our clothes and placed them on the table, with the Queen's likeness on the coin always facing up. I also had brought my *talit* and *tefilin* with me. The servants did not know what to do with the *talit*. They thought it was my wife's, so they laid it out on her bed, next to her nightgown. Nonetheless, I must mention that a special stand for *netilat yadayim* [washing the hands before breaking bread] had been placed at the entrance to the banquet hall! This invitation was considered to be of the highest importance, and everything was done with the greatest elegance, with the organizers seeing that everything was prepared in advance, down to the smallest detail. It is of interest that when dining at the Queen's table, she is not toasted, and so the problem of *yein nesech* [the wine of non-Jews, which may not be imbibed by Jews] did not arise. During the course of the banquet, the Queen stated that she would be happy to visit Israel, but this has not happened yet. The Duke of Edinburgh, however, has visited the country. His mother, who comes from the Greek royal family, saved several Jews during the war and she is buried in Jerusalem. The Queen told me that during her trip to America she noted several Jewish phenomena about which she told me, mentioning that New York Jews figure prominently in many avenues of life. She is indeed a keen observer.

Did you also talk about politics?

One must be careful in talks with the Queen, since delicate political matters are not discussed with her because of her position and standing. With other members of the royal family, on the other hand, the situation is different. Even the Queen Mother is freer. My wife told her how significant the visit was for us, as Holocaust survivors who were privileged to be the guests of the most important royal palace in the world. The Queen Mother responded: 'We have many guests, and they all are grateful for the opportunity to visit the royal palace, but I have never heard a sentence like this, and I am capable of appreciating its significance.'

And the Queen's husband?

I had a number of debates with the Duke of Edinburgh about the birth rate in the world, which he considers to be too high. In his opinion, encouraging more births poses a danger to the future of humanity. He was very surprised when he heard that we have more than 30 grandchildren. I told him that this constitutes a serious problem in certain countries, since there is not sufficient food for everyone. If someone was to come from there and ask me in my capacity as a rabbi: 'What is the moral position regarding births?' I would reply that it is permissible to use birth control methods, since, according to Judaism, the saving of life overrides everything, and hunger is life-threatening. As regards Jews, however, we do not have such a problem. To the contrary, we suffer from under-population, and even from vanishing Jews. Consequently, each society and people must be treated in accordance with its particular situation.

What about Margaret Thatcher?

I had a very cordial relationship with Mrs Thatcher, the Prime Minister and 'Iron Lady'. I met her for the first time when she held the post of Education Minister in the government of Edward Heath. In a conversation with her, I spoke of the centrality of education in Judaism, and

I told her that on the door of every Jewish home is affixed a *mezuzah* in which it is written: 'Teach them to your children' [Deuteronomy 6:7]. I added that, from our viewpoint, the Minister of Education is the Minister of Defence, 'and you are the true Minister of Defence of the country'. She did not forget this and she reminded me of it years later, when she was already the Prime Minister. From then on we have enjoyed a warm relationship, and in her memoirs she praises me as a 'wonderful man', adding that it would please her if the English would learn from Judaism, which places emphasis upon mutual aid and personal responsibility. She visited our home several times, with her husband, and once even was a guest in our *sukkah*. When she was Prime Minister, I wrote to her on the subject of terror (she had a similar problem, in Northern Ireland), and I expressed the opinion that terrorists were not to be given the 'oxygen of publicity', since they thrive on this. If there was not so much publicity, they would have died of thirst long ago. She used this expression in one of her speeches and drew my attention to this. Mrs Thatcher is a woman who is very open to new ideas and is a genuine friend of the Jewish people and the State of Israel. She was the first British Prime Minister to visit Israel while in office. She wrote in her memoirs that this visit made a lasting impression upon her. When she returned and saw the dirt in the streets of London, she turned to the officials in charge and told them: 'Perhaps you should go to Israel and see how it is possible to clean the streets.'

Many receptions were held for various occasions, and I had to attend because of my position. Once a conference on educational subjects was held and I was invited to speak. I mentioned that there are people in our community who will not allow television in their homes, out of their concern for their children's education, since they consider it a waste of time, and so they do not introduce smut into their homes. Several months later, one of the government ministers (later to become the Education Minister) said to me: 'Your influence upon the members of my household is greater than that of my Cardinal.' I asked how this could be. His reply was: 'I have a six-year-old daughter and, since you spoke, we have no television in our home.'

Were there instances in which you were asked to act on behalf of the Jewish people with the British government?

I made no secret of my views, and they knew that my approach was a moderate one. Government officials in England appreciated me for this. I often received requests from organizations dealing with the subject of Russian Jewry to intercede and use my good offices with the British government on behalf of the Prisoners of Zion, and of course I always agreed. Before her trip to Russia, Mrs Thatcher received from me a list of prisoners and acted on this matter. Also when it was necessary to intervene on behalf of Israeli prisoners of war, I met with several parents of the prisoners and interceded on their behalf, on humane, and not political, grounds.

How did you become a lord?

Although I was close to Mrs Thatcher, I never dreamed that I would ever be included in the Queen's honours list of those receiving titles, which appears biannually. It was therefore a great surprise when I received a confidential letter from Mrs Thatcher (in 1981), which stated that she intended to recommend that the Queen award me a lordship – an honour which had not been conferred on any incumbent Chief Rabbi before. She asked if this was acceptable to me, and obviously the offer was very flattering and exciting. My wife was in America at the time, and it was forbidden to speak about this before the official publication of the list. I called her and asked: 'Would you like to become a Lady?' She understood what this was all about, and of course she agreed. I replied to the Prime Minister that I would be greatly honoured by this, and it was published in the New Year's honours list. What was remarkable about this was that the Prime Minister herself had recommended me, instead of others recommending me to her, as was the general practice. My success in being close to her was a result of my position on social issues.

In 1986 the Archbishops of Canterbury and York had appointed a committee of clergymen on inner-city, low-income neighbourhoods, that were in difficult social straits, due to immigration from the British Commonwealth. They suffered from crime, prostitution, drugs and such like. The clergymen sought to solve the problem in the spirit of Christianity, but they sent me a draft of their proposal and requested my opinion. I saw immediately that their approach differed from ours. They charged the government with not having taken action on behalf of the underprivileged classes, with emphasis placed mainly on the government's shortcomings. They said nothing about strengthening the family, nor did they mention the intrinsic value of work. They omitted stating that the members of these classes must themselves take the initiative and take action of their own to change the situation for the better. Since I had been asked to respond, I devoted thought and labour to this, in order to address issues of the family, work and society, according to the world view of Judaism. I wrote about 20 pages and sent my response to the Archbishop of Canterbury, as a personal reply, without knowing that this would be published. He answered that he had received my letter and, although he did not agree with everything I had written, he suggested that it be published. I therefore contacted the *Jewish Chronicle* and offered this essay, on condition that it be printed without any omissions. My request was accepted, and I was told that this was the first time in the newspaper's history that it would publish a three-page article. My statements were later copied by the general press. Furthermore, a resolution was submitted with the signatures of more than 150 Members of Parliament, to thank the Chief Rabbi for his essay. As all this was happening, I saw that it was within my power as a rabbi to contribute something to matters pertaining to the society at large. I wrote that, according to the Judaic tradition, work has intrinsic value, and is not merely a means. I cited the medieval dictum that work is kingship. When Adam was placed in the Garden of Eden, he was told 'to **work** it and to guard it' [Genesis 2:15]. I noted that when the Jews had come to Britain, they had not come with demands to the government. Rather they themselves gave their children education more intensive than was the norm, and they worked harder than others which led to their success. They did not remain wretched, with no hope. They attained what they attained, not by protests and demonstrations but by their own labours. Today as well, it must be said that the solution lies primarily in the efforts of the immigrants themselves. I also mentioned the role of the family in this process. Success is difficult without normal family life; Judaism stresses the family, and therein lies the secret of its success. My views were generally accepted, although some criticism was levelled as well, mainly by Jews. Thus I went from the private domain of Jewry to the public domain of English society. This influenced the government and Mrs Thatcher, and from then on I enjoyed a certain standing in the general English society.

Some time later, another opportunity presented itself for expressing an opinion on general matters, although there were some – mostly Jews – who opposed my actions. In 1988, when I was offered the title of 'Lord' and this was made public, most of the community officials wrote me that this was an honour for the community. Some individuals, however, advised me not to accept the title, stating that, as Chief Rabbi, I should not be involved in politics. One of the leaders of the community, who had been close to me until then, also held this view and from then on he became one of my opponents, possibly also because he himself did not receive this honour. (Some years later he was offered and accepted an honour.)

In my maiden speech in the House of Lords, on the subject of immigration, I noted – even though it was customary not to speak on controversial subjects in one's first speech –that it was said that I was the first rabbi to have been appointed to the House of Lords. In actuality, however, I had been preceded by another rabbi – Moses, after whom the adjoining room for the Lords is named, the Moses Room. Moreover, the large painting in which Moses receives the Tablets covers one of the walls in this room. The House of Lords is the source of legislation, I said, and Moses was the first lawgiver, whose spirit inspires all legislators. I concluded by stating that we must all know that we have received the right to stay in this world for only a limited time; the time will come when this permit will expire, and we will migrate to another world.

Was the title personally conferred on you by the Queen?

Yes, and this was not all: I also received a parchment scroll, written in a scribe's hand, in a special box with the wording: 'My beloved Immanuel Jakobovits ...' Even before this, when I was knighted, I had to present myself before the Queen and declare, 'Cursed be the one who thinks ill of the Queen ...'

Wasn't it necessary to kneel before her?

When I received my knighthood, I had to kneel, but I did so on only one knee, and they knew this beforehand. In addition, I merely took an affirmation, and not an oath.

How many Jewish lords are there in the British Parliament at present?

About 30 Jews are presently sitting in the House of Lords, out of the approximately 1,200 lords. In most instances, they are hereditary titles. This custom has been abolished and the title now is given only on a personal basis (life peerage). In one of my speeches in the community I stated that at present we cannot say that we have Jews who have won the title 'Jew' on a hereditary basis. Now, either they are Jews on their own merit or they are no longer Jews.

Do you frequently appear in the House of Lords?

There are two types of peers: the churchmen (bishops), who sit in special benches in one wing, and alongside them the peers from the government. In the other wing sit the peers from the opposition parties and between them, on the cross benches, sit the independents, including myself. I said once that this was the only cross that I bear. Once a year, when the Queen comes to open the session of Parliament, one must appear in the official robes of a Lord, but not in the other sessions. One must also have a special invitation to this session, since there are no more than 300 seats in the hall, and the number of peers greatly exceeds this. The members of the House of Commons must stand outside as they are not permitted to sit in the House of Lords. To now, I have attended three such opening ceremonies and I go to the regular sessions once every two or three weeks when there is a subject of interest to me. For instance, I like to be there when matters pertaining to societal and medical ethics, and relating to Israel and the Middle East are debated. In the past there was a fierce debate concerning war criminals' trials, and I took part in the discussions. I am similarly interested in new educational legislation. The Education Law contains sections regulating religion and prayers in the elementary schools. I supported the new legislation that favoured providing religious education within the framework of the school. Although the law spoke of this education being Christian, since Christianity is the state religion, I received assurances that minorities would be given the right to educate according to their religion, on condition that sufficient pupils would request this.

I am in the minority of Jews on this issue. In my opinion, it is better for us that the non-Jews receive a Christian education than not to receive an education about religion or ethics. As Abraham said to Abimelech: 'Surely there is no fear of God in this place, and they will kill me' [Genesis 20:11]. All this is conditional, of course, that the Jewish students will not participate in these classes.

Did the initiative for this legislation come from the Church?

No. But it was very active in this direction. I also took part in this and insisted upon the rights of the minorities. Additionally I participated in the issues of fertility treatment and artificial insemination. The debate centred on the question of the permissibility of conducting experiments on foetuses. I opposed this if these are experiments for their own sake, although in principle I do not oppose medical experimentation. For example, in the case of patients suffering from a hereditary disease, it would not be possible to find a cure without genetic experiments that would prevent such illnesses. In other words, in order to save life, it is permitted, in my opinion, to conduct experiments on foetuses. The question also arose, whether it is permissible to register children conceived using artificial insemination with the name of their non-biological father. Parliament voted in the affirmative. I opposed this, since it would not be possible afterwards to know the identity of the child's brothers and sisters. This was the first time that Parliament adopted a bill according to which official documents would knowingly contain false information.

Are there major differences between the stance of Judaism on this issue and that of Christianity?

Yes. For example, regarding artificial insemination from a stranger: Judaism opposes this, and it unquestionably opposes the registration of such children with the name of their non-biological father. This is a lie! The identity of the father **must** be known, in order to prevent incest. This is also true of medical experiments; the purpose for which they are conducted is significant.

You mentioned legislation regarding war criminals.

This subject came to England on the initiative of the Simon Wiesenthal Center in Los Angeles. I was not enthusiastic about it and would have been happier if the issue had not been raised. It is difficult today to find witnesses to events and crimes that occurred over half a century ago. Look what happened in America, in Canada, in Australia and also in Israel! There is a danger that this may be counterproductive. Since, however, the issue came to England and the government supported the bill, it was passed in Parliament by a large majority. In the House of Lords, in contrast, the majority opposed it on technical – not moral – grounds, and the bill was defeated. The bill was returned to Parliament, where it nevertheless passed, and it is now the law of the land. Despite my apprehensions, I spoke and voted twice for the bill. I said that I was not so interested in finding these criminals, but rather that the law would accuse them and pursue them for all eternity.

There also were debates on granting residence rights in England to immigrants, and I participated in these as well. The subject of *shechitah* [the ritual slaughtering of animals for kosher meat] was also discussed. One member of the House of Lords, from the Royal Society for the Prevention of Cruelty to Animals, opposed the slaughtering of animals without first stunning them. The *poskim* [deciders of Jewish law], however, oppose this for various reasons. This issue had begun in Germany, a few months after the Nazis took power. At that time it was my father, in his capacity as head of the rabbinical court, who was involved in the controversy, both in the exchange of letters with the leading Torah scholars of the time – headed by Rabbi Hayyim Ozer Grodzinski – and in the conducting of experiments in Holland, to establish if the animal became non-kosher (by causing a hole in the membrane enveloping the brain) as a result of the electric shock. My arguments were accepted in England and *shechitah* is permitted there, in contrast with Switzerland, Sweden and Norway, where Jewish *shechitah* is prohibited and the Jews must import kosher meat from other countries. I argued in the House of Lords that those who are concerned for animals (causing distress to animals is forbidden by the Torah) usually make light of human life, as was already expressed by the prophet Hosea: 'They that sacrifice men kiss calves' [13:2]. Thus, Cain refused to offer a sacrifice from his flock but he did not refrain from killing his brother Abel; so too in Egypt, where 'all shepherds are abhorrent to Egyptians' [Genesis 46:34], thousands of Israelite children were drowned. In Germany they protected the animals against the 'cruelty' of *shechitah* but killed millions of human beings in the gas chambers and the crematoria.

Are you given the right to speak in the House of Lords on any issue?

If there is an ordinary debate (second reading), one must sign up the day before and then a lottery is held to determine the order of speakers. The first to speak are from the government, who are then followed by members of the opposition. In the debate regarding war criminals, for example, 80 speakers were registered and I was number 18. One may speak for a quarter of an hour, and those present may interrupt. The members of the House of Lords do not have to be re-elected, since they are peers for life, and therefore they can address the issues directly; this is not so in the lower house, where the debate is more unruly. Consequently, the discussions in the House of Lords are always on a higher level. All the participants are experts in their fields, and the lower house generally accepts the changes proposed in the House of Lords and prepares a bill accordingly. The members of the House of Lords also are entitled to introduce and renew legislation, but this is a lengthy procedure. Sessions are held five or six times a week, Monday to Friday, corresponding to the sessions of the lower house. The first session of the House of Lords each year is opened by the Queen, and the deliberations in Parliament begin at the same time. This is not merely a matter of ceremony; these rules afford stability to the country and an attitude of civility towards tradition, in which the English take much pride.

If a referendum were to be held today on the question of cancelling the monarchy, would there be a majority for this?

Certainly not. What will be in the future? I do not know.

11 *Leaders and Heads of State*

'Gorbachev is the only individual who had such decisive influence in the twentieth century, by bringing about the liquidation of Communist rule in the USSR and its satellites.'

Did you have interesting meetings with national leaders?

In 1964 I met with President Lyndon Johnson in the United States. A programme for Jewish institutions to receive support from the American government was on the agenda. Mr Zeev Wolfson dealt with this; he organized a religions delegation to attend a kosher reception in the White House. I took the opportunity to read to Johnson the prayer for the welfare of the President. He was unaware that people prayed in synagogues on his behalf. By doing so, I sought to bring to the President's attention the fact that Jews have a religious attitude towards the government.

I also had an interesting meeting in my home with the Dalai Lama. He visited London, and asked to meet with the religious leaders, including me. He insisted that the meeting take place without the presence of any women, not even my wife. Although he is a person of simple ways, he came with a large army of attendants. He was certain that he would return to Tibet, which has not been the case to the present. He naturally favoured peace and interreligious understanding, and revealed understanding of and sympathy towards Judaism.

In addition I participated in a conference in Moscow organized by Mikhail Gorbachev. Half of the participants were members of Parliament, and the other half were religious leaders. I fit into both categories, as a rabbi and as a member of the House of Lords. The venue of Gorbachev's concluding address was the Kremlin, close to the Sabbath. We were about 30 rabbis and other observant Jews, including Rabbi Arthur Shneyer from New York, Rabbi Moshe Rosen, the Chief Rabbi of Rumania, and the Chief Rabbi of Russia, Rabbi Shayevitz. We found a place to pray [the Friday evening service of] *Kabbalat Shabbat*, with much singing, within the walls of the Kremlin. This naturally received wide coverage. It seems to me that not even during the time of the Tsars did anyone dream that the time would come when Jews would pray publicly in the Kremlin!

Did you meet Gorbachev?

Yes. A year later I received an honorary degree from Bar-Ilan University, at the same time as Gorbachev. On this occasion I reminded him of that conference. Gorbachev delivered an outstanding speech then. In my opinion, this was one of the most important documents of the twentieth century, but the newspapers here [in Israel] are not cognizant of spiritual processes, and did not grasp the significance of this. 'We erred', he said, 'when we declared, as Communists, that religion is the opium of the masses, since society cannot exist without religion and without religious sentiment.' This was almost the speech of a penitent. In my opinion, Gorbachev is the only individual who had such decisive influence in the twentieth century, by bringing about the liquidation of Communism in the USSR and its satellites.

When did you first visit the USSR?

In 1975, after the Helsinki Conference, when détente reigned in the world. The Soviet authorities sent to me a Jewish Communist professor who wanted to meet me. He told me that we have to see that there is detente with the Jewish people as well, that reciprocal visits should be arranged and, accordingly, 'the Jewish community there would be pleased if you were to accept their invitation to visit the Soviet Union'. This was obviously done with the knowledge, or even under the supervision, of the Soviet authorities, and certainly with their consent. Since I was the first Chief Rabbi in the West to receive such an invitation, I replied that I would have to think about the matter. Already at that point, however, I added that I would accept the invitation only on condition that I would be able to see whomever I wished to visit. I consulted with several organizations and leaders in Israel, and also Rabbi Soloveitchik in America. In London and in New York I was told that I should accept the invitation – which I did – and only the Israelis were hesitant. I accepted the invitation, on my terms, that included the possibility of meeting with refuseniks. When I informed the professor of this, I did not receive a clear-cut answer. Some time later, however, I received an official invitation which I accepted.

I went with my secretary. When we arrived in Moscow we were greeted with great respect and a suite in the Russiya Hotel, the largest hotel in the world, was placed at our disposal. My itinerary included visits to the Jewish communities in Moscow, Leningrad and Kiev;

meetings with the heads and members of the communities; and also with members of the government and local officials.

Immediately after our arrival in Moscow, we met in the hotel with the leading refuseniks, and especially with Professors Ashbel and Lerner. We talked in Hebrew and in English. They said that they were waiting for exit visas. They didn't exhibit any fear at all and when I hinted to them that perhaps we should be careful about what we said, they replied: 'We know very well that everything that is said is recorded, but we want things to be heard.' They were in favour of clamorous propaganda on behalf of Soviet Jewry, and they demanded that I continue with this.

My itinerary also included visits to Russian Orthodox religious institutions in Leningrad and in Zagorsk (the Russian Orthodox Vatican, about 25 kilometres from Moscow). I also insisted that I would travel to Leningrad and to Kiev by train and not by aeroplane, so that I could gather an impression of everyday life. They agreed to this, and sent with me, as a 'watchman', the head of the Moscow Jewish community. I was given a sleeping car, next to which was some literature and newspapers, where I found a small pamphlet in German about Birobidzhan. I read it and discovered that it was 'Paradise' there. Following the visit, upon our return to London, I met with the First Secretary in the Soviet embassy. His first question was: 'What about the little pamphlet on Birobidzhan?' It obviously had been placed there intentionally, because they assumed that I would look at the only booklet that was in German and not in Russian.

In Leningrad I was received by the heads of the community and also by the refuseniks, who asked me to deliver a lecture in the scientific seminar that they had organized. When I told this to the heads of the congregation, they were not enthusiastic about the idea. They placed at my disposal an official vehicle, and wanted me to visit the cemetery, as well as the memorial to the victims of starvation during the war. This was a gigantic monument, as big as a football pitch. I agreed, but I insisted that I also visit the homes of the refuseniks. They travelled with us, and this was the first time that the heads of the community met with the refuseniks. They hardly wanted to talk to each other, since each was regarded as a traitor by the other! The heads of the community spoke in Yiddish, and the refuseniks in English or Hebrew, and I was the 'intermediary' between them. When the ice had been broken, the refuseniks also invited the community heads to come to their homes. They accepted the invitation, and they saw how the refuseniks were learning Hebrew and singing Jewish songs which made a great impression upon them. On our way back they thanked me profusely for this.

In the morning, I was told that we were to have returned to Moscow on the night train, but that they had not succeeded in obtaining reserved tickets. They therefore asked me to remain in Leningrad for the Sabbath, especially since 'the Jews there would be very happy to see me'. They knew fully well that I had arranged meetings on Sunday with refuseniks in Moscow, and they wanted to prevent these meetings from taking place. I told them that this was not possible, and I suggested that we call the British consulate in the city to make arrangements. Half an hour after this 'proposal', room on the train was suddenly found ...

In Leningrad I also visited the seminary for Russian Orthodox priests, and I had a lengthy conversation with the director of this academy. I asked him how it was possible to live a religious life in Russia. He answered by saying that everything they did was with the permission of the authorities. He said that about 800 students were studying in Zagorsk and in Odessa, even though the studies for the priesthood took eight years! They asked me if I wanted to meet some of them, and I naturally said I would. With the aid of a Russian interpreter, I spoke about the unity between us as the children of one God and about religion as a moral force. I asked if any of them spoke English. I was answered that there was one young man who did, from one of the Mediterranean countries. He came over to me and said that he held an Israeli passport. It transpired that he had been born in Greece, had studied in a Christian seminar in Jerusalem and engaged in additional studies in Leningrad. This was the only Israeli I met during all my trips to Russia.

I found that members of the Russian Orthodox religion in Russia enjoy much greater freedom than the Jews, and that they even publish a serious religious journal. I mentioned this to the president of the Leningrad Jewish community, and I asked why the Jews do not demand equal rights. He responded to this: 'The authorities will probably not agree.' I told him that in my meeting with the head of the Ministry of Religions I would voice the demand that the Jews be given the opportunity to publish a journal of their own, but then he tried to be evasive and claimed that, 'we don't have any writers'. I said that I would find the writers, to which he replied: 'I don't think that the attempt will succeed.'

I was in Moscow on the Sabbath. In the synagogue I was not told until the last moment whether I would be allowed to deliver a sermon, although they knew of my coming and there were more worshippers there than was usual. Before I left London, the representatives of 17 Jewish youth organizations in England gave me a document containing greetings to the Jewish youth in the USSR. They asked me to find an opportunity to present the document, and I brought it to the synagogue on Sabbath eve and I concealed it. The next morning, in the middle of the service, Rabbi Fishman came over and invited me 'to say a few words' to the congregation, which numbered close to

1,000 people that Sabbath. I regarded this as a great moment, to say something to the Jews. A few weeks before the visit I had already asked myself what I would talk about. This was the Torah portion of *Miketz*, and I mentioned the episode of Joseph and his brothers. His first words to his brothers, whom he had not seen for decades, were: 'Is my father still alive?' I asked what is significant about this. My response to this followed: The first question of Jews who were distant from one another for a long time, is: Is **that** father, as I remember him, still alive? I came, I said, to see if the Father who unites is still alive in your midst and in your homes. I added that according to the law in the *Shulchan Aruch*, the response to every good tiding is the '*Shehecheyanu*' blessing or the '*Ha-tov veha-metiv*' [who is good and does good] blessing, while for bad tidings one says, 'Blessed be the true Judge.' The *Shulchan Aruch* adds that there are instances in which the two blessings are recited together. For example, if a person's rich father died, he recites, 'Blessed be the true Judge' for the death and 'Who is good and does good' for the inheritance. The *Magen Avraham* commentary adds here that, 'one who was compelled, due to his poverty, to marry a rich woman who did not arouse him recites, "Blessed be the true Judge" for the woman, and "Who is good and does good" for her wealth.' I said to my audience that on my visit to Russia I recited the two blessings: 'the true Judge' for the terrible destruction of Jews and Judaism that I saw and the 'Who is good and does good' blessing for the miracle that once again in Russia there is the aspiration to live as Jews and to immigrate to Eretz Israel, with unparalleled self-sacrifice. When I finished, after about half an hour, I presented to the head of the community the document that I had received in London from the Jewish youth there, and I asked him to give it to the representatives of the Jewish youth in Moscow.

On Sunday I visited Zagorsk, the repository of the treasures of the Russian Orthodox Church, where there are wonderful cathedrals in which many choirs chant. They seated me at a pulpit, where it was difficult to leave in the middle of the service, apparently so I would cancel my visits to the refuseniks in Moscow later that afternoon. Specifically for this reason, however, I cut the visit short, and they had no choice but to return me to Moscow. Anatoly Sharansky was also present during one of the classes with the refuseniks. Years after his arrest and following his release, he said in an interview in the *Jerusalem Post* that from my lecture he had heard for the first time in his life that there is such a thing as medical ethics in Judaism. His wife Avital visited our house in London several times during her campaign to free her husband.

In Moscow I also met with high officials of OVIR, the department in the Ministry of the Interior responsible for exit permits from Russia. I gave them lists of refuseniks who had been waiting to leave for years and they assured me that they would take care of the matter. They added, however, that this processing would take about five years, which was the case. I also met with the Deputy Minister of Religions, who also promised that the authorities would be lenient concerning the religious and cultural situation of Russian Jewry. In practice, however, I did not discern significant changes in the years following my visit.

We travelled from Moscow to Kiev. When we arrived, I saw that the pressure on the Jews there was much more severe than in Moscow and in Leningrad. I met the leading refusenik there, who was an active and loyal Jew. Of course, my itinerary also included a visit to Babi Yar. In preparation for this visit they took me to a school of the arts, where I met the person who planned the memorial in the Vale of Slaughter. I asked him how the Jews were memorialized in the statue. He said that at the top of the monument is an allusion to the Jewish victims. You see there the figure of a woman with her baby, and the woman is breathing her life into the baby. He added that they received the idea for this from the Vatican, where the *Pieta* statue (in which Mary is holding her son Jesus) is on display, and this is a symbol of Judaism ... I must note, however, that a special additional statue was later erected to commemorate the murder of the Jews. When I recently visited Kiev, I was told by the local rabbi that several weeks before the liberation of Babi Yar by the Russians, the Germans had brought thousands of workers to the site, in order to burn the bodies of those who had been murdered so that no traces of what had happened there would remain. There was a large flood in 1962, and many skeletons were washed up there.

On the last day of my stay in Moscow, one of the old people came to me in the synagogue and said: 'I have two questions for you. First, there is a great hue and cry among you, that they let us go to Eretz Israel. We, however, cannot leave, because we live in a Communist country, and flight from it is regarded as treason. You in the free world, on the other hand, may immigrate to Israel without an exit visa and without fear of being exiled to Siberia. Why don't you immigrate to Eretz Israel?' I answered him: 'I do not have an answer but I will pass the question on to Jewish communities in the Free World' – as I subsequently did in four continents. His second question was: 'At present, many Jewish tourists from Western countries visit us, but when we honour them by calling them up to the Torah reading, they don't even know the blessing! You demand that we be given permission to educate our children in the spirit of Judaism, and it is known that we live under a regime that denies every religion. But why don't you yourselves ensure Jewish education for your children?' To this as well I responded that I did not have an answer. I mentioned these questions in many speeches that I delivered in subsequent visits all over the world.

In 1993 I visited the former USSR once more, going this time to Minsk and travelling from there to Vilna, Volozhin and Radin. In Volozhin the Jews received from the authorities the building of the *yeshivah* [in which Bialik had studied]. Only about 25 Jews remained in the city, and in Radin only a single Jew was left. The building of the formerly renowned *yeshivah* there is now used as a town hall. We also visited the home of the Hafetz Hayyim, which was very neglected. The non-Jews who live in it still remember something about 'Rabbi Israel Meir'. Recently we European rabbis travelled once again to Kiev upon the invitation of the rabbi of the city, Rabbi Yitzhak Bleich from New York (who is a Karlin-Stolin Hasid). We were about 15 rabbis from Europe and Israel (including Rabbi Yisrael Lau [the Chief Rabbi of Israel] and Rabbi Simhah Kook of Rehovot). In conjunction with our visit about 35 heads of Jewish communities in the Ukraine also arrived. For the Sabbath we went to a summer camp, where there were 250 youths. From our conversations with them, we learned that only a small portion of them think about immigration; the majority to Germany or America, and only a minority to Israel. According to them the situation of the Jews has improved compared with the past. At present a Jewish school with 600 pupils functions in Kiev, and is recognized by the state which supports the institution. The level of Jewish studies there may be compared with that of good Jewish schools in the West. Likewise in Berditchev, there is a *yeshivah* today. In addition to religious studies, they also learn Hebrew there, with emphasis placed on Eretz Israel studies. In Russia today there are circles that reveal great self-sacrifice on behalf of Jewish education.

Do you foresee a future for Jewish life in Russia?

Certainly. It is correct that there are great dangers, but there are tens of thousands of Jews who must not be neglected. Obviously, efforts must be taken to persuade them to immigrate to Israel, but at present we are obligated to ensure that they will live there as Jews. It appears that even the number of Jews in the former USSR is much higher than we had thought, and may possibly go as high as five million people! Experience has proven that only those who have received some sort of Jewish education in Russia, and who aspire to live as Jews in the full sense of the word, will immigrate to Israel instead of remaining there, because they want a Jewish environment. This reason is stronger than material security and social happiness, but does not apply to the many who will stay there.

It is no secret that there is a severe problem of intermarriage among immigrants to Israel from Russia. What is the solution to this problem?

To the extent that it is possible to convert them, this is being done. Halachically speaking, there is some relief regarding their Jewishness, because they did not marry according to Jewish law in Russia. There-fore they may be permitted to remarry without a proper Jewish divorce and without fear of the *mamzerut* [the status held by the children from unions which could not be sanctioned by Jewish law] of their children. Nor are they required strictly to observe the 613 commandments, but rather they must have a knowledge of the main principles of Jewish belief. Most rabbis make do with this. When I was in Russia, I was happy to see rabbis from the Jewish Agency also dealing with spiritual absorp-tion, and not only with the subject of immigration. My friend Mendel Kaplan, the Chairman of the Jewish Agency Board of Governors, who himself is a traditional Jew, also is active in this direction.

Are you optimistic?

Yes. Patently, most of them will not be pious Jews, at least not in this generation, but in America the losses are even greater. More than half of the marriages of Jews there are mixed, and there is a danger that within two generations Jewry will almost vanish there.

Are you pessimistic regarding the future of Jewry in the Western world?

My prognosis is that at present we are losing large numbers of Jews and the number of Jews is decreasing, but the qualitative part of the Jewish people is increasing in a manner unparalleled in Jewish history. The demographic increase of observant Jews is six times that of the others! Eventually, 'the Eternal One of Israel does not lie' [I Samuel 15:29], and within a few generations we will once again grow, numeri-cally as well.

There is no danger that there will be a falling away from the religious and ultra-Orthodox circles as well?

There are no indications of this at present. To the contrary, they are getting stronger. I am certain that in the future the religious and ultra-Orthodox will constitute the majority of the Jewish people. Also possible is that there are prospects today that a synthesis will be found so that all those who wish to live as Jews in the modern world will be able to do so successfully.

12 Notable Personalities in Israel and throughout the World

'I heard from Nahum Goldmann that if Ben-Gurion had taken his advice and waited with the establishment of the State, he [Goldmann] would have effected a reconciliation between the Jews and the Arabs, and the State of Israel would have been established without a war.'

Did you meet with Israeli government ministers?

I met with almost all the Prime Ministers, from David Ben-Gurion (with whom I spoke in New York) to Yitzhak Rabin, with whom I had many contacts in Jerusalem and in London, both in writing and orally.

At the beginning of the Lebanon War I had an interesting and very polite conversation with the Prime Minister, Menachem Begin, of blessed memory. He held rabbis in high esteem, and I had already met him in London. Begin received me in his office very hospitably. He brought a map of Eretz Israel and showed me how small and narrow the country is (as if I did not know this …).

We spoke then about the terrorists possessing tremendous quantities of weaponry that were capable of destroying Israel, and about the incursion of 40 kilometres into Lebanon. I accepted this argument and I even appeared on television and in the press along this line. Afterwards, however, when things developed beyond this and the response of the entire world became very hostile (including among the Jews), I also began to have doubts, especially after the Sabra and Shatilla incident. The President, Yitzhak Navon, proposed the establishment of a commission of inquiry into this matter then. I wired him my thanks for his proposal. Until then, I had not come out in public against the Israeli government, but rather against the religious circles who express uncompromising positions on peace and the territories. I wanted to show that there are also moderates among Torah Jews

Earlier I had also met with Golda Meir. She was interested in our educational enterprise, and I wanted her to support us. In a banquet in the synagogue, in honour of the 'Prime Minister's Delegation', Golda said, among other things, that despite her not being religious, she supports religious education, so that the youths will at least know what they reject! ... This aided me in my activity among my congregants. Generally speaking, however, I was not an admirer of her policy. She may possibly have brought a disaster upon us in the Yom Kippur War, and missed a golden opportunity to make peace. Golda Meir had declared that she was willing to talk on any subject with the heads of the Arab states, 'without any preconditions', but she immediately added: on condition that Jerusalem is not for discussion, and that the borders will remain as they are. Notwithstanding this, Golda was a very interesting individual. She had more charm than Dayan. When she died, a memorial service was held in London, and Mrs Thatcher, who was the head of the opposition at the time, was present during the eulogy I delivered.

Did you meet Moshe Dayan?

Yes, and in 1977 I wrote him a personal letter in which I noted that, as I saw the situation from afar, Israel's main problem is the Palestinians, and without a solution to this issue, the question of Israel's relations with the Arab states also would not be resolved. I asked him: Why don't people think to cede most of the territories conquered in 1967, on condition that this would be preceded by a period of between five and ten years, in which normal relations would be in effect with the Arab states and with the Palestinians? If it would transpire, as a result of this, that there was a possibility of coexistence, the territories would be given to them, with border adjustments, obviously with the demilitarization of the territories. At any rate, I wrote, we must make the offer and assure them that the possibility of coexistence exists. I did not receive any meaningful response from him.

How did Dayan impress you?

In 1973, several months before the Yom Kippur War, I came in a delegation of the leaders of English Jewry, and Dayan was one of the government ministers who spoke with us. His statements on the security situation ruled out the possibility of the Arabs attacking us, because of the strength of the IDF. 'They don't even dream of this,' he said. The impression I gained of him was that finally, here was a true hero and we spoke to him with great respect. Shortly afterwards, however, we saw how greatly he had been mistaken!

After the Yom Kippur War (and also in the summer of 1994), I also met with Rabin. I told him that the struggle for the physical power of the state was not sufficient, there was also a need for a spiritual struggle, which would centre around the goal of Israel's existence. However I did not receive a meaningful answer from him. I wanted Rabin to understand the danger of assimilation, and be sure that he would be sensitive to this, so that he would say, especially to the Orthodox, that he too was aware of this threat and feared it, but I doubt whether I was successful in this. He lived in a totally different world. I said to him that I was one of the few Orthodox rabbis who fundamentally supported his policy line and hoped and prayed that he would succeed, despite my doubts and worries. As is well known, the great majority of the Orthodox, especially the religious parties and the [Israeli] rabbinate, oppose his policy, and those not in opposition are hesitant to express their views publicly. This is so even though in the past the Mizrachi, Agudath Israel, and the Chasidic rabbis were always moderate in matters pertaining to politics, even on the question of the partition of the Land of Israel.

What explanation is there for this?

I have no explanation for this turnabout. Nonetheless, I must state that they do not oppose the government for religious and moral reasons, but out of nationalist fanaticism. They argue that we cannot rely upon Arafat, and Israel will have no security if there is any surrender of even a single step from the country's borders, as if they, as observant Jews, are greater experts on the security of the State than the leaders of the government and the army! Moreover, they fear that after the establishment of peace, there will be increased alienation from Judaism, because they believe that the aim of Zionism is to be like all the peoples. Indeed, it will be more difficult to be Jewish here, under assimilatory conditions. Let us not forget, however, that we have not suffered for thousands of years so that we will possess what every other people has. If we do not have the ability to make a unique contribution to humankind, perhaps we should truly say that the end has come, and we will assimilate among the other peoples.

I also met with Peres. I tried to find channels to him as well, but he was not attuned to Jewish matters, which was not the case with Begin who possessed the soul of a Jew. He told my brother-in-law, Rabbi Fabian Schonfeld that he became the outstanding disciple of Jabotinsky because his father, who lived in Brisk, once saw a Russian soldier beating the local rabbi, and in response he struck the soldier. When Begin asked his father, 'How do you dare? They will kill us!' his father replied: 'They will kill us, and then we will die for the Sanctification of the Name of God. This is what Jews have done in all generations.' Since then, Begin maintained that only by force is it possible to defend the Jewish people, and the honour of the rabbi is so great that it is necessary to die for the Sanctification of the Name of God.

I also met with Shamir in London, but I was not overly impressed by him.

Who, among the many notable individuals with whom you met, did make an impression on you?

I was close to Sir Isaiah Berlin, of whom it was said that he was the 'foremost brain' in England. He visited our house several times and made a great impression upon me. He possessed profound under-standing and far-reaching vision. Berlin was one of the few who sup-ported me throughout my term in office as Chief Rabbi in England. He wrote to me, on his initiative, and congratulated me on my positions on political matters, and even wrote an introduction to my English book, *Zionism in My Life*. He truly was an outstanding individual. His historical understanding was enormous, and his writing was excellent.

In contrast, I also heard Chaim Weizmann deliver a speech in London, but I was not especially impressed, especially since his book *Trial and Error* contains slurs against faithful Judaism, which I did not like. When Weizmann testified before the Peel Commission, he said that the Bible is our mandate over Eretz Israel. He, however, did not believe in the Bible as a divine source, but rather viewed it as a historical narrative. If so, of what significance is this? It is shameful that he imposed on the non-Jews a religious obligation in which he himself did not believe!

You mentioned that you met with Ben-Gurion.

Yes. When I was in America, but I did not have the opportunity to engage in a meaningful conversation with him.

Were there Jewish Members of Parliament who made an impression?

I had known Emmanuel Shinwell, who had been Minister of Defence in Britain. Lord Young, the Trade Minister, who was very close to Mrs Thatcher, also was an important person and we regarded his opinion highly. Thatcher writes in her book that there were Jews in each of her Cabinets, because she sought ministers blessed with intellectual ability and influence. The present Foreign Minister is Malcolm Rifkind, a traditional Jew who comes to the synagogue on the Sabbath.

Is it not true that the non-Jew usually thinks that the Jew, because of his Jewishness, is smarter than he is?

This is a myth in which many believe, especially in business affairs, and also in the realm of science.

Who were the people in the world of Torah who made a special impression upon you?

It is impossible to draw a comparison between leading Torah scholars and Jewish scientists, and obviously they cannot be compared to the leaders of the non-Jews. Among the great Torah scholars, I will mention Rabbi Joseph Baer Soloveitchik. I knew him well, and during my time as a rabbi in New York, over the course of eight years, I attended most of his public lectures. I found him captivating. I also met with him personally, and I asked his advice, for example regarding my first visit to the USSR in 1975. Some argued that the Soviets would take advantage of this visit for their own purposes, and the visit would thus prove to be counterproductive. In Israel as well there was opposition to this visit, while Rabbi Soloveitchik told me then that I had to go, albeit with certain conditions. He advised me to impose a condition on the USSR authorities that I could meet with whomever I wished. He was very worried by the clamorous anti-Soviet propaganda from the Jewish communities in the Free World, and feared that this would harm Soviet Jewry and USSR–American relations. He was of the opinion that we Jews, as a small people, should not provoke the superpowers.

Soloveitchik was an individual totally immersed in the world of Torah. He was an outstanding individual, but it was difficult to be close to him in personal matters. He was blessed with vision encompassing broad horizons, and many times saw phenomena that escaped the eyes of others. He was not always right, but there were no rabbis like him in our generation. His influence was very great, and to this day he is extensively cited, everywhere.

While still in Dublin I was closely acquainted with Rabbi Joseph Kahaneman of the Ponivezh *yeshivah*, as well as his wife and son. He was a wonderful and broad-minded person. Practically speaking, he was the father of the *yeshivot* in Eretz Israel after the war. When I contended that *yeshivah* students are not interested in communal life and do not want to be rabbis, he told me that I was right, 'and I too am pained by this, but what can I do? I don't have the strength to swim against the present-day current.' Thus he argued against those who opposed flying the State flag in the Ponivezh *yeshivah* on Israeli Independence Day. He held the view that the State has religious significance, and that we should at least be thankful for having been able to establish a *yeshivah* such as Ponivezh, after it had not been possible even to think of such a thing after the destruction in Europe. Rabbi Kahaneman was a very sensitive person and he let you feel as if you were his son. His behaviour drew you very close to him. When he was in our home, I would accompany him when he left, but then he would always walk me back to my house!

I also met Rabbi Menahem Kasher, the author of *Torah Sheleimah*, and I was very close to him. He was my guide in matters in the rabbinic literature with which I had difficulty. Once I received an invitation from the organization of plastic surgeons in New York to deliver a speech on cosmetic surgery according to Judaism. The chairman of the organization said in his opening remarks that it sometimes happens that a woman comes to him and asks him to refashion her nose, so that she will have a Liz Taylor nose … In another instance, someone asked for surgery on his nose. The surgeon asked him: 'Why? Your nose is perfectly all right.' To this he answered: 'I am not Jewish. I have a Jewish girlfriend whom I want to marry, but her parents are opposed because I don't have a Jewish nose.' I came to Rabbi Kasher and said that I could not find any sources, not even responsa, on this subject, and I asked for his advice. He responded immediately: 'In my *Torah Sheleimah* there is an unattributed midrash that asks why Abraham, who observed the Torah in its entirety even before it was given, did not circumcise himself prior to the giving of the commandment of circumcision.' The answer was that the implementation of such an operation without being so commanded harms the act of Creation, and man is forbidden to cause damage to himself. Consequently, in the absence of a commandment, and with no obligation to undergo plastic surgery, it would seem that it is forbidden to perform such an operation. I said in my lecture, that if a person had been in an accident that disfigured his face, then it was permitted to correct the flaw, as part of the process of his healing, and also if his livelihood were dependent upon this. A woman, so that she will find a husband and so that she will be a good-looking bride, also is permitted to undergo such surgery. An operation for beauty for its own sake, as both Joseph and Absalom did when they curled their hair, on the other hand, is forbidden.

Dayan Yehezkel Abramsky was also close to me. He was a very impressive individual. When you were near him, you felt that you were in the presence of a great person. You could not ignore him. I heard several lessons that he gave, and I remember that when he delivered a new teaching that he liked, he always said that he first told it to his wife, and she would say, '*Dos shpilt vi a fidl* [This plays like a violin].' He elevated the status of the rabbinical court in London to a world centre, until it became the most prominent court throughout the Diaspora, and in several matters it even surpassed the rabbinical courts in Eretz Israel. There were matters in which he was lenient, while he was stringent in others. For example, he was lenient regarding the kashrut of gelatin that was made from animal bones. On the other hand, on the question of whether it is permitted to conduct a marriage ceremony for someone who is not circumcised, he responded negatively, assuming that this refusal would cause the person to undergo circumcision. He also was stringent in accepting prospective converts. He took an interest in general studies. I was privileged to receive from him the last best wishes for the New Year that he wrote before his death. I was told this by his son, Professor Shimon Abramsky, when he concluded the *shiva* [mourning week].

I will also mention Rabbi Aaron Kotler, whom I visited several times. He was the first link in the chain of the renewal of the *yeshivah* world and Orthodoxy in America. What Rabbi Joseph Kahaneman did in Eretz Israel, with the establishment of the Ponivezh *yeshivah*, Rabbi Aaron Kotler did in America, with the founding of the Lakewood *yeshivah*. Without him, Orthodoxy in America would not have got to where it is today. I went to see him several times. For instance I consulted him about the construction of an *eruv* [a legal 'wall' permitting carrying on the Sabbath] in downtown Manhattan. There was a serious disagreement on this question at the time. Rabbi Kotler opposed the construction of the *eruv*, while I was of the opinion that an *eruv* should be built for Manhattan, to make life easier for the elderly and for young couples with children. Rabbi Leo Jung also held this opinion, and was the chief spokesman in favour of the *eruv*, and in his old age he did indeed establish it. Rabbi Menahem Kasher, the author of *Torah Sheleimah*, also supported this. Rabbi Kotler, in contrast, had reservations, because, in his view, all large cities now have the status of a public domain, by force of Torah law. When I asked him: 'Then why are there *eruvin* in all the cities in Israel?' he responded that he doubted whether one could rely upon these *eruvin*. Nevertheless, he told me that he would not take part in the propaganda against the *eruv*.

I also visited Rabbi Moshe Feinstein many times. He too was involved in the *eruv* controversy. He had written in the *HaPardes* journal a few years ago that although he personally opposed the construction of an *eruv*, those who ruled leniently could find support for their position. Then one day I received a telegram in his name stating that it is definitely prohibited, by Torah law, to establish an *eruv* in Manhattan, which surprised me. I went to him, showed him the telegram, and asked if this was really his opinion. It transpired that he knew nothing about the telegram, which had been sent in his name … This is what people do there!

I experienced something similar many years later. In 1980 I spoke about peace between Israel and her neighbours, even at the cost of a compromise and a withdrawal from the territories. The extremists attacked me, accompanied by slurs and falsifications, and they wrote in the *Jewish Press* as if I supported a Palestinian state with Jerusalem as its capital. They even 'quoted' strong protests against me in the name of Rabbi Joseph Baer Soloveitchik and Rabbi Moshe Feinstein (I know who fabricated the 'quotes'). I knew that these rabbis were more moderate than I was, and I turned to them, to discover what they had really said. Rabbi Soloveitchik told me explicitly that he had not even heard about the declaration by me, and that he had said nothing. Furthermore, he added that I must continue to speak and make my views public, without paying attention to the critics. In a conversation with my son Yoel, Rabbi Feinstein spoke in a similar vein. Thus hatred can spoil things and lead to lies and falsifications.

Rabbi Eliezer Silver also should be mentioned. He considered himself to be the Chief Rabbi of America, even though there is no such position. It was said that at a border crossing between the United States and Canada he was once asked who he was by the customs officials and his secretary answered that he was the Chief Rabbi of America. Silver heard this and added, 'Of Canada too.' He truly was a rabbi – and not a *yeshivah* head – who properly saw life as a whole. He deserves to be mentioned in the same breath as Rabbi Leo Jung, who already was a friend of my father, and he installed me as rabbi of the Fifth Avenue Synagogue in New York. I also knew rabbis Lookstein and Belkin, the heads of *Bar Ilan* and of Yeshiva University in New York.

What about the Lubavitcher Rebbe?

The Lubavitcher Rebbe was a constant visitor to the home of my wife's family in Paris during his studies there. When we met in New York, he mentioned my father-in-law. I went to him several times for *yechidus* [personal meetings], and he even met with me at nine o'clock at night, making an exception to his usual practice of receiving people at midnight. After I was appointed Chief Rabbi in England, my wife received an invitation from his secretary to come to a meeting with him, with no reason given. When she went, the Rebbe told her that he had heard that our eldest son Yoel, who was studying at the time in the Ner Israel *yeshivah* in Baltimore, wanted to study medicine. He wanted to deter him from doing so, on the grounds that at present there is a danger in non-Jewish studies, especially in medicine. He consequently advised her to have a heart-to-heart talk with him, to persuade him not to study medicine. My wife said: 'But the Rebbe himself studied in a university!' He replied to this: 'Times have changed.' (Nevertheless, our son came to London, studied medicine, and returned to be the physician of the Ner Israel *yeshivah*.) He also wanted her to give me a message concerning my rabbinical career and that I should stress educational matters. In fact, I spoke in support of Habad institutions and their activities on five continents. On matters concerning Eretz Israel, on the other hand, we parted company. Some of his views seemed strange to me. Thus, as I have already noted, on the question of 'Who is a Jew', there may never have been such aggressive propaganda in the Jewish world as on this question. Habad emissaries were always present in meetings of European rabbis. They had been sent to exert pressure so that we would support the position of Lubavitch, but I always opposed this. In the end, the entire matter was forgotten.

What about Jewish scholars?

Among Jewish scholars, I will mention Martin Buber. Once I listened to a lecture of his in London. I had heard a great deal about him, but I was disappointed. I am distant from his 'dialogue' and his 'I-Thou' (or, in the language of the rabbis, 'I and Him', based on 'This is my God and I will glorify Him' – Exodus 15:2).

I was more impressed by the Jewish historian Salo Baron, the author of the monumental work, *A Social and Religious History of the Jewish People*. I held him in great esteem. He and his wife were guests in our home in London once. I found much wisdom and discernment in his writings. He writes, for example, at the beginning of his work that all the holidays in the Torah are properly observed to the present, but *Rosh Chodesh* [the beginning of the Jewish month] has been virtually forgotten, although this was a very important date in the time of the Bible, as it is written: 'And on your joyous occasions, your fixed festivals and new moon days' [Numbers 10:10]; 'It is neither new moon nor Sabbath' [II Kings 4:23]; 'Your new moons and fixed seasons' [Isaiah 1:14]; the banquet given by King Saul in honour of *Rosh Chodesh* ('Tomorrow will be the new moon' – I Samuel 20:18), and other passages. Baron explains this as follows: all of the holidays, such as Passover – the festival of Aviv [i.e. spring], Shavuot – the harvest festival and Sukkot – the festival of ingathering – were initially connected with Nature. As time passed, when we parted from our soil, these holidays acquired a historical coloration and became 'the time of our freedom', 'the time of the giving of the Torah', and just 'a remembrance of the exodus from Egypt'. Because of this, they remained living and have been preserved to this day, which is not the case for *Rosh Chodesh*, which is dependent solely upon Nature and the cosmos, and therefore has almost been forgotten and has practically disappeared. The same is true of Jewish history: if the Jewish people had been subject to the rule of Nature, like any other people, we would have vanished long ago, in accordance with natural law. But in the constant struggle of history with Nature, Israel has prevailed and has remained in existence, like the festivals. Inherent in this struggle is the key to the secret of Jewish survival: history vanquishing Nature.

Among the other prominent people in the world whom I knew well was Lazarus Goldschmidt, the translator of the Talmud into German, who lived towards the end of his life in London. He told me once that he would burn the concordance to the Talmud that he had composed, with more than a million entries, if he would not receive the proper sum for its publication (the concordance appeared only in part, in Copenhagen).

I likewise once heard a lecture by Dr Isaac Breuer, in which he declared that the Mizrachi transgresses 'You shall have no other gods beside Me', because it affiliates itself with both the Torah and Zionist camps. For some time I was also a constant visitor in the home of *Morenu* (a rabbinical title conferred on him *honoris causa*), Jacob Rosenheim, the president of Agudath Israel, when he lived in London. He was an eminent leader, in both Torah and general knowledge.

I was also well acquainted with Nahum Goldmann, who was a Jewish statesman of the first order after the war. I heard from him that if Ben-Gurion had taken his advice and waited with the establishment of the State, he [Goldmann] would have effected a reconciliation between the Jews and the Arabs, and the State of Israel would have been established without a war. He founded several important international organizations, including the World Jewish Congress and the Claims Conference, based on an agreement between him and Chancellor Konrad Adenauer of Germany. In this manner Goldmann received hundreds of millions of marks, that were paid to individuals whose possessions had been stolen, to communities that had been destroyed and to the State of Israel. When I was asked if such reparations are justified, and should be accepted according to Torah ethics and law, I replied that these monies do not belong to the Germans, but rather to the Jews, and the command 'he must return the stolen article' [Leviticus 5:23] must be fulfilled, with this restored to its owners. Nonetheless I added, the Jewish people would pay a stiff price for accepting the monies. Once I said, in Goldmann's presence, that while the Germans contribute to the Jews, the Jews give to the Germans by enabling them to win recognition in the world, despite their crimes.

In recent years I heard Goldmann when he spoke – almost as a repentant – with special esteem for faithful Judaism. In a public dialogue with me in London, he said that, in his opinion, only the Orthodox Jews would remain in the future, due to their strong sense of mission and their high birth rate, in comparison with the other portions of the Jewish people. When it was my turn to speak, I asked him: 'If you really believe that and I have heard you state this before, then why don't you conduct yourself in accordance with the *halachah*, observe the Sabbath and put on *tefilin*?' Goldmann answered: 'You are right, but what can I do? I don't have any religious belief, and without it one cannot be observant.'

His argument is valid and he, numerically speaking, represents the majority of the Jewish people at present.

This is correct, but he admitted that in the future I will be the one who will represent the Jewish people, and I already see this now with my own eyes, for example in America. Most American Jews are assimilating. The families are too small and mixed marriages are increasing at a rapid pace. On the other hand, the religious and the ultra-Orthodox in America – and in Israel as well – are growing rapidly. Consequently, I have no doubt that, in the final analysis, we will live as Jews. Moreover, the ultra-Orthodox also will change their ways. The moment that responsibility for managing the country and the army will fall upon them as well, they will be forced to contend with the need to maintain ties with the world at large. The primary goal of the Jewish people is to be an instrument with which we will show to the entire world the moral path, the purpose of life and the right road. The Holy One, blessed be He, said to Abraham: 'all the families of the earth shall be blessed through you' [Genesis 12:3], which was his task as the first Jew, even before he entered the Land. This was reiterated by the prophets, who also assigned to the Jews a special role in the history of humanity. If we abandoned this purpose, perhaps it would be preferable if there were no Jews. In the final analysis, who will cry if there will be no Jews left in the world, unless we still had something unique to contribute.

Two great writers, both in the religious camp, were my faithful friends: Herman Wouk, who was one of the founders of the Fifth Avenue Synagogue in New York, and Eli Wiesel. Wouk told me once that he wrote his book about Judaism, *This Is My God*, as a sort of atonement for his novel *Marjorie Morningstar*, which is an extremely secular book.

I knew Eli Wiesel well in America, through a mutual friend, Herman Kahan of Oslo, one of the leaders of the community there, who was with Wiesel in the extermination camps. Both of them came from Sighet in Hungary. In Oslo Kahan was close to the people who decided upon the awarding of the Nobel Peace Prize. I wrote a number of times to the prize committee and recommended Wiesel as someone worthy to receive the prize. In response to my invitation, Wiesel came to London twice as the guest of honour of the Jewish Education Fund that I established, mainly for the construction of schools, thus aiding us greatly.

13 *Religion and State*

'The Chief Rabbi of Israel, Yisrael Lau, told me explicitly that he was a government official, and he could not freely express all his views.'

Where are there greater chances for Jewish life – in the East or in the West?

In the meantime, certainly in the West, and especially in Israel, in which the productive force is much greater. I will mention, for example, the major encyclopaedias. This is also true in the realm of Torah novellae. On the other hand, this is not original literature, as it had been in the past. The ultra-Orthodox circles today have their reservations concerning a new approach. At present there are no movements of renewal such as Hasidism, the *Mussar* movement and the *Haskalah* movement, which left their mark on the history of the Jewish people. My teacher, Professor Isidore Epstein (of Jesus College in London), once explained to me the difference between ultra-Orthodox Jews and their opponents now, as compared with the situation in the Middle Ages. When the Karaites disagreed with Rabbanite Jews and did not accept the Oral Law, they produced many important works of their own. The entire fields of philosophy, grammar, poetry and history were completely new realms for the Rabbanites, created as a response to the Karaites in their dispute with them. The same held true even earlier. The Talmud is, to a great degree, a response to the teachings of the Sadducees, who did not accept the Oral Law. The need arose then to strengthen the Oral Law, by means of the Talmudic literature. Today, in contrast, there are no new creative works in the Torah world, as a response to the new situation. Rabbi Samson Raphael Hirsch and also Rabbi David Tzvi Hoffmann, in their struggle against Reform Judaism, may possibly have contributed something in this area. At present, however, the spring has run dry, and we are causing a great loss within the Jewish people.

If so, then you are in favour of the seclusion of the ultra-Orthodox from the other groups within the Jewish world?

There are reasons to fear the encounter of the ultra-Orthodox world with the outside world, and we must take them into account. In my opinion, this is still a result of the great disaster that occurred in the Holocaust. Faithful Judaism lost about 90 per cent of its adherents, and the others 'only' a third. Those remaining accordingly considered themselves obligated, first of all, to rehabilitate their world. Another cause can be explained by the law of Isaac Newton, that for every force in Nature there is an opposite force of the same strength. The secular force, which consists mainly of life without morality and without values, has led to the creation of a counterforce of even more pious life. One must know and understand the causes, and thereby interpret the rising streams in our day, directions the likes of which did not exist in the past, in both camps. There obviously are reasons why the majority of Jews in Israel are not observant, but not enough is being done to study and understand the situation.

What do you think about the religious parties?

When I was in Kiev not long ago, I met with the Chief Rabbi Yisrael Lau and we discussed the issue of the territories and peace. Rabbi Lau told me explicitly that he was a government official, and he could not freely express all his views. Such a situation in which a rabbi cannot express his opinion on matters that pertain to his work is impossible, and is incomprehensible to me as a rabbi in the Diaspora. I have declared many times that a rabbi or the rabbinate, or even all of faithful Jewry, must choose one of two possibilities: to attain influence or to win power. The rabbinate in Israel has much power, from the State and by force of law: in matters of *kashrut*, personal status laws and so forth, I, in contrast, as the Chief Rabbi of the British Commonwealth, have no power. If someone does not desire to accept my rulings, for example, in matters of personal status, I cannot impose my decisions on him, and he has alternatives, with the Reform or in civil marriage. On the other hand, I do possess influence. The Jewish leadership in England consulted with me on everything, even on topics that do not directly bear upon the rabbinate; for example, on everything pertaining to the attitude towards non-Jews and towards the royal family. I also have marked influence in educational matters, and concerning the curriculum in the Jewish schools. In Israel, in contrast, it is difficult to indicate any influence in these spheres. Consequently, it is not possible to attain both power and influence, and a choice must be made between them. I am of the opinion that the Israeli rabbinate would be much more influential if it did not derive its power from the government.

If so, you support the separation of State and religion?

When we examine the history of our people and how things have developed, we see, following Nachmanides, that the Hasmoneans were the first to join religion and state together – by uniting the monarchy and the priesthood – which was contrary to the spirit of Judaism. So, already in our ancient history we find a precedent for this current-day issue. The question arises: in order to acquire influence, must we seek a place within the establishment or not? In the early days of the State, it may have been necessary for the religious to participate in the establishment – in the government and the Knesset, in the special [religious] parties – in order to fight for achievements in different realms, especially on the issue of education and religion in the army and similar matters. But this has turned on us. In my opinion, the leaders of religious and ultra-Orthodox Jewry should now waive their status as separate parties, with the aim of there being religious representatives in every party, thus enhancing religious influence in the Jewish society in Israel. Under the present situation, that of the existence of religious parties that struggle to conquer new positions of power, widespread circles are apprehensive, if not afraid, of religious coercion. Many have no desire to live in a country that is foreign to them, and fight for their rights.

In present-day Israel, putting on *tefilin* is a political act, and not a religious one. The person who puts on *tefilin* is perceived as a member of some religious party, and the secular therefore feel that they must oppose the putting on of *tefilin* for political reasons. Already years ago I wrote – and it still seems to me – that the influence of faithful Jewry upon the Jewish society at large in Israel would be much stronger without the religious parties. Then politics would not be intertwined with religion. I patently do not oppose a Torah state, but this goal will not be attained by means of religious parties. I do not want to separate Judaism from the State, but Judaism from partisan politics. I greatly fear that despite a rise in the strength of ultra-Orthodox Jewry, this will prove to be counterproductive. The influence wielded by religious figures will not expand in the future, but hatred towards them will increase.

You sound as if you support the arguments of the secular!

My feeling is that the secular as well are in a state of crisis at present. Their philosophy and world view that Eretz Israel is merely a political refuge for the members of the Jewish people, possessing no spiritual mission, is bankrupt. They too sense that something is lacking. People are searching, but they find no answer among the religious circles, because they regard these as a power that threatens them. If we would take pains to ensure proper education, things would be different. Today, most of the children in the State of Israel have never prayed and have never seen a prayerbook with their own eyes. They are totally alienated from all the sources of Judaism. We brought here much more of Jewish life in the Exile than we export at present from Eretz Israel to the Diaspora. In the Diaspora, in contrast, every child who is within the system of Jewish education receives some religious education.

The 'match' between religion and State is therefore, in your view, a curse and not a blessing?

I believe that this 'match' is bad for both sides. Both religion and politics are corrupted. The loss for politics is that the small parties – generally the religious ones – enjoy power and influence far beyond what they deserve on questions such as the formation of the government and its policy, similar to the healthy cows that were swallowed by the thin cows in Pharaoh's dream. This gives rise to the charge of religious coercion that is responsible for animosity towards both religion and the religious. Faithful Jewry itself, on the other hand, suffers in that most of its forces are directed to political disputes and deals, in which its people certainly possess no greater expertise than the members of other parties. Then, what will be the fate of the Torah? I do not refer solely to Torah study, nor even to the normative observance of the commandments; rather I speak of spiritual values, of raising the level of society and the environment from the filth that have adhered to them, and of integrity and broad-mindedness, to the extent that there will not be anyone without merit, and 'there is no righteous one who does not accept the truth from whoever utters it', as Maimonides writes in his introduction to the tractate of Avot.

The ultra-Orthodox subscribe to the view 'I have saved myself', with society at large being of no interest to them.

This was the way of Cain, who said, 'Am I my brother's keeper?' but we must be responsible for each and every Jew, because the future of the people and the State is dependent upon this. If the ultra-Orthodox will live their lives and the others will live theirs with no contact between the camps, then I greatly fear for our future, in terms of the State and in terms of Judaism. If the ultra-Orthodox behave in this fashion, 'for this I weep'. This is not Jewish life when people say, 'I have saved myself'! According to my philosophy of life, I am responsible for every Jew, wherever he is, and I am obligated to find some connection to him and to influence him. It is true that the ultra-Orthodox built here a network of *yeshivot* and Torah centres, but they have also lost a great deal. Based on what they have established, they should take an additional step forward, not necessarily by means of the religious and ultra-Orthodox parties.

Would you recommend a single educational trend, in Israel, in place of the general state education and the religious state education?

In principle, I support this approach. Every Jewish child is entitled to receive religious-spiritual education. Those who are desirous of more intensive Jewish education must be given the opportunity. A single general system should be founded, with different trends, including one for reinforced religious studies. At present, the lives of most children in the State of Israel are no different from those of a non-Jewish child in the West. The dress, the music, the dances – all are the same!

Jews in Israel argue that, abroad, religion is what separates the non-Jew from the Jew, while in Israel Jewish nationality is sufficient, without a religious component.

I have heard this argument, but I do not accept it. I believe that 'from Zion Torah will go forth'. It is from here that influence must be exerted on all the Diaspora communities. The prophets already warned against any tendency to 'let us be like all the peoples'. The prophets of Israel have a place in world culture, but nothing remains of the works of the kings of Israel! There is a danger at present that our return to the homeland and the formation of a Jewish society, not only on the basis of a Jewish state, but rather with leadership and government without Jewish content, will lead to a situation of 'the House of Israel like all the peoples'. If we will follow this path, there is a very great danger to the future of the country; nor will the non-Jews accept such a state of affairs. We will not succeed in maintaining a state of Canaanites here. In other words, the fact that we live in Eretz Israel is not sufficient to transform us into a people. If this will come to pass, the link between the Jews of Israel and the Jews of the entire world will be severed; nor can Israel survive without ties with world Jewry.

We must impart to the world values that are essentially Jewish. From my experience and from my meetings with government officials from different countries, I know that they think of the Jews as a spiritual force as well. Thus, for example, after I came to England to accept the position of Chief Rabbi, I participated in a reception in the course of which someone who worked in the Foreign Office came over and told me that he had had a hand in the drafting of the Balfour Declaration.

I asked him what the British government had thought at the time: was the Declaration issued only on the basis of political calculations or was there also a religious motive at work? The British are known to appreciate the Bible. His answer was: 'Certainly! The Bible was the main point!' On another occasion, when I was on one of my speaking tours in America, I spent a Sabbath in Kansas City as the guest of Rabbi Morris Solomon, who was close to Truman. He asked me if I wanted to visit the Truman Library in Indianapolis, Missouri. I answered in the affirmative and we went there. There was an exhibition there of all of the gifts that Truman received while president, including a Torah scroll that he had been given by President Chaim Weizmann, next to a bust of Weizmann. Rabbi Solomon told me: 'In the first years of the State [of Israel], I received a request from Member of Knesset Rabbi Shlomo Lorenz to arrange a meeting with President Truman for him. The meeting was held in the White House, with Rabbi Solomon translating. During the meeting, Lorenz noticed the bust of Weizmann on the President's desk. When he asked Truman about this, the latter told him that he had received the bust as a present, and he decided to place it in the Oval Office, since it reminded him of a Jew in Independence, whose house he had entered every Sabbath as a *Shabbas goy*, to turn on the light on Friday night. Truman added that he had great respect and esteem for that Jew. During this meeting, Lorenz further asked the President why the United States had decided to recognize Israel on the day it came into being, despite the opposition of his advisors. Truman replied: 'That day I thought that Divine Providence had commanded me to complete the Balfour Declaration.'

Years later, Sir Geoffrey Howe, the British Foreign Minister at the time, visited our home in London. During the meal I asked him: 'As Foreign Minister, you conduct negotiations with many governments. Is Israel something special for you or is it just another country?' He looked at me wonderingly and said: 'I was born in Wales and in my childhood I knew only two maps: the map of Wales and the map of the Holy Land, and I obviously cannot act towards Israel like any other country!' We see from these incidents that the non-Jews sense that the State of Israel is not just one more country, like all the other countries. Furthermore, not only do they want us to be different from all other countries, they also demand this of the leaders of Israel. If we do not regard this as a vision that we inherited from the prophets – even if the vision will come to pass only in hundreds of years in the future – then how can we win recognition from the non-Jewish nations?

Today, the religious circles and their leaders lack a prophetic element regarding what happens in the world and in Israel. As in the words of the prophet, 'what the Lord requires of you: only to do justice and to love goodness, and to walk modestly with your God' [Micah 6:8] in the realm of morality; 'for I desire goodness, not sacrifice' [Hosea 6:6] on the relationship between the rite and its place in society; or 'Zion shall be saved by justice' [Isaiah 1:27] and 'Not by might, nor by power, but by My spirit' [Zechariah 4:6], regarding the conquest of the Land. Today it is the religious, more than others, who believe that the country's security is dependent upon the location of the borders and the strength of the army. On the verse, 'The sceptre shall not depart from Judah' [Genesis 49:10], Nachmanides comments that this was the punishment of the Hasmonean kingdom, whose heads fell by the sword of their enemies and the entire dynasty was extirpated, because they were both priests and kings. They thereby transgressed the rabbinic injunction, 'priestly kings are not to be anointed', because the crown of Torah and the crown of kingship are distinct, and political power and the rule of the Torah are not to be intertwined.

14 *The Rabbinate in Israel*

'The average rabbi must possess knowledge and learning in both worlds.'

If you were given the opportunity to found a rabbinical seminary in Israel what, in your opinion, should be the curriculum of such an institution?

Emphasis must unquestionably be placed on the students being at home in both worlds. Rabbi Soloveitchik told me once, in regard to the expression '*Ramatayim Tzofim* [Ramathaim of the Zuphites]' [I Samuel 1:1], from where Samuel the prophet came, that these are two mountains somewhat distant from one another. Nevertheless, the Jew must feel at home on both, even if they cannot be joined. He thereby disagreed with the author of the teaching 'Torah with *derech eretz* [i.e. secular education]', Rabbi Samson Raphael Hirsch, who thought of a **synthesis** between the two worlds. According to Soloveitchik, we should not seek a synthesis between the two, but one should be familiar with both worlds.

First, the rabbi must patently be a Torah scholar, and a *posek*, at least on matters concerning his community, and not only in matters of the *Yoreh Deah* [one of the books of the *Shulchan Aruch*], such as *kashrut*; especially so, since nowadays most rabbis do not encounter this, since the meat comes from the butcher already koshered. On the other hand, there are questions relating to prayer, the Sabbath, holidays and mourning, and he must display expertise in these areas as well, and not solely in pure Torah scholarship. The rabbi must be erudite and at home in matters of Jewish law but he must also learn Jewish studies, such as Jewish history, Bible commentaries and literature and philosophy, such as the *Guide of the Perplexed*, the *Kuzari* and other such books. Besides this, if he wishes to be a rabbi and guide for the confused in his congregation, then he must be familiar with science and politics also. A rabbi who is also a professional in a non-Jewish field, such as non-Jewish literature, history, law or even medicine is to be preferred; in my opinion, he is not only capable of finding solutions to problems that arise in the halachic realm, he will also demonstrate to all that there is nothing that is totally alien to the Jew. I once heard from my brother-in-law, Fabian Schonfeld, that according to the rabbis, 'it is permissible to engage in non-Jewish studies only at an hour that is neither day nor night', for it is said regarding Torah study, 'but meditate in it day and night' [Joshua 1:8]. Since, however, we live in confusion today, in a time that is neither day nor night, from a point of view of ethics, morals and standards, it may very well be permitted to study other matters, and not only at twilight.

Does this include other religions?

I am not speaking about other religions but rather about non-Jewish knowledge to which we must relate. If we wish to receive under-standing and esteem from laymen and from the university-educated young, this will not be possible without knowing what is happening with them and their intellectual world. Patently, some will concentrate and specialize in only one realm but the average rabbi must possess knowledge and learning in both worlds.

What institution do you see in your mind's eye as a model?

The rabbinical seminary in Germany, and possibly also Yeshiva University in America and perhaps also an institution such as the Harry Fischel Institute in Jerusalem. It also may be that studies in a rabbinical institution should be combined with university studies.

None of this exists today in Israel!

Accordingly, in practice, no rabbinate exists in Israel as it is known abroad, where there is a bond between the rabbi and his congregants and he is their advisor. If it were not for this lack, the Jewish community in Israel might possibly be more open to Jewish matters. Nonetheless, I am certain that things will develop in this direction in the future.

We have been promised that we will arrive 'to the resting place and the inheritance' [Deuteronomy 12:9], even though these two things are presumably contradictory. If we want an inheritance, we do not find, in the annals of our people, rest; and if we desire rest, it would seem that we will not attain our inheritance. Once there was a Jew who had two daughters, one named Menuchah (rest) and the other named Simchah (joy). After years had gone by, the daughters married. Simchah had a child every year while Menuchah was barren. The father said about this: 'From Simchah I have no rest (*menuchah*), and from Menuchah

I have no joy (*simchah*).' The Jew must choose between joy and rest. Most Jews select the latter, so that they can live in peace, but there are some who do not seek rest, but rather joy. This is so in Eretz Israel as well.

If so, why don't you seek joy and try your hand at establishing a rabbinical institution in Israel in accordance with your philosophy?

There are many difficulties involved in this. At my age, I am no longer certain about this. Many before me tried and were unsuccessful. The leading Torah scholars opposed this. If I were to see that conditions were ripe for this, then, together with others, I would join such an undertaking, even if it were to face opposition, but I don't see that the conditions for this have been created. In the meantime, there are rabbinical seminaries abroad. I encourage such a direction and position in Israel, but 'the work is not for you to finish' [Avot 2:16].

Let us turn to another subject, one that pertains to the Diaspora. In your opinion, is it impossible to cancel the second Festival day of the Diaspora?

To the contrary, today, more than ever, there are reasons to maintain the second Festival day of the Diaspora. First, this gives some special sort of honour to Eretz Israel, as if we were to say: 'If you want one holiday, move to Israel.' In the Diaspora, however, where we live in a non-Jewish environment, we need more of our own holidays as a response to the surrounding world. A double portion is necessary in order to attain the same goal. Second, it should be recalled that those who live in the Land of Israel enjoy extra sanctity. Centuries ago it was already possible to find an allusion to these calculations, that inspiration is greater in the Land of Israel than in the Diaspora, and one Festival day in the Land of Israel attains the same sanctity as the two days in the Diaspora.

How do you personally conduct yourself when you are in Israel?

Each time that I came I asked the opinion of the Chief Rabbi in Jerusalem, Rabbi Kolitz. He ruled that I must observe the stringencies of both places: that is to say, not to pray in the synagogue, so as not to shame the holidays, but neither to put on *tefilin*. Even though I do not recite the weekday prayer, I do not recite *Kiddush* on the second Festival day. This is how I act, even though I have doubts concerning these practices.

As long as I am not a permanent resident, I find myself in 'no man's land'. Every time that I come to Israel I hope that the day will come when I settle here for good, and then this problem will be resolved. At present this is still not a viable option, among other reasons, because I am a member of the House of Lords and I do not desire to waive this position, since it is of benefit to the community and to the Jewish people as a whole, and I can influence public life in general.

In your opinion, should the division caused by two Chief Rabbis serving in Israel be continued?

It is my view that each group maintain its version of the prayers and its customs. The midrash on, 'Who split apart the Sea of Reeds' [Psalms 136:13] states that each Israelite tribe had its own passage. The *Magen Avraham* on the *Shulchan Aruch* comments on this that whoever has a fixed custom must maintain it, and this is so at present as well. I think that this contributes to the vitality of the people, despite the differences of opinion. During all times, from the days of the Bible to the present, there have been different streams in Judaism. On the other hand, there must also be uniting components shared by all Jews wherever they are. In London the Hacham is the religious head for the Sephardim and the Chief Rabbi for the Ashkenazim, with each responsible for his community, unlike the situation in Israel. Here the two rabbis are responsible for the entire public, and this is a source of dispute because 'two kings cannot wear the same crown'. Nonetheless, it is good that there are two rabbis – the Sephardi and the Ashkenazi – as long as each serves the members of his community.

Do you think it would be a good idea to have a Chief Rabbinate in America?

Yes, but it is too late to institute this. There is no possibility that such an institution would be accepted. The rabbi's power is derived from the members of his community and if they oppose such an institution, it would have no possibility of acting. American Orthodoxy is divided, and I do not see any practical possibility for this. An attempt was made in this direction in New York when Rabbi Jacob Joseph was accepted as Chief Rabbi of the city, but this attempt also failed. There was a proposal in the nineteenth century to appoint Meir Loeb ben Jehiel Michael Malbim as Chief Rabbi in America but by the time the conditions were right for this, Malbim had passed away. Almost at the same time, in 1844, Rabbi Nathan Adler became Chief Rabbi in England. Rabbi Samson Raphael Hirsch had also been a candidate, one of four in the running, but was not accepted. Cecil Roth wrote in one of his essays that if Hirsch had been selected for the post in London, and likewise if Malbim had been appointed Chief Rabbi of American Jewry, how different the course of Judaism would have been in the English-speaking world!

What is the level of contact between the Chief Rabbi in England and the Jewish communities in the other member states of the British Commonwealth?

I visited almost all the communities in Australia and New Zealand. Once I had a *din Torah* [case tried by *halachah*] by facsimile communication concerning a dispute between a rabbi in Sydney and the members of his congregation. There also was a controversy regarding the *eruv* in Melbourne in which I intervened and eventually prevailed (today there is an *eruv* there). Queries from individuals and from rabbis there were also directed to me. Before I replied to them, I usually consulted with the members of the Beth Din in London.

Are there pronounced, major differences between Australia and South Africa and its Jews?

South Africa was never formally affiliated with the rabbinate of the British Commonwealth, but I also had close ties with the rabbinate there, which is constructed in a format similar to that of the British Commonwealth. In Australia and in South Africa there are a Chief Rabbinate and rabbinical courts, and they widely use the prayerbook as we do in England. In Australia, relations between the Sydney and Melbourne communities are tense. The Sydney community is closer to the English pattern, because the first Jews there came from England. In Melbourne, on the other hand, most of the Jews trace their origins to Eastern Europe, and they therefore have a different approach. Organizationally, nonetheless, they are similar to the communal structure in England. Most of the Jews in South Africa are of Lithuanian descent, but the Chief Rabbis came from England.

Is there a noticeable difference regarding intermarriage?

Unfortunately, the numbers are equalling out of late. The percentage of intermarriage there comes to about one-quarter, half of the accepted figure in America.

Are you optimistic regarding the chances for survival of the Australian and South African communities?

I have no doubt that they have a future, because established Jewish day schools are active in both places, to a much greater degree than in England. In England, 30 per cent of the children attend Jewish schools, while 90 per cent of children do in Australia and South Africa! The schools there are at the centre of Jewish communal life. The number of Jews in Australia has grown in recent years, while in South Africa there is a general problem of immigration, due to the change in government. I was also in Wellington, New Zealand, where 2,000 Jews live – out of the 5,000 in the entire country – and they told me that 10 per cent of them came from the former USSR and are not absorbed in the Jewish community.

There also is a problem regarding education for immigration to Israel!

There certainly is opposition by a portion of the parents, but we found a balanced solution. There are realms in which the Diaspora influences Eretz Israel, because the rabbis in the former have greater influence than in Israel, and obviously Eretz Israel exerts an influence upon the Diaspora. In my opinion, as long as one needs the other and they are dependent upon each other, we will be one people. The moment that Israel will be independent and the Diaspora communities also will no longer be dependent upon Israel, a danger will arise of our being two peoples, because the interests – apart from the religious sphere – will be different.

In your opinion, are the ties between Israel and the Diaspora strengthening or weakening as time passes?

They are weakening, although we cannot make generalizations. Identification with Israel rose when the State was endangered but today, when there is perceptible stability, the link no longer is so close. On the other hand, many more Jews visit Israel at present, in comparison with the past. Young people and youth groups have programmes for visits and studies in Israel, and these programmes expand from year to year. The number of *yeshivah* students from England who study in Israel also has increased so that ties have been strengthened, but trends of alienation also are discernible. A polarization process is occurring, and it is increasing among all parts of the Jewish people.

15 *The Faith of Judaism*

'Faith will come from the act; true faith from a profound sentiment and from inner sight.'

It is said that rationalism is the greatest enemy of Judaism. Do you agree with this?

I do not accept this hypothesis. It is not rationalism, but rather paganism and secularism in the form of materialism that are the primary enemy of Judaism. Humankind at present possesses no spiritual vision. The goal is to live, with the slogan, 'eat, drink and be merry, for tomorrow we die'. I have stated many times that, according to Judaism, we do not live to have a good time but to make the times good. On Rosh Hashanah we do not ask for a 'happy year', but a 'good year', and good is a moral concept. A people and society that lack such a vision do not have an assured future. In the words of Proverbs: 'For lack of vision a people perishes' [Proverbs 29:18]. Even in the State of Israel there will be no stability if we do not remain faithful to this vision.

Perhaps the tactics of the ultra-Orthodox world, that flees from and opposes the outer world, proves that Judaism in its traditional sense is not capable of contending with the outside world?

I have already stated that I regard the current tactics of the ultra-Orthodox world as something temporary, that is based on logical reasons. After the Holocaust, the ultra-Orthodox remained as a small part of the Jewish people and they lived in surroundings far removed from the environment in Eastern Europe from which they had been uprooted. They feared that they too would assimilate and be lost, like the majority of those who came from the east and settled in the Western countries in the nineteenth century. Those remaining therefore concentrated upon the renewal of their world. Today, it must be admitted, they have succeeded in this in an outstanding manner! Forty years ago, no one could have imagined that ultra-Orthodox Jewry would rehabilitate itself to such a degree. In the Mir *yeshivah* in Jerusalem, for example, about 1,600 students learn! In the past, not more than 300 students had been in Mir. The ultra-Orthodox have attained such accomplishments only because they concentrated on the building of their world. The time will undoubtedly come, however, when they will feel sufficiently strong and confident to contend with the non-ultra-Orthodox Jewish world, and even with the non-Jewish world. Maimonides states in the Laws of Repentance that a person should always regard himself and also the entire world as if half meritorious and half liable. If he performs a single commandment, he tilts the entire world to the side of the scale of merit, or the opposite. I once asked about this passage: Didn't Maimonides remember a verse that explicitly contradicts this? In his dialogue about the destruction of Sodom, Abraham argues with the Holy One, blessed be He, and asks: 'Suppose ten [innocent people] should be found there?' [Genesis 18:32]. We learn from this that ten people are capable of saving an entire city, even if half the inhabitants do not turn the scales to the side of merit. I answered: Ibn Ezra, on this same chapter, states: 'If I find "in Sodom ... within the city", I will forgive the whole place for their sake.' In other words, if this is done in secret and the righteous person enwraps himself in his own cloak, then half the population, or humankind, is needed to save everyone. If, however, the good deeds are done in public, 'within the city', then ten righteous ones will suffice to save all of Sodom with its wicked people. The question is not whether the ultra-Orthodox are a majority or a minority, but rather if there are ten righteous ones who influence the entire community 'within the city', publicly. At present, unfortunately, they do not even seek influence in this spirit, but the time for this will undoubtedly come.

My apologies for the direct question, but what is your belief?

Regarding Nahum Goldmann's claim that he had no religious belief and therefore could no longer put on *tefilin*, I would say to him, if he were not so very old, that doing for the sake [of the commandment] comes from performance not for the sake [of the commandment]. Faith will come from the act; true faith from a profound sentiment and from an inner sight. I was privileged to grow up among believers, and faith was almost self-understood for me. But the gates of repentance are open to all.

Consequently, Judaism is more a way of life than belief?

Belief is not expressed solely in the observance of the commandments. I once heard my teacher, Rabbi Eliah Lopian, who was a master of *Mussar* [ethical teachings], speak on the verse, 'what the Lord requires of you: only to do justice and to love goodness, and to walk modestly [literally "in secret"] with your God' [Micah 6:8]. He interpreted this as follows: when the hypothesis of the existence of a Divinity is accepted, the Holy One, blessed be He, gazes upon a person even in what is concealed, in the innermost chambers. The main component of faith is not in its public expression, but in man's inner feeling. The question is, whether man senses that there is a Divinity and knows that he will have to give an account of his lifetime, every year or at the end of his life. In other words: man is not abandoned and he must justify his creation, based on the assumption that there is a Master of all creation. We accordingly recite on Rosh Hashanah: 'Today is the birthday of the world, today all creatures of the world will stand in judgment.' Because man was created, he must stand in judgment and fulfil the will of his Creator. When a person finds a shell on the seashore, he does not ask why it is of such and such a shape. He accepts this as a fact, that after thousands of years this is its shape. If, however, he were to find a clock, he will certainly ask who made it and for what purpose was the clock and its hands made? It is inconceivable that the clock created itself or was created with no purpose. So, too, regarding man: with the awareness that he was created above all other creatures, he must give an account to his Creator.

Do you regard Divine Providence as a personal matter for every individual human being?

Yes, but reward and punishment belong to another category. I accept that there is no reward or punishment for **individuals** in this world. As the rabbis formulated this: 'There is no reward for [the observance of] a commandment in this world.' That is to say, when we recite in the *Shema*: 'If, then, you faithfully keep … you shall eat your fill. Take care not to be lured away … and you will soon perish from the good land', the reference is to the people as a whole. As *Rashi* comments on this passage: 'A warning to the public.' Reward and punishment are a communal matter and not an individual one; consequently the analogy was chosen of rain from the sky that descends on both the righteous and the wicked. This is also true for the punishment of Exile, which is decreed for the community and not for individuals. I would add that in every place in the Bible that speaks of collective reward and punishment, the intent is only to Eretz Israel. For example, it states in the reading of the *Shema*: 'So that you … will long endure on the land that the Lord swore to your fathers to give to them', and also in the ten commandments. Later as well, we recite in the prayers: 'Because of our sins we were exiled from our land.' In Eretz Israel we are charged with the responsibility of living as Jews and, if not, 'the land will spit us out'. The responsibility for fashioning the way of our lives falls primarily in Eretz Israel, because in it – and only in it – are we masters of our fate. This is not so abroad, where we are subject to foreign rule.

Is this also your response to the Holocaust?

With regard to the Holocaust, I have no questions against Divine Providence, because all the promises of Divine Providence regarding reward and punishment in this world were given only in reference to Eretz Israel. For example, there were many anti-Semitic persecutions during the Crusades, and these are expressed in *kinot* [lamentations], but these troubles were never interpreted as 'because of our sins', since they occurred outside Eretz Israel. The Jews in the Diaspora did not feel that they were responsible for these actions. In Eretz Israel, on the other hand, destructions were understood as the consequence of idolatry, illicit sexual behaviour, bloodshed, gratuitous hatred and the like. This does not constitute a response as regards the Holocaust, but what happens in Eretz Israel cannot be compared with events in the Diaspora. If every good deed was rewarded in this world, then they would be of no value or merit.

If so, then the answer to the issue of 'evil befalling the righteous, and good being the lot of the wicked' lies in the World to Come?

The answer is that there are righteous whom evil befalls, and this does not contradict my philosophy regarding Divine Providence. This is not a bank in which a sum of money is deposited and from which the money can be withdrawn when the time comes. Nonetheless, I am responsible for all my actions and I will have to account for them, I truly feel this. When the time comes, when my last day draws near and I will be asked if I conducted my affairs faithfully, if I engaged in the commandment to procreate and if I set times for Torah study – I will have to give an answer to this.

And what about the belief in the resurrection of the dead and the advent of the Messiah?

I am not concerned with this. Maimonides already stated that a person should not engage in this. I oppose, and I am afraid of, the Messianic propaganda that is being conducted at present. The internal history of Jewry has known no greater disasters than false Messianism. I do not maintain that, 'Behold, he is right behind the door.' I don't know. Furthermore, the primary belief in the Messiah – which is one of Maimonides' Thirteen Principles – does not maintain that he is already on the way and that he will come at a fixed time. To the contrary! It is said only that we must believe in the advent of the Messiah. The hope that he will come is part of my faith, but the belief that forcing the End of Days will bring him is not based on the teaching of Maimonides, and this is highly dangerous. This is so because, if, Heaven forbid, he were not to come, there would be such great frustration. Who knows what the consequences would be? Accordingly, I therefore keep my distance from such a belief and regard it as entailing serious damage to faithful Judaism. I was recently in Zhitomer, where about 10,000 Jews live at present. The rabbi there is from Chabad, and a large sign hangs in the synagogue there, proclaiming 'Welcome, King Messiah', with a picture of the Rebbe, and I cannot agree with this.

At the time I was quite close to the Lubavitcher Rebbe, but today I have a serious problem with the current Messianic movement that is emerging from Chabad, and I do not know how this happened.

Was this done with the Rebbe's knowledge?

No, I cannot conceive of this; rather his followers are more Catholic than the Pope himself. Nonetheless, I wonder why he did not protest against their activity or foresee where this would lead. Accordingly, I never accepted in the Prayer for the State of Israel the wording 'the beginning of the flowering of our redemption'. I do not know if this is so. This may be stated only after the fact. Generations believed that they were on the threshold of the Redemption, but this did not come to pass. If so, then how is it possible to prophesy and state as a certainty and established fact that this is already 'the beginning of the flowering of our redemption'? In England, I advised those who wanted to adopt this wording to add **'that it will be** the beginning of the flowering of our redemption'.

In conclusion, I believe in the coming of the Messiah but not to the extent that we have already arrived at the End of Days and that we are standing on the threshold of the complete Redemption. I still do not see any signs of this. After the Second World War, when the United Nations organization was established, with the vision of imposing a world morality, a sort of eschatological atmosphere reigned, but it is a fact that we have not reached this and we are still distant from world peace. When the Messiah will come, he will be the Redeemer of the Jewish people and of all humankind. The separation between the fate of the Jewish people and that of humankind as a whole is contrary, in my view, to the vision of the prophets. Every time that they spoke of the Messianic age, they also included the non-Jewish nations in this era. Furthermore, the entire concept of peace is between all the peoples and throughout the world. The statement that the Messiah will come only for us, the Jews, is opposed to the spirit of Judaism, and I cannot accept it. There must be hope for the entire world that the day will come when we will attain life with a purpose: 'In all of My sacred mount nothing evil or vile shall be done; for the land shall be filled with devotion to the Lord as waters cover the sea' [Isaiah 11:9].

How do you interpret the concept '*halachah* [given] to Moses from Sinai'?

Everything is inherent – potentially, if not in actuality – in the Torah from Sinai. If not, this is not Torah, nor is it eternal. There are corner-stones on which the Oral Law is to be constructed. If these codes are observed and are drawn upon, they clearly are part of the Oral Law. The tradition never was static and frozen, but rather dynamic.

When you speak about Torah from Heaven, do you understand this literally?

Yes. But how did things come from Heaven and how did Moses receive the Torah, by dictation or by inspiration? We are not to concern ourselves with such matters (as Maimonides has already ruled). I accept that the source of the Torah is Divine. Otherwise, not only could I not be a rabbi, I could not be a believing Jew. This is among the basic principles of our faith.

What do you understand from the term 'revelation'?

That the Creator of the Universe is not capable of creating mankind without presenting it with a goal of some sorts that is embodied in the question: Why was man created? This purpose necessitates the finding of a way to connect the Creator with humans that is expressed by some form of revelation. How did this happen? This question is not of great importance, but there is virtually no escape from the conclusion – if there is any significance to life – that the Giving of the Torah was an event perceived by the human intellect and that is logical.

Can man reach the conclusion that there is no purpose to life?

If he does, then he is no better than a beast! I don't understand how one can look upon Nature as a phenomenon which has no purpose and no goal. It is difficult to accept the view that the universe was created from itself, as it were, without cause, reason or consequence. My human intellect does not accept the assumption that everything was not created but is instead random. When one sees the wonders of the Creator, as Maimonides formulates this in the Laws of the Fundamental Principles of the Torah, 'he immediately loves, praises and desires to know the great Lord'. Without this, the entire world may be compared to, 'He flies away like a dream' [Job 20:8].

What is your understanding of the expression 'the Chosen People'?

In every place in the prayers in which it is written, 'You have chosen us from all the peoples', it is stated immediately afterwards, 'and You have sanctified us with Your commandments'. That is to say, by our being chosen, more commandments and more obligations are imposed on us, and not more rights that we demand from others. We have never viewed being chosen as being privileged in comparison with other peoples. Thus we also say in the blessing for the Torah: 'Who has chosen us from all the peoples, and has given us His Torah.' Every people must aspire to having a special role in the world. The Romans were given the task of ensuring order and a legal system, and of building roads; the Greeks, of developing philosophy and aesthetics; and in our time, the British and the Americans are the standard-bearers of democracy and parliamentarianism. And just as every individual must say, 'the world was created for me' so, too, each people must set a goal for itself. There is nothing wrong with our regarding ourselves to be 'the Chosen People', because we were the ones who gave to the world the values of monotheism and morality. If we were to claim we deserve more rights because of our being 'the Chosen People', the peoples of the world would be justified in opposing us but we make no such argument. To the contrary! The prophet Amos declares: 'You alone have I singled out of all the families of the earth – that is why I will call you to account ...' [Amos 3:2] – we are the Chosen People in our relationship with the Creator.

But common people understand this as the Jew being essentially better than the non-Jew, standing above other humans.

Even the *Kuzari*, which emphasized the chosenness of Israel, does not claim this.

Even non-Jews say that there is a Jewish genius, and that the Jews are smarter than other peoples!

They think that in certain realms Jews have the ability to contribute something to humanity, and regard the Jewish people as a means to elevate all humankind to a higher level.

All this is true when speaking of the Western world, but most of the world's population today is in Asia, Africa and other places that 'did not know' – and do not know – 'Joseph'. Doesn't this constitute Jewish egocentrism?

We do not represent the majority of humankind, and we have no dreams today that we will attain this. Our aim is not to become the majority of the human race, but rather to hope that the idea of the Oneness of God will be accepted by humankind. The concept of the chosenness of the people of Israel is not to be measured quantitatively, because we are 'the least of all peoples', but we nevertheless have a role and mission to all humankind. The truth is that Jewish influence was mainly upon Christianity, and afterwards upon Islam. Interestingly, both these religions viewed Judaism as the root of human development. Even though the majority of the world's population today is not Christian or Muslim, it cannot be denied that these religions led the world. We too, despite our being a small people, have been greatly influential. There are still Jewish values that have not lost their relevance and it is our task to disseminate them throughout the world. If only the majority of the Jewish people would see this as its duty, especially in the State of Israel, in which it is possible to live according to Judaism, not only as individuals but as a people, and, as a public, to create Jewish life within it. We must not say that after attaining security and a good economic position that we have achieved our goal. I cannot accept this as a Jew and as a rabbi I protest against this.

16 *The Eternal One of Israel*

'We would not have been selected as the Chosen People if we did not have an eternal mission.'

Do you believe with complete faith that, 'the Eternal One of Israel does not deceive' [I Samuel 15:29]?

Certainly! We would not have been selected as the Chosen People if we did not have an eternal mission. History teaches that peoples and empires were destroyed and vanished from the world, leaving no trace, while the people of Israel continues to exist. Thus, for example, a Jew who visits Rome sees the Arch of Titus with its depiction of the Temple *Menorah*, and he knows that the Romans built this arch in order to show the world that once Jews existed in the world. But today, we stand there as Jews, while the Romans are only a chapter in ancient history. Does this not attest to the eternity of Israel? The Nazis also spoke of the 'Final Solution', and began the construction in Prague of a museum that would provide testimony to the fact that once there were Jews in the world. And now, we stand, still alive, on the graves of the wicked.

Do you not see a danger in the creation, specifically in Israel, of a distinction between secular Jewish nationalism and Jewish religiosity?

In order to be a people like all others, there was no need for us to suffer as we did. If this is the goal, what did we gain from the entire experience in Eretz Israel? This alternative was always open to us. The Christians in the Middle Ages told the Jews: Convert and you will be like us, and you will no longer suffer persecutions and discrimination.

They will say to you, we will not be like all the peoples, but like the best among them.

This is impossible, and becomes increasingly evident every day. It is not possible to be more moral than the non-Jews without being more Jewish. Either we will live as Jews and we will find values that we wish to express as members of the Jewish people, or we will be like all the other peoples without any such aspiration, and as time passes not a trace will be left of the people of Israel.

Are you apprehensive that the Jewish people will disappear from the earth?

I am certain that without Torah, we are speaking of the end of the Jewish people. We cannot live as a people without the Torah of Israel. Larger peoples than us have departed from the world without humankind shedding a tear over the loss. Only to the degree that we possess values that are based in Judaism, values that contribute something to the world as a whole, is there justification and recognition – from the non-Jews as well – for our continued existence. It is a fact that the non-Jews, of all peoples, think that the Jewish people has something special to contribute to humankind.

They will say that the Jewish people has contributed to humankind great scientists such as Einstein, but this is not a Jewish contribution to the world. Judaism, as it is at present, contributes nothing to the world!

I therefore say that our contribution is not Einstein. His contribution was that of an individual, and is not related to the fact that he was a Jew. My intent is to a Jewish contribution that will influence all of humankind, in terms of how one looks upon life and its meaning. Consequently, Abraham was already told, 'And all the families of the earth will be blessed through you' [Genesis 12:3; 28:14], which is the entire vision of the prophets. The mission of the people of Israel is to function as a signpost for the whole world. We may possibly have tired of the realization of this vision, but without it, what purpose is there in our continuing as Jews?

Do you really believe that faithful Judaism is capable of assuming this role?

This entire development will extend over time. This is not a question of pushing a button and seeing immediate results. As the eternal people, we have time, even though time is pressing. But this must be our goal and our aspiration. This is Messianism. That is to say, that the Messiah will come and change the life of the Jews and the life of all humanity. This is the vision of the Jewish people. We must devote to this will and thought, so that we will be privileged to see a goal and purpose in life. If everything is limited to the very desire for life and defence of life, of what use is such an existence? At present most Jews think that the purpose of their lives as Jews is the battle against anti-Semitism or the struggle for Israel's security. This is a negative goal. The true question is, what to **do** in life.

Then why don't you regard the State of Israel as 'the beginning of the flowering of our redemption'?

We already spoke of the significance of this slogan. *Vis-à-vis* the State, I am a Zionist. I do not accept the opinion of the majority of the ultra-Orthodox, who attribute no religious meaning to the State. In my view, this is an event caused by Divine Providence. I wonder why the leading Torah scholars at the time of the establishment of the State did not consider this to be a significant event, although one could possibly find a reason for this attitude. *Rashi* comments on the verse, '**This** is my God and I will glorify Him' [Exodus 15:2]: a handmaiden at the Sea of Reeds saw what Ezekiel son of Buzi did not see in his vision. What happened at the Sea of Reeds was a tangible occurrence, and the handmaiden was amazed upon seeing something that exceeded the normal bounds of Nature. The prophet, in contrast, was not moved by this because this was a material, and not spiritual, phenomenon. Afterwards, at the Revelation, it is said about the people that, 'they stood at a distance' [Exodus 20:15]. The people saw nothing but Moses as a prophet saw God face-to-face. Thus it is also at present. What happened upon and following the establishment of the State is mainly in the material realm, and this is still not a Torah state. Accordingly, the leading Torah scholars still cannot say, 'This is my God and I will glorify Him.'

Do you speak with them about this point?

Certainly. I asked them and they argue that until there is the rule of Torah here, they are not certain that this is an instance of the 'finger of God'. They await a spiritual awakening; I myself, however, regard the establishment of the State to be the greatest event in the history of our people after the destruction of the Temple.

How is Israel Independence Day commemorated in England?

The first time that this issue arose, I served as Chief Rabbi in Ireland. I assumed this position in 1949, and the JNF organized a large party, with musical accompaniment, in honour of Independence Day. This was in the middle of *Sefirah* [the semi-mourning period of the counting of the *Omer*], and I still did not want to rule how one should act without consulting with the Israeli Chief Rabbinate. I wrote to Rabbi Herzog (my predecessor) and asked for his advice. He replied that he would bring the query to the Council of the Rabbinate. I received an official answer that the mourning of *Sefirat ha-Omer* cannot be overridden by the celebration of Israeli Independence Day, and that the performance by an orchestra was not to be permitted. Later, in 1967, when I came to London as Chief Rabbi, it was already the accepted practice there to celebrate Israel Independence Day with many participants and accompanied by musical instruments, and I accepted the local practice. For years a festive prayer has been held on this day to commemorate the establishment of the State, in which the leaders of the community participate. I also accepted that the *Hallel* prayer is to be recited. Since, however, Chief Rabbi Unterman ruled that *Hallel* is not to be recited on Israel Independence Day with a blessing, I acted accordingly. On the other hand, he ruled that *Hallel* should be recited with a blessing on Jerusalem Day (Iyyar 28), which was marked by more miracles than Independence Day. I followed this ruling in America.

Do you think that it is possible to run a state in accordance with the *halachah*?

This certainly is not something easy. The *halachah* must be developed, so that it will be possible to apply it under conditions different from what was accepted until now. It is one thing to rule in accordance with the *halachah* for individuals and even for communities, and something completely different to issue rulings for a state. For example, properly observing the Sabbath entails great difficulties, due to the need for essential services. It was generally ruled that, in order to ensure the existence of the people, it is permissible to operate certain services. At any rate, this question must be thoroughly examined and the *halachah* must be expanded in order to provide state-oriented solutions. It is of much greater importance, however, to ask how, in a halachic state, the *halachah* influences topics that exceed the narrow bounds of the observance of any specific commandment. In other words, will all life in such a state really be influenced by the ideals of Torah and Judaism – for example, the entire educational system? Today, unfortunately, a large part of the educational system is run without any reference to the

Torah and Judaism, not to mention the observance of the commandments. The *halachah* is not merely the keeping of a commandment and refraining from transgression, but also the fashioning of thought, so that it will be effected by the Torah, and we must hope that this too will come.

> **Yeshayahu Leibowitz argued that the main problem of the *halachah* today is that it can act within the context of a society that accepts upon itself from the outset the yoke of the *halachah* but not within the context of a society that does not assume this principle, and today the majority of the Jewish people falls under the latter category.**

The crisis began during the time of the Emancipation. We must relate to the situation as it is, even if this is painful. The society must be influenced so that it will accept the rule of the Torah. This is much more essential than legislation in the Knesset regarding Sabbath observance or autopsies. The main thing is to gain influence over the majority of the population so that it will regard Judaism as something exalted, the acceptance of which is worthwhile. It should not be forgotten that the majority of the new immigrants after the establishment of the State, especially those who came from Eastern countries, were observant when they arrived. Nevertheless, most of them threw off the yoke of the commandments, both because they did not receive religious education and because faithful Judaism alienated them more than it attracted them, and in this the ultra-Orthodox are responsible.

> **You say that education is more important than the enactment of laws in the Knesset, and now, the question of the importing to Israel of non-kosher meat has arisen once again. What is your opinion on this issue – that the religious parties not try to fight this phenomenon by legislative means?**

I have given much thought to the subject of religious coercion. I generally do not support it, because in this manner we drive away more than we draw closer, and this is counterproductive. Currently the image of the observant is very bad and unattractive, and many people do not come closer to Judaism for this reason. We have lost many due to religious coercion. If, however, it is possible to struggle for the acceptance of laws against the importing of non-kosher meat, within the context of the status quo, then I am in favour of such action because this is acceptable to the secular as well. Nonetheless, we should not aspire to attain new legislation, new pressure and new decrees that are in complete opposition to the majority opinion, are not worthwhile and that are counterproductive. Great care must be taken not to intensify the gap between the secular and the religious in the country. The same holds true for civil weddings. I do not see any great profit from the fact that only religious weddings are conducted in Israel. In practice, this does not work. Many live without standing under the wedding canopy and others marry in civil weddings outside Israel. Is this better? The Supreme Court Justice Haim H. Cohn married a divorcée in America, contrary to Torah law. At the time I said: 'Shall not the Judge of all the earth not deal justly?' [Genesis 18:25]. This is also true for public figures who eat non-kosher food. What impression does this make on those non-Jews abroad who aid us in the struggle concerning ritual slaughtering and *kashrut*? I am glad that El Al now publicly observes the Sabbath and *kashrut*, and even the non-Jews are impressed by this. It also transpires that the company has not suffered an economic loss, either.

> **This is the case for the religious kibbutzim, whose economic condition is better than that of the other kibbutzim, despite their Sabbath observance.**

We learn from this that those on a religious mission are not harmed.

In this context, can democracy and *halachah* co-exist?

This question was already examined by the author of *Sefer ha-Chinuch*, in his discussion of the commandment, 'so as to pervert it in favour of the multitude' [Exodus 23:2]: 'this choice by the majority … applies when each of the contending camps possess equal knowledge of the wisdom of the Torah; we do not say that a small group of scholars should not outweigh a large group of the ignoramuses, even [in numbers as great] as those who went forth from Egypt'. In other words, as regards the *halachah*, democracy is in effect and the majority view is followed only if both camps – the majority and the minority – are Torah scholars and observant.

I heard once about a Jew who was travelling by train, and a priest who was with him argued against him: 'It is written in your Torah, "so as to pervert it in favour of the multitude", and the "multitude" here are the Christians; consequently, the Jews must accept Christianity.' The Jew replied: 'You are right, and so I will become a Hindu, because they are even more numerous.' In America it is impossible to enact legislation that is contradictory to the Constitution, while for us the Constitution is the Torah. Against those who argue that in every case the majority opinion is to be accepted, Job already declared: 'It is not the many who are wise' [Job 32:9].

Nonetheless, even in the ultra-Orthodox society, each one chooses his own halachic authority, and they do not observe 'so as to pervert it in favour of the multitude'.

Over the course of time, however, the rulings acceptable to the majority of halachic authorities are accepted.

Is what is accepted by the majority really accepted, in general?

Yes. For example, the *Shulchan Aruch* accepts, as the *halachah*, the view of the majority of the major halachic authorities – Maimonides, Rabbi Asher ben Jehiel and Rabbi Isaac ben Jacob Alfasi.

And in our times?

This is also the case at present. What is accepted by the majority of the halachic authorities now will eventually become the *halachah*. For example, in the realm of medical ethics, on the question of determining the time of death. Is the deciding factor brain death, which is determined as final death, and from that moment on it is permissible to remove organs for transplants from the body of the person who died, or is the determining time that of the cessation of heart activity? This question has not been decided and the legal authorities still disagree on the matter. The rabbinical court of the Chief Rabbinate has already issued a ruling in the former direction, while rabbis such as Rabbi Shlomo Zalman Auerbach oppose this and do not allow 'putting to death' such a patient, because they maintain that life is dependent upon the heart. I tend towards the opinion of those who do not accept this ruling, because the heart still functions unaided, as well as the circulatory system, and it is difficult to say that this is already absolute death, because the person still breathes, even if aided by an artificial respirator. If the time will come when medical science will provide conclusive proof that brain death is in actuality, in the view of physiological experts, the end of life, more and more halachic authorities will accept the opinion of the experts, and the majority will in practice decide the law.

Following in this line of thought, there are rabbis who argue that the opinion of the majority of halachic authorities is that it is forbidden to surrender territories in Eretz Israel. What is your opinion on this matter?

I heard about this from the Chief Rabbis, after they received an invitation to participate in a rabbinical assembly in which this would be declared. They accepted the invitation, but when they heard that a resolution against [the Rabin] government policy in the territories would be passed, some rabbis did not come.

> **This is proof that it is not good for the Rabbinate to be a government institution, which is not free to rule without outside considerations!**

This is correct, and I weep over all the ties between the rabbinate and the government. On the other hand, this is not a question for which an unequivocal ruling can be issued. It entails many calculations that are beyond the bounds of the *halachah*. Already in the time of the Bible there were disagreements concerning peace with the neighbouring peoples at the price of extensive territories. The Book of Judges states that the tribes did not dispossess the inhabitants of the Land, but instead of this, 'the land was at peace' for decades. And so during the time of the Talmud and in the Middle Ages: there is a disagreement regarding the positive commandment to settle in Eretz Israel 'at the present time' [i.e. after the destruction of the Temple] between Maimonides, Nachmanides, *Rashi* and others, and this argument prevails in our time as well.

17 *Israel and the Territories*

'Most of those among the religious who oppose the peace agreement ostensibly for security reasons base their calculations on wholly secular concerns. Being religious makes them no greater experts on security than anyone else.'

Is the topic of the territories a halachic issue at all?

There undoubtedly are ties to the *halachah*. In connection with this I entered into sharp disputes which reverberated throughout the world. I did not argue with the policy of the Israeli government but I opposed the position held by the leaders of the religious and ultra-Orthodox parties, from the religious aspect. I always spoke and wrote as a rabbi, and not as a political or security expert.

Yitschak Shamir, who was a former Prime Minister, criticized the government while in America, so why are you careful in your criticism of Israel and its policy?

I do not regard his making these statements abroad as the most important matter, because we live in one small village today. This may have been a breach of etiquette, but not beyond this. Great care is taken about this in England, but in Israel as well it should be learned that propriety is important. Otherwise 'people would eat each other alive', including leaders and politicians. This is the problem, it does not lie in his expressing his opinion, which is known in any case. My main problem, during my term in office as rabbi, was when to keep silent and when to speak up. I delineated red lines for myself, when to speak my mind and when to keep quiet. The claim, that has been raised more than once, that I strengthen the enemies of Israel with my criticism of Israeli policies is unacceptable to me. On the other hand, there were those who maintained that my remarks were liable to cause damage to the unity of the community, and I do take this argument into account.

Did this occur in the community?

Many members of the communities did not agree with the extreme positions held by the rabbis. They also wanted to hear other views, and it was possibly me, with my moderate positions, who saved the honour of the rabbinate. I received responses in this spirit, even though as a rabbi I do not speak in accordance with what the public wants to hear. This is the case also when I speak about Sabbath observance. The prophets of Israel did not speak in the name of the people of Israel, but they nevertheless are acknowledged by us to be the leaders of the people. This is also true of our attitude towards the non-Jewish nations. There are conditions under which the sensibilities of the non-Jews must be taken into account, even if regarding the beliefs and views that we hold as Jews we are not to consider of the opinions of others. For this reason we are Jews.

In 1978 the first public 'affair' arose in England regarding my position on the territories. I was quite friendly with the editor of the *Jewish Chronicle* at the time, Geoffrey Paul, and he told me that he intended to write a leader based on the ideas that I had expressed. He asked me if I would agree later to write a letter to the newspaper, adding points in support from a religious perspective. I agreed, which led to the unleashing of a strong attack against me. After this came the *Al-Ahram* affair, which made its way into the *Evening Standard*. The representatives of the Egyptian newspaper falsified an interview with me, attributing to me statements that I did not make that were contrary to my real views. Moreover, in the first-page headline they wrote that I had said things that were 'embarrassing' to Israel. And so three versions of what I had 'said' were created: what I **had** actually said, what was printed in the newspaper and what the editorial board of the newspaper wrote to me in a personal letter as statements that I had allegedly said. I opposed negotiations with the PLO, because its members championed terror, were not willing to acknowledge Israel's right to exist and were not willing to amend the Palestinian National Covenant. I held similar views regarding Northern Ireland. I maintained that as long as the opponents of negotiations with the British government did not cease terrorist activities, negotiations with them could not be initiated.

Is this really a halachic question?

This definitely pertains to the *halachah*. It is not easy to issue a ruling on such topics, in contrast, say, to matters relating to the Sabbath or *kashrut* – because they are not explicitly stated in the *Shulchan Aruch* and not even in Maimonides. Nonetheless, the *halachah* and the spirit of Judaism have something to say on these subjects. For example, the love of peace: if there is no peace, there is nothing, as *Rashi* comments on the verse, 'I will grant peace in the land' [Leviticus 26:6], and many other sources. It follows from this that there is a religious ideal of attaining peace. Besides this, the way to attain this ideal must be in accordance with the spirit of Judaism. Currently, however, most of those among the religious who oppose the peace agreement actually oppose peace, and their thoughts and calculations are wholly secular. As Jews, incumbent upon us is the obligation to find ways to bring peace closer, based on the fundamental principles of the Torah. Thus we must weigh the value of the territories in 'Greater Eretz Israel' against the dangers of war and terror, which are liable to exact a price of thousands of victims, and there are additional problems related to the peace process that pertain to Jewish law and Israelite thought in accordance with the Torah.

Today – perhaps for the first time – the religious have a sense of power, which leads to their thoughts and responses.

In a very basic sense, they are not believers! We say twice every day: 'Take care … lest you will soon perish from the good land.' They say this, but do not believe that the existence of the people of Israel is also dependent upon this stipulation. Specifically those who present themselves as the keepers of the faith have less faith than a part, at least, of the secular community. The latter believe in the vision that perhaps the time has come for understanding and reconciliation with the Arabs. The religious and the ultra-Orthodox, in contrast, are not concerned about change in the character of the State. If they were to concentrate on raising the spirituality and morality of the people, and were to see themselves as responsible for that, the situation would change for the better, but these realms are distant from them. In practice, they are among the extremists who do not incorporate spiritual considerations in their calculations regarding their relations with the Arabs.

In this respect, I was a nonconformist among the Orthodox rabbinate; perhaps less in England, but certainly in the United States. I am still a member of the Rabbinical Council of America, but when these episodes occurred, and I sought to convene a meeting of the Council's Executive Board so that they would hear my views first-hand from me and not from the press, they told me that I was mainly concerned for 'what would the non-Jews say', and that we should not take this into account. Where is it written, 'what would the non-Jews say'? I asked them this and it transpired that there is no such verse. To the contrary! It is said: '**Why** should the nations say?' [Psalms 79:10]. That is, that the nations **will not** say, 'where is the God' of the people of Israel. They did not even think about the fact that they distorted the verses in order to bring proof for their positions; in actuality, I did not receive any answer from them.

> **The disagreement is whether the saving of life takes precedence over territories or not. Those who argue that it does not say that the intent is only to the individual, but not to the people, regarding which there is the obligation of *milchemet mitzvah* [a religiously ordained war], even in a place of danger.**

It is true that some make this claim, but I can in no way accept this. They say that there is a ruling in *Minchat Chinuch* that says, in reference to *milchemet mitzvah*, that the law of saving a life does not apply in time of war. Use is made of this, primarily by Rabbi Goren, but in my opinion there is an error here, because this was stated only regarding those who actually fight in a war. If, however, the existence of the entire Jewish people is endangered, this danger undoubtedly must be considered! In other words, if our not reaching a peace agreement with the Arabs gives rise to the danger of additional wars and additional victims, then it is clear that the law of saving life applies to the entire people and not only to individuals.

It is also claimed that there is a religious obligation to defeat the Arabs, so that the territories will be ours, and the number of casualties is not to be taken into account. I say that this is not in accordance with the *halachah*. To the contrary, if there is danger to Jewish life, that is a consequence of their thinking that all the territories must be in our hands now, and as a result there will be more wars and more casualties, the saving of the life of the people is certainly relevant. There is no obligation to fulfil now the commandment of the conquest of the Land. And so it was at the beginning of our history: neither Joshua not Ezra conquered all of Eretz Israel.

> **If so, then we are not talking about a *milchemet mitzvah* at present?**

I do not maintain nor do I accept the philosophy of, 'I am, and there is none but me' [Isaiah 47:8 and other verses], and their claim that only their way of thinking is correct. There has been a dispute on this question throughout all Jewish history. Rabbi Johanan ben Zakkai, after the destruction of the Temple, was already willing to make concessions – even to surrender Jerusalem – in order to ensure the continued existence of the people, in his statement to the Emperor Vespasian, 'Give me Yavneh and its sages.' On the other hand, there was also Rabbi Akiva, who supported Bar Kokhba and who fought Rome to the end, and even thought that he was the Messiah. So there were different opinions. Nachmanides was of the opinion that the conquest of Eretz Israel and immigration to it are positive Torah commandments to last for ever, while Maimonides did not concur. Therefore there are precedents. I myself do not see any necessity for translating these views into current-day obligations, especially not if this entails the repression of millions of Arabs. I do not want us to be responsible for the lives of so many non-Jews who are not our allies, with all that this entails – hatred, terror and war. In my opinion, we will be more secure in Israel if these territories will not be under Israeli rule. Then we might possibly attain a reciprocal agreement by division [of lands], as the Mishnah determines in the case of: 'This one says, "It is all mine", and the other one says, "It is all mine" – they divide it' [Bava Metzia 1:1]. It is impossible to find a compromise without concessions; each side must waive something. The Talmud says about a young couple that desire to obtain a divorce: 'Whoever divorces his first wife, even the Altar sheds tears for him.' Why the Altar? Because it symbolizes sacrifice, and if they divorce it shows they were not willing to sacrifice something which makes it impossible for them to live together. So too regarding the State. If the two sides are not willing to contribute their part in concessions, it is impossible to make peace. And so when we say, 'who makes peace in His heights' at the end of the *Amidah* and the *Kaddish* we go three steps backwards because there is no peace without withdrawal. Obviously, I also am aware of the great difficulties but I take care not to say – which one hears a great deal – that, 'it is a *halachah* given to Moses from Sinai that Esau hates Jacob'. At present we are not speaking of Esau but of Ishmael, and this was not said about him. To the contrary! There were times, in the Middle Ages, when we were very close to Ishmael, and Jews and Arabs together produced important works for the good of humankind. One must make concessions and one must take care.

It is argued, on the other hand, that if the territories are already in our hands, we may not waive them.

The main thrust of this argument is that we are obligated not to give over to non-Jews parts of Eretz Israel, without taking into account the casualties. In my opinion, this is a distorted view, but I am not an expert on security, and I know that there are differences of opinion among IDF officers on this question. This is not a matter of *halachah* but of reality, as in medicine, for example; you might ask is it **possible** to save such and such a life? Consequently, the discussion cannot be determined by stating that, according to the *halachah*, it is forbidden to withdraw from the territories.

And what about our right to Eretz Israel? This is an argument that is not accepted now by international law. Besides this, the Arabs also claim that this right is theirs.

The Torah was given to the people of Israel and not to the non-Jews, and we must demand of the Jews that they accept it. If we maintain that we have the right to Eretz Israel, then this is an internal claim, directed to ourselves, but it cannot be used *vis-à-vis* the Arabs. This claim cannot be forced on the non-Jews! We therefore must understand the Arabs and, to the degree that this is possible, influence them and convince them that there is something in our arguments. I will bring an example from a completely different place, Australia. There are tribes that lived on this continent before the arrival of the Europeans, and they now demand independence and rights, as is the case with the native Americans; and everyone is beginning to understand these arguments. We too have similar claims, that we were here before the Arabs. Notwithstanding this, we cannot say to them that we have the sole right, that everything is ours. We have always been connected with this land, as we see things, but we must also take their claims into consideration. In the final analysis, the world is not judged by history. We must be aware of what is happening in the present, not only of what took place thousands of years ago. Nonetheless, we do have a right to Eretz Israel, since the Creation of the world. I believe this. The question is, to what degree are we to insist on our right at this point in time.

There are religious Jews who say that international law is not our concern.

In my opinion, this is nonsense. It is a fact that we received approval to establish the State from the non-Jews, and we are dependent upon their desires. So that what we do will be legal, we must observe what is accepted throughout the world. Also applicable here is, 'If it were not for the fear of the ruling power, men would swallow each other alive' [Avot 3:2]. To say that we do not care about the world's laws, and that 'Let them think what they want, we will do what we want', is not serious. A distinction must be drawn between commonly accepted conventions in the world and what is not related to United Nations' resolutions. There are matters on which we can act by the principle of 'a people that dwells apart' [Numbers 23:9], but this principle does not apply to other things.

Did you take up such issues with the Israeli Chief Rabbinate as well?

After the Six Day War I spoke with Rabbi Goren, who was the Chief IDF Chaplain at the time. He invited me to visit Mount Sinai, together with a group of army rabbis. We flew in an air force aeroplane to Sharm-el-Sheikh and travelled from there through the desert to Mount Sinai. Immediately after the war he also began to write a Torah scroll on Mount Sinai, and during our visit he completed the writing on the top of the mount. In this way, only he and Moses received the Torah at Sinai …

Did you feel at ease with this performance?

Goren claimed that he had indications that this was indeed Mount Sinai. There is an uninterrupted tradition from the second century CE that Jebl Musa is Mount Sinai. Second, he found there stones with a burnt shape resembling a bush, and every time that such a stone is broken, the bush shape is still visible in it. He relied upon the commentary of Rabbi Moses of Narvonne (from 800 years ago) on Maimonides in the *Guide for the Perplexed*, who wrote: 'Indeed, we found such stones.' I was in good relations with Rabbi Goren at the time, but since I expressed my opinion on the territories years later, and he maintained that, according to the *halachah*, we must rule that it is forbidden to give up even a single step – and even asked me to be a signatory to such a ruling and I refused – our relationship took a turn for the worse. I still think that if there is a possibility of **true peace**, it is permitted to surrender territories, as occurred in the distant past. According to the *halachah*, true peace is more important than territories, especially since more than two million Arabs live here and we rule them against their wishes.

Years later, Goren came to England and I was his host. A conference of rabbis was held and he demanded that they sign a declaration forbidding the giving up of territories – which I opposed. Ever since, he was so angry with me that when my opinion on matters concerning the territories appeared in the press, he falsified my statements – despite his knowing what I had actually said! – and created the impression that I support the PLO. An article appeared then on the front page of the *London Times*, in which he expressed his view that the community must 'vomit me out' but in the end this was his fate, to be got rid of by his community, even though I certainly was not happy about it. There were additional clashes between us but later on, in a public event in Israel, he came to me and shook my hand. He did not ask my pardon, but he did give me regards.

Goren was not the only one in Israel who opposed my philosophy in such a sharp and public manner. In America as well there were many who fought me, especially the Lubavitchers, albeit not the Rebbe himself, whom I regarded as an outstanding and extremely influential leader. He himself wrote to me that he was not responsible for the propaganda against me. Those in his inner circle, however, were very angry with me and they attacked me in a crude manner, to the extent that I received an invitation to the Chabad rabbinical court for a *din Torah*, because I had uttered, as it was written there, 'things against the people of Israel'. I agreed to appear, on condition that proofs would be brought for what they claimed I had said, and that I would be given the opportunity to defend myself with witnesses. 'But', I wrote to them, 'if you do not succeed in proving your charges, you must ask my forgiveness.' I never heard from them after that. They were interested only in publicizing the fact of my having been summoned by them to a *din Torah*.

You told me about the response of the rabbinical courts in America, who were not interested in a real *din Torah* concerning your views but only in propaganda, and also Rabbi Goren's conduct. What is your opinion about this?

I am concerned for the honour of the rabbinate and am grieved by this, but I never publicized a response that was liable to harm the honour of the rabbinate and the leading Torah scholars. We are paying a heavy price for these disgraceful actions, but they too are human beings and they must be understood. They regard these topics as being of paramount importance, and if someone does not agree with their philosophy, he causes them sorrow. Just as hatred spoils things, love also spoils the order of things and distorts what one sees. Goren, for example, did not even attempt to hear what another is saying. He lived under pressure and saw that even among the religious the majority did not accept his opinion, and he regarded this as an inauspicious portent. There were disputes through all of Jewish history, but to claim that one's opponent is not fit to be a rabbi ... I do not find any parallel to this among those who accepted the tradition of faithful Judaism. Even in the Talmud it was said to Rabbi Akiva: 'Grass will grow through your jaws [i.e. you will be dead and buried], but the son of David [the Messiah] will still not have appeared.' Rabbi Akiva believed that the Messiah had already come – and this is much more than what is said today – but the rabbis nevertheless were loyal to one another (despite their differences). Once I asked: 'Why do we observe, to this very day, the mourning customs from Passover to *Shavuot*, because of the deaths of Rabbi Akiva's pupils?' The answer is because 'they did not treat each other with respect'. They had to raise the banner of the honour of the Torah and, because they did not do so, the Bar Kokhba revolt failed – and the same holds true today. The problem is not the very disagreement, but rather it lies in the fact that Torah scholars do not treat each other respectfully. This is liable to bring a catastrophe upon us, today as in the past.

Did you visit settlements [beyond the Green Line]?

Yes, even though each time I heard about a new settlement in the territories I was alarmed lest, Heaven forbid, it would be abandoned and destroyed, as happened during the withdrawal from Sinai. I was very interested in visiting settlements, expressing my concern about the security of their inhabitants and hearing from them why they live where they do. My first visit was to Elon Moreh, as the head of a delegation of European rabbis, several months after they settled there. One of the heads of the settlement, Nehamah Porat (whose daughter was later killed), is my uncle's granddaughter. I asked them: 'What did you think when you came to a place that invites trouble, near Shechem? Did you come here on behalf of Israel's security or in order to demonstrate that Jews have the right to settle in all parts of Eretz Israel?' Their response was that they are not security experts. 'We are not generals. We are here only because we have rights to the entire land, and we must show this to the Arabs and to the whole world in general.' I did not forget this, and this troubles and pains me to this day.

Another time I visited Karnei Shomron, where I also have two nieces, who were among the first settlers there. I was very impressed by what they had built from nothing, without forcing out the local Arabs. I told them this, despite my not being able to agree with their arguments. But there were some among them who would not be present when I spoke because they were familiar with my views. Later, I told them that I wanted to hear their arguments and we conducted a polite debate.

I also received an official invitation to visit Kiriat Arba, which I accepted. I met with the leaders of the settlement. Also I visited Beit Hadassah and Tel Rumeidah; there too I was affected quite emotionally by what I saw, but was also full of anxiety. They told me that there is a *minyan* [quorum prayer service] at the Cave of Machpelah every Sabbath, with more than 300 worshippers in attendance. This was the portion of *Shelah Lecha* ('Send [literally, "send for yourselves"] men to scout the land' – Numbers 13–15). I said that *Rashi* comments on this verse: 'Send for yourselves – according to your own judgment.' *Keli Yakar* states on this: 'According to your own judgment, Moses, send men whom you think are fit. But these people hated the Land, because they returned and said: "Let us appoint a leader and return to Egypt" [Numbers 14:4]. "It is My opinion," said the Holy One, blessed be He, "that it would have been better to have sent women instead of men, because they love the Land, as it is said about the daughters of Zelophehad, that they asked of Moses: 'Give us a landholding'"' [Numbers 27:4]. In response to this, the leaders of the settlers told me: 'You are right. The women did indeed tell us and pressured us to stay here, and if it had not been for them, we would not have remained here.' This time as well, the debate was conducted in a polite manner. My hosts even sent me an aerial photograph of Hebron, which is a present that is very dear to me. I am truly interested in becoming close to them, and I am willing to accept some of their arguments, although I do not agree with most of them.

My main argument is that there is not enough patience and tolerance between us. There is much talk about dialogue, so that there will be mutual understanding. At present, however, the problem is not speaking but, rather, listening. For us the main thing is 'Hear, O Israel', and not 'Speak, O Israel.' Currently, everyone speaks at the top of his voice, but there is no one who hears. I know that it is not in my power – and nor do I want – to demand that the other accept my view. Nonetheless, I was happy to visit them and to show them that I am not a 'traitor' to Eretz Israel.

And therefore they attack you?

It is said: 'Deliver me, I pray, from the hand of my brother, from the hand of Esau' [Genesis 32:12]. My father, of blessed memory, believed that to say, 'deliver me from the hand of Esau' is one thing, but if he is my brother this is more difficult. They are my brothers so attacks by them are difficult and pain me; I make efforts in order that they will at least understand my arguments, even if they do not agree with them. Notwithstanding all this, enough of demonstrations and impoliteness. Fanatics do not need to explain themselves, and so it is much more difficult to be a moderate than a fanatic. In my opinion, some of the settlers are currently active without these actions being based on the intellect; for example, in their claim that they are not willing to receive orders from the government. This is a situation that is liable to lead to destruction! None of them has said what is the practical alternative to government policy.

The transfer of the Arab population!

Do they really believe this? These are false dreams! Especially in our period. I, at any rate, do not accept such philosophies, nor an approach that relies on miracles. The two million Arabs under our rule will patently cause internal ruin in the Jewish society, and the destruction of Judaism.

Did you express your opinion in this direction?

When the Israeli government decided to annex the Golan, doubts were aroused in my mind – not only regarding its policy but also regarding the religious sentiment. I asked myself if this is in tune with the spirit of Judaism. On the one hand I wanted to say something in this spirit; on the other hand I was apprehensive that the government would not understand what I wanted to say and I would thereby arouse controversy and quarrels. I finally decided not to say anything, although I felt within me the need. This had been the case even earlier, when the law annexing Jerusalem was enacted. I had inner doubts whether to speak out or not. Clearly, I – like every Jew – wants the entire land to be under our control. This goal, however, cannot be attained immediately, and I thought that as a rabbi – who is obliged to express the spirit of Judaism and Jewish thought – I must express my views. However I knew that this would spark public controversy, so in the end I therefore refrained from speaking. I made my views known only in a few instances, and every time I later heard much criticism. Notwithstanding this, there were instances in which I felt that I could not be silent. This is the price that I pay for the honour I receive as a rabbi. The struggle, however, was continuous and was not easy for me.

And now, when you are no longer burdened by the yoke of an official position, do you feel freer?

Today as well there are restraints, albeit in a different form, even if currently I am neither accountable to the congregants who elected me nor to my rabbinical colleagues. Rabbi Jacob Emden, the rabbi of Altona, who did not receive a salary from his community, was completely independent. He said once that every morning he recited the blessing, 'who has not made me *alef-bet-dalet* [the head of the rabbinical court]' [instead of the usual blessing, 'who has not made me an *eved*' – *ayin-bet-dalet* means a slave]; I too recite a similar blessing every morning. Blessed be the Lord, that this burden has been removed from me. Nonetheless, I am still responsible to my community, so I am careful not to say things that would not be properly understood and are liable to cause controversy. I must weigh the scales, especially now when such important matters are on the agenda. I still do not feel that I can say everything in public, for example, concerning the peace agreement with the PLO. Obviously, I know that there are weighty considerations on each side. Matters are still unclear, and I am careful not to express my opinion. I have hopes and I have concerns regarding the peace agreement.

Like everyone.

No. There are some who do not hope for peace, and I weep for them. If they too were to have hope, I would agree with them. But specifically among the religious and the ultra-Orthodox there are some who do not pray for the rescue of the process. They are those of small faith; their calculations and thinking are secular. They put their trust solely in the strength of the army, with the philosophy of, 'my own power and the might of my own hand' [Deuteronomy 8:17], which is surprising. How is it that circles of Mizrachi, Agudath Israel, Lubavitch, Gush Emunim and others lack religious feeling springing from Judaism, and all their arguments could be spoken by any secular Jew as well? I cannot accept this.

On the other hand, I also see the doubts. My *yeshivah* head, Rabbi Elijah Lopian, once said on the verse, 'Let Your mercy, O Lord, be upon us, as we have put our hope in You' [Psalms 33:22], that the mercy of the Lord will be in accordance **as** we put our hope in His mercy. If we do not put our hope in the mercy of the Lord, mercy will not come, and many of the religious do not put their hope in mercy. The entire religious community does not now contribute what should grow forth from the spirit of Israel.

Perhaps this is because of the mingling between nationalism and religiosity?

Without a doubt. I see secularism, and possibly even idolatry, in the worship of the Land. On the other hand, as I noted, I accept the potential – if not actual – religious significance of the State of Israel. This is in contrast to Yeshayahu Leibowitz, for example. Over the course of time, the State has the potential of giving birth to something based on the vision of Judaism, but I am not a prophet so cannot know if the time has already come. If they do not put their hope in and await our success in this direction, then there is no hope for the future of the State of Israel. We must live in this part of the world, and if people say that we have no choice but to live by our sword, then we have no hope for the future. We are a small people, and if today, when there is modern weaponry and borders are not greatly significant as regards security, we will not even dream of reaching an agreement with our neighbours, then why must we remain here? If I were not certain that the time will come when we will live in peace with our neighbours, I would say that we must salvage what is possible and we must eliminate the State! The assumption that we will never attain an agreement with them means that we cannot establish here a state of Jews. To the contrary, each and every one is in danger in such a situation, and the lives of the entire people cannot be endangered. Now, the centre of Jewish life is in Israel, and if, Heaven forbid, something were to happen there, there would be repercussions for the entire Jewish world. Consequently, even if I do not yet live there on a permanent basis, this is important to me. I know that this assumption is not universally accepted, but the ultra-Orthodox circles also still see a difference between what happens in England and events in the State of Israel. This is acknowledged even by Satmar Chasidim, who are quite strong in England.

Their previous Rebbe, Rabbi Joel Teitelbaum, was a wise and intelligent person, and I heard that after it was decided to call the State Israel and not Eretz Israel, he quoted the verse from Jeremiah: 'Why is **the land** [*ha-aretz*] lost?' [Jeremiah 9:11], that is to say, until now we had Eretz Israel and now only Israel. He replied: 'Because they forsook My Torah' [*ibid.* verse 12]. But they are not an important factor. The *yeshivah* world, Belz and Gur Chasidism and others, regard Israel as the centre of Torah, even if they do not consider the State to be a Jewish centre. Moreover, they strengthen the Jewish community there, and there is a large *aliyah* from these circles. Many of the secular abroad, however, have no connection nor relatives in Israel, and this is how they relate to Israel and to the State.

But the fact that Israel is now the Torah centre is of no interest to the secular?

I am not sure. They also may possibly want all parts of the people to regard the State as some sort of centre for Judaism. Even if we are speaking about a centre of Torah, this is of value and importance for them as well, at least so that they will know what they do not accept, as Golda Meir said once. The secular in the Diaspora also feel that this strengthens the centrality of the State.

It seems at times that the ultra-Orthodox image drives away from the State many secular Jews outside Israel.

Religious life, and especially ultra-Orthodox life, may possibly alienate these circles, but a considerable segment of the people regards the State of Israel as the centre of its life. A distinction should be drawn between what appears through secular eyes as religious coercion and its influence in Israel on the one hand, and the acceptance of Israel's centrality for all parts of the people on the other. Thus, for example, secular emissaries as well use the argument that the religious regard Israel as the centre of the people's life, and this is accepted.

Is there no danger of polarization between the various parts of the people?

There undoubtedly is a great danger, but such a threat exists throughout the world, and not only in Israel. At present there already are visible separate neighbourhoods in Israel, which is not so abroad. I greatly fear for the unity of the people. We must find unifying elements, such as the centrality of the State, which is important for the unity of the people. What is important, besides tolerance, is that each side will recognize and understand the fears of the other camp. The ultra-Orthodox are apprehensive that if they open the walls encompassing them, they will lose their youth, as has happened since the Emancipation. The secular must understand this and provide assurances that this will not happen, and that they will be able to continue living their lives. The secular, for their part, fear that as a result of the increase in the numbers of the religious and the ultra-Orthodox, due to their high birthrates, they will not be able to live in such a society. They would not be able to drive on the Sabbath or to go to movies, and they fear that they will be strangers in their own land. The religious must promise them that they will respect the secular, who will be able to live as they choose. Until everyone will accept one Torah, we will not be a stumbling block for the secular. Both sides must give mutual assurances, but the opposite is the case – each side makes life more onerous for the other, which entails great danger.

Perhaps in matters of manners we have to learn from the non-Jews?

It is already written in the Torah that the non-Jews do not possess Torah, but they do possess wisdom. This belongs to wisdom: how to live together, how to increase peace between the different groups. On the other hand, the decisions that a Western statesman has to take are not as fateful as those in Israel. There are many more decisions made in Israel now on which the future of the State rests than in England or France. The tension here is greater, because of these factors.

Do the politicians in England understand this as regards Israel?

I have the impression that they generally understand that Israel is still dependent upon world politics, much more than England, for example, where there already is a sort of status of *chazakah* [presumed establishment]. They also understand that Israel lives among enemies, which is not the case for England. Even if there is a spot in Northern Ireland that causes problems, this does not relate to the existence of the English people. Those who are friendly to Israel – and there are many in England – understand this. I attempt to strengthen this sentiment and generally find a positive response. On the other hand, there are some – even among Israel's friends – who argue, certainly until recently, that not enough is being done in Israel to find a solution. They maintain that there are moderate elements among the Arabs as well. There is a demand for a new approach, that takes into account the new facts that have been created. They patently cannot dictate Israel's policy, but it is also impossible to disregard public opinion in the non-Jewish world. The world is becoming smaller; today, all nations are dependent upon one another. One cannot live by the slogan: 'There is a people that dwells apart, not reckoning itself among the nations' [Numbers 23:9]. There is no justification for this philosophy. My father, of blessed memory, told me as a young rabbi that 100 friends are too few and a single enemy is too many. This thought guides me to the present day.

18 *Who is a Jew?*

*'It is more important to return Jews to their source than to convert
non-Jews who desire to become Jewish.'*

**There are rabbis who are searching for the remnants of the
Ten Tribes throughout the world. What do you think about
this?**

What we have is quite enough. 'I am looking for my brothers' [Genesis
37:16], so that they will live as Jews. There are those in England who
claim that the term 'British' comes from [the Hebrew words] *brit-ish*,
meaning 'a man of the covenant'. I do not accept this, and I have no
interest in it. We must find Jews who were born as Jews and make Jews
out of them. This is also my position on the issue of conversion. It is
more important to return Jews to their source than to convert non-Jews
who desire to become Jewish.

And what about Ethiopian Jews?

From the outset it seemed to me, based on what I had heard, that the
problem began in the nineteenth century, with Dr Feitelovitch. Now,
however, after they have been accepted as Jews by the Chief Rabbinate
of Israel and they too consider themselves to be Jews, then they are to
be accepted after the fact. At present, when they are already in Israel,
everything has to be done so that they will live as Jews, in accordance
with Jewish tradition. Notwithstanding this, if I were in charge of
making decisions here, I am doubtful if I would have encouraged such
a movement from the outset.

The question of Jews from Ethiopia arose only after the sources of *aliyah* from other countries were blocked. Would they have been brought here if the Russian immigration had preceded them?

There is talk about the future of the Jewish people and ways are being sought to increase the Jewish population, which I find strange. It is assumed that the number of Jews in the entire world in the Middle Ages did not exceed one million, and many of them were persecuted, killed and burnt. The entire responsa literature, however, contains no allusion to efforts expended on the issue of the future of the Jewish people, which seemed assured. Currently there are about 13 million Jews in the world, who live in greater freedom and prosperity than ever before, but doubts regarding the future of the Jewish people nevertheless arise. I think it is the rabbis who were supposed to provide a sense of security concerning the future of the people. But they do the opposite! They disseminate feelings of despair that there will not be peace in Israel. They thereby undermine the people's confidence and its hopes. This is more important than a war against the importing of non-kosher meat to Israel, even though this is undoubtedly important. For not by coercion shall the Jewish man prevail but rather by the spirit of influence.

What is your position regarding Reform Jews?

The charge that their intentions and arguments are foreign to Judaism is unacceptable to me. A most strange development can be seen here. When the movement began in Germany in the early nineteenth century, the Reform arose as a group that was interested solely in matters concerning the synagogue ritual, such as reciting prayers in the vernacular and playing the organ. Later on, they also began to intervene in matters of personal status and the observance of the commandments; for example, the cancellation of the second Festival day abroad, along with many halakhot which, in their opinion, have no validity now. They took an additional step when they cancelled Jewish divorce, saying the non-Jewish courts sufficed to dissolve marriages. This step sowed deeper dissension, and by the birth of *mamzerim* [the issue of a union forbidden by Jewish law], they created, 'a twisted thing that cannot be made straight' [Ecclesiastes 1:15]. Nonetheless, they claimed that they still accepted the ethics of Judaism. Today, it seems to me, they have abandoned this value. They maintain, for example, that people guilty of homosexuality are to be accepted as rabbis. We receive our ethics from the *halachah*, but since they do not accept the *halachah*, their morality also is waning. Even the non-Jews speak of morals in connection with sexual relations, while the Reform disavow even this.

They will say that there were disagreements among the Jewish people in the past.

Regarding the general observance of the commandments, I cannot accept that those who observe the Sabbath, on the one hand, and those who desecrate it, on the other, merely belong to different trends within Judaism. One who believes in the sanctity of the Sabbath cannot accept that one who desecrates it merely belongs to another trend within Judaism. I told them many times that by their not accepting the basic principles of faith and the commandments, they have the status of those who have no portion in the World to Come, as the Mishnah states. This is not a disagreement, such as those between the School of Hillel and the School of Shammai. In the latter case, both schools believed in the Heavenly origin of the Torah, based on a shared faith, which is not so today. Accordingly, I could not participate in their prayers or take joint action with them on educational matters. I could not regard this breach as a disagreement for Heaven's sake or a sort of internal quarrel within faithful Judaism.

The Reform claim that if it were not for them, many Jews would have abandoned Judaism long ago.

There is some justification in this argument. It is true that were it not for the Reform movement, many Jews would have already been far outside the camp. Furthermore it is my contention that even regarding those Jews who do not live in accordance with the Torah, their children and grandchildren may very well return to authentic Judaism. If so, the existence of the Reform is somewhat beneficial. It is preferable that they be Reform than completely removed from Judaism, maintaining that there is no connection between Judaism and religion. There is something in this movement that retards complete assimilation, but I speak only about those born as Jews, and not their converts who never were nor will be Jews by halachic standards.

They claim that intermarriages increase the number of non-Jews who join the Jewish people.

This is not so, not even statistically. Seventy per cent of the children one of whose parents is not Jewish are not raised as Jews. Only a small minority is interested in raising their children as Jews. There is no benefit in this, because they will not become observant, and we should not deliberately increase the numbers of Sabbath desecrators among the Jewish people.

This argument is quite applicable today to the majority of the Jewish people.

That is something else. For example, if I am a citizen of some country and I was born in it, even if I become a criminal, I will still be a citizen of that country, and it must accept me. Parents cannot deny the existence of their children, nor a country its citizens. We are talking, however, of people who come from outside. Generally speaking, parents will not adopt a child who is not healthy or whom they fear will be a criminal. Accordingly, we must not accept someone who we know from the outset will violate all that is sacred to Judaism and become a sinner. To be a Jew is more than the acceptance of nationality. True conversion is not a new passport! Someone who becomes a Jew has, as it were, undergone heart surgery. This is something very sensitive and it cannot be done casually.

The secular will say that it is enough if a person feels that he is a Jew.

Can someone say that he is a member of some club because he feels that he is? Every society and every club is entitled to determine who is a member and who not, based upon its regulations. Someone claiming that he is Jewish still does not make him a Jew. Those who want the Jews to accept them as Jews and who seek to be recognized as such must create the conditions under which every Jew will regard them as a brother. But if this is not possible – and this is only a unilateral phenomenon – this does not constitute affiliation to the Jewish people. During a Knesset debate, Menachem Begin said that a Jew is one who is accepted by the Jews as such. In other words, this is something mutual. Moreover, we are talking about a phenomenon of tradition. In the final analysis, we are not a new people on the stage of history, we have ancient roots, and whoever says that he is part of the Jewish people without taking this into account is acting improperly. We must not sever ourselves from our past and from what was commonly accepted until now, and say that now there is a new Jewish people and the past is of no interest to us. This is the negation of the Jewish people's roots.

The youth in Israel says that it is first and foremost Israeli, and only afterwards Jewish.

This is a grievous error. It is not for me to determine the definition as regards the question of who is a Jew. Also in England there are Jews who argue that they are first of all Englishmen, and this is unacceptable to me. I attempt to persuade them, to the best of my ability, to accept

Judaism as something more serious than just simple nationality, and this is certainly so in Eretz Israel as well. We did not return to the Land so that we would receive an Israeli, and not a Jewish, passport! I cannot accept such a line of reasoning.

> **Questions of conversion abroad can be solved on an individual basis but it is more difficult to act in such a manner in Israel, even though it may be assumed that the majority of converts will not be observant after their conversion.**

This is an extremely thorny problem and I too see that the situation in Eretz Israel is different from that in the Diaspora. If there is someone in Israel who regards himself as Jewish, the question is: What are we to do with him? For example, if the wife in a mixed couple is non-Jewish and her children are not Jewish, we cannot tell her to send them to Arab schools. These children live in the State of the Jews, and it therefore may be hoped that they will grow up in a Jewish environment, which is not the case abroad. I accept Rabbi Goren's opinion in this matter. He said that opposition to conversion is much more noticeable in the Babylonian Talmud than in the Jerusalem Talmud. The Babylonian Talmud declares: 'Converts are more difficult for Israel than a sore on the skin', but there is no parallel in the Jerusalem Talmud. This is so because it is easier to accept converts in Eretz Israel since the environment is Jewish. Abroad, in contrast, people who will not be observant will unquestionably not live as Jews – and their children, even less – and we therefore must take greater care to determine if their intentions are pure.

When I wrote to the Lubavitcher Rebbe concerning his uncompromising war for conversion **according to the *halachah*** in Israel, I told him that specifically abroad the pressure on rabbis would increase if they were to act leniently, as would still be the case in Eretz Israel, even with this amendment to the law. People would say to these Diaspora rabbis that they need not be more Catholic than the Pope. There is a tradition of strictness regarding conversion in England. They were already stringent in this matter in the eighteenth century but, notwithstanding this, there are dozens of true converts every year. Many non-Jews come to us in England and ask us to convert them. In most instances, we discover that they do not intend truly to accept the yoke of the kingdom of Heaven and the yoke of the commandments. We obviously reject such individuals. A resolution in a similar spirit was accepted by the Conference of European Rabbis. In America, the situation is different; there are even Orthodox rabbis there who are lenient regarding conversion. In this as in many other realms, chaos reigns in America.

And does your rejecting those seeking to convert put an end to the matter?

It happens that they go to Israel for a week and return with a very nice conversion certificate, a proper Orthodox certificate!

This is a serious accusation.

This is what I said. The names of the rabbis who act in this manner are known. We have many troubles from conversions conducted in Israel. I do not want Israel to accept converts that we reject. In Israel, they rule in accordance with the political situation, and not to correspond to the situation as it is in other places.

What do you think about the attitude of the ultra-Orthodox to the State courts, which they regard as 'non-Jewish courts'?

I do not see any problem in the ultra-Orthodox having difficulty in accepting the authority of the State, which is not based on the laws of the Torah. The problem is that of the State and of the Jewish society in Israel, which is not conducted in accordance with the Torah. Nonetheless, I am cognizant that more and more subjects of legislation, based on the rules of Jewish jurisprudence, are included in the laws of the State. This will take time, because the conditions today are different from those that prevailed 2,000 years ago, when Jewish independence was lost. In consequence the body of law pertaining to governmental and societal matters in accordance with Jewish law remained static. We must continue from the point where this was interrupted. There are disagreements regarding the issue of 'the law of the land is the law', based on Nedarim 28a. *Ran* [Rabbeinu Nissim ben Reuben Gerondi] states that the intent in the Talmud is not to Israelite kings, but to non-Jewish monarchs whose law is binding, since the land is theirs and they possess it. This is not the case regarding Israelite kings because all Israel has a share in Eretz Israel; consequently the law of an Israelite monarch is not binding in this respect. What the *halachah* terms *takanot kahal* [communal regulations] may possibly have state-political validity also according to the *halachah*, if the majority of the people accepts them as authoritative. If so, then the verdicts of State courts are not to be totally negated, even if they are not based on Torah law. Their validity is at least as great as that of *takanot kahal*. I therefore would not say that the ultra-Orthodox have clear justification not to take into account these verdicts, because they too are part of the community and they therefore must accept its authority.

What about women's status? Can you conceive of a situation in which, in accordance with Torah law, women also will serve as rabbis?

There is a ruling by Maimonides based on the verse, 'Be sure to set as king over yourself' [Deuteronomy 17:15] – '[it is written] "king", and not "queen", and so to all the functions in Israel only a man may be appointed'. This applies to positions of authority but regarding everything pertaining to equal rights for men and women, the latter may do whatever men do, in the professional arena for example, and this is commonly accepted at present in religious circles as well. The *halachah* does not oppose this. On the other hand, men cannot do what is uniquely feminine, such as giving birth and raising children. Consequently, the demand to see women functioning as rabbis does not constitute equality but discrimination against women. This will lead to the woman having two tasks, which the man does not. In this manner the woman's unique tasks will be neglected, which will bring about the destruction of the family, even in ultra-Orthodox circles. In their society as well, the wife engages in some secular studies while the husband 'sits and learns'; in the final analysis the wife is better educated than her husband which creates tensions. It happens that such a wife demands from her husband more than he is capable of giving her, thus creating a crisis, and the number of divorces is rising, in the ultra-Orthodox society as well. This is an unnatural phenomenon, and if people live such artificial lives Nature takes its revenge on human beings, who pay a high price for this.

Once again, do your statements contain criticism of the ultra-Orthodox society?

In this realm, yes. The fact that they educate their sons in a completely different manner from how they raise their daughters is fraught with great danger. Our tradition states that only one of a thousand who enters the study hall goes forth to Torah as his profession, but the rule, 'He did not create it a waste but formed it for habitation' [Isaiah 45:18] applies to the rest, and whoever is not engaged in the 'improvement of the world' is invalid as a witness! Those who live solely within the four cubits of the *halachah*, at the expense of their fellow man and without contributing to society are not creative people. Theirs is a reaction against those who completely abandon Judaism. Extremism leads to extremism, and neither is beneficial. Notwithstanding this, I am certain that the time will come when the ultra-Orthodox circles also will live a more balanced life.

Do you see the possibility of women also participating in congregational life?

I am not opposed to this. There are women in England who are members – and even leaders – of the communal organizations. Thus, for example, in Manchester, Leeds and Glasgow, the representative organizations were led by chairwomen, and I agreed to this. On the other hand, I would oppose a woman occupying a position pertaining to synagogue management.

And if women pray in a women-only prayer service?

In my opinion this is nonsense. Why should they remove themselves from the community? They argue that they are to be accepted within the congregation, while in practice they exclude themselves from the public.

The women will say: 'Accept us with equal rights and then we will not leave the community, but if we are not granted rights we have no choice but to leave.'

Today there are *minyanim* like this, with the approval of the Chief Rabbi in England who succeeded me, Rabbi Jonathan Sacks, on condition that they would not read in the Torah, and they accept this. Also, they do not recite *Kaddish* or *Kedushah* because these require a quorum [of men].

But the sources state that a woman may not be called up to the reading of the Torah out of respect for the public, and this has certainly changed today!

One can find an opening for this. But what do they gain by this? This is not public prayer, according to the rules and fine points that govern it. Several women students from Cambridge had come to me and requested to organize a prayer group. I permitted this, on condition that they would not recite any portions of the prayers that required a *minyan*. They agreed to this, but the *minyan* was later cancelled.

And what about the question of a woman being invalid to deliver testimony?

According to the *halachah*, if both sides accept relatives to testify, then the testimony of a woman also may be accepted.

But it is clear that, in general, both sides will not accept a woman's testimony!

Generally speaking, this is not a practical obstacle. One of the reasons why we do not accept testimony by a woman ensues from the court not wanting to impose upon her the burden of testifying. She should not waste her time in court, nor is this to her honour.

Isn't the reason why a woman is discriminated against essentially sociological?

I agree with this, and this is in accordance with Nature. If the Creator had wanted to create man and woman equal, He would have done so. The man and the woman have different functions and we are not to blur such differences; this would be against Nature and against the *halachah*. The existence of the human race cannot be guaranteed if the laws of Nature and the Torah are violated. Such confusion is liable to destroy the Jewish home.

Nonetheless, in a society like ours, shouldn't women be granted the same rights as men?

On condition that neither the woman nor the man neglect their respective main tasks. My wife, for example, is very occupied in communal affairs, and she never maintained that she was critical of not being able to be called up to the Torah. This is even strange to her. She has other duties which she regards as her calling in life, as well as the honour, recognition and appreciation that she receives. This is also true regarding my four daughters, all of whom are engaged in public affairs. I never heard any of them complain that they do not have 'equal rights', because they do not do what men do.

Do you support Torah study – even the study of Talmud – for women?

Yes. There is already a disagreement about this in the Talmud. One party maintains that if a person teaches his daughter Torah, it is as if he teaches her wantonness, while the other party argues that this is obligatory, at least concerning topics pertaining to women. Now, however, I am in favour of women studying even Talmud, if they so desire. The revolution in this realm began in Poland, in the Beit Yaakov educational network, and this is accepted at present even in ultra-Orthodox circles.

What is your opinion about women serving in the IDF?

This is a serious, delicate and painful subject. Speaking for myself, I would like to see a role for every girl – as for every boy – in the defence of the people but possibly not within the context of the army because this poses difficulties halachically. Girls should be drafted for National Service; even within the army. Their exemption, with no sense of responsibility for national security, is not justified. At present, not only do [religious] girls not serve, most *yeshivah* students do not serve in the army. I regard this as highly dangerous, something that deepens the breach within Israeli society and which also leads to fraternal enmity. The distinction between one person's blood and another's, with all the excuses of the *yeshivah* population that they are protecting the people by their Torah study, creates divisions and polarization. Notwithstanding this, I understand – at least in part – the arguments of the ultra-Orthodox. They cannot preserve their way of life if they are put to the test within the framework of the army since they live in seclusion, separated from secular life. They do not see this life and do not experience it; they fear that if they will be exposed to this new life, many of them will fall victim to their environment. In order to narrow the gap, each side must understand the other, which will already be half the remedy. Bridges to a solution must be sought on the basis of these facts. The problem today is that neither side is willing to understand the problems of the other camp.

What about the solution of *yeshivot hesder* [that combine military service and *yeshivah* studies]?

I endorse such a solution. If my sons had to serve in the army, I would encourage them to serve within this framework. I was very close to Rabbi Meir Schlesinger from the Shaalbim *yeshivah* and to Rabbi Chayim Goldwicht from the Kerem be-Yavneh *yeshivah*, who were the first to establish this framework, and I encouraged them. At present, however, the atmosphere militates against any compromise in this as in all other realms.

Do you talk about this with the ultra-Orthodox circles?

Yes. They know my opinion but they oppose any exposure to the outside world. They called Rabbi Herzog 'Dr Herzog', to the extent that his widow told my wife that Rabbi Herzog had died of grief because of the way the extreme ultra-Orthodox circles had mistreated him. It is difficult to reach mutual understanding in Israel. Religion and politics are too intertwined and there is no desire for compromise. I regard this as highly dangerous to the stability of the people.

**What about *shemittah* [the Sabbatica
agricultural activity is prohibited by To**

I attempt to understand both sides: on the one ,
sell [the lands of Eretz Israel to a non-Jew, thereby
activity during the Sabbatical year] by Rabbi Ko
only to the Sabbatical year; and on the other hand
this permission. It is strange that we sell the lands
foreigners, contrary to the commandment of, 'Give the.
techanem]' – you shall not grant them an encampmen.
Eretz Israel; nevertheless I see that it is specifically by s
that the Land is sanctified and we remember that there is a
the Land and that we live on hallowed earth, not in a norma
The earth has intrinsic sanctity and this must be remembered
we are not capable of observing the commandments dependen.
[i.e. that may be performed only in] Eretz Israel. The idea that 'the
and the fullness thereof is the Lord's' [Psalms 24:1] and that F.
Master of the land is a sublime and important concept. Therefore – ev
though I accept the permission to sell of the rabbinate (I have a son wh
lives here and who does not rely upon this permission, and he
purchases fruits and vegetables from the Arabs) – ways must be found
to ensure we will not forget that this is sacred land and that we must
conduct ourselves accordingly.

**Perhaps this is still an inheritance from the atmosphere in
Eastern Europe which is expressed, for example, in the
attitude to Zionism?**

Possibly, but there the Sabbath observers and the non-religious could
live separately. The situation is different here. Now we have a State and
a society, in which all are 'among my own people' [II Kings 4:13].

**In my childhood in Jerusalem, Communists who wanted to
reform the world and ultra-Orthodox lived side by side
much more than today!**

The polarization is intensifying, outside Israel as well, but mainly in
Eretz Israel which, in this case, influences the Diaspora. The entire
ultra-Orthodox world is influenced by Israel, although the extremism
in America may possibly be even greater than in Israel. Furthermore,
in my opinion, the political extremism among the ultra-Orthodox
originates in America. The movement of Meir Kahana, as I view the
situation, could have been born only abroad; Lubavitch Chasidism,
Satmar Chasidism and even Gush Emunim are influenced by America.
When I found myself in a dispute regarding things I said – or that I did

– concerning the territories, it was difficult to live in America
se of the threats. I was warned that at one of my lectures there
l be demonstrations and fliers against me, and the organizers
lled the event. Such an experience I never had in Israel!

In your opinion, should religious life in Israel as well be built of a communal basis?

ertainly. I weep about this every day. In Israel there is neither a rab-
inate nor communities as are common in all the Diaspora countries.
The rabbinate there – beginning in the time of the Mandate – is for
representative and supervisory purposes, and not to provide spiritual
leadership. In my opinion, this is a vacuum that must be filled. One
cannot exert influence upon the public without rabbis and intellectuals;
the problem in Israel, however, is that not even the rabbis regard
themselves as influencing the masses. They are not engaged in the
great issues of the State and its character, and if there will be peace with
the neighbouring countries, a vacuum will be created also regarding
relations with Diaspora Jewry.

Is the public willing to accept the influence of the rabbis?

In my opinion, the majority in Israel would already now accept as a
given that every Jewish child is to be given a Jewish education, that is
to say, religious guidance and understanding. It is evident to all that
secular education is bankrupt. Under current conditions, however,
people fear this, assuming that education in accordance with Judaism
would lead to consequences in the polling booth. It would make the
parents vote for the 'wrong parties' – therefore the secularist majority
must oppose religious education!

But it is a fact that Judaism is in crisis at present.

Undoubtedly. Influence must be brought to bear upon the Jewish
people, to persuade it that incumbent upon it is the mission of
contributing its share to all humankind. Until we attain this, we will
continue to experience a crisis. We have a role *vis-à-vis* the world in the
realm of ethics and spirituality. I do not understand why the majority
of the people has such difficulty in comprehending that there is no
meaning to life – neither for the Jewish people as a whole nor for the
individual Jew – if we do not make this our prime concern.

In conclusion, the pressure to institute changes in the spirit of
Reform is comparable to a ship at sea. One night, the sky is overcast
and the captain cannot set his course by the stars. There is a tall mast

on the ship and he thinks that if he will place a lamp at the masthead, he will be able to determine his direction and set his course, even without relying upon the stars. But he patently is mistaken. In other words, if we do not have fixed stars in the sky, everything will go wrong. The Torah is of eternal nature and through it we are aware if we are travelling on the correct path; and so too these changes [by the Reform are similarly fickle]. We live in a very exciting period, and every day new matters arise. Nonetheless, there are fundamental principles that are stable and that show us the way. One who accepts that solutions to problems must be found in this spirit will indeed find these solutions. Samson Raphael Hirsch said that Judaism will never adapt itself to the times, until the times adapt themselves to Judaism. If we indeed are the eternal people, our mission is to find something that is eternal and to contribute to mankind elements from within which it too will know if it is proceeding on the correct course. This holds true for Reform, women's rights and other matters. If there is nothing in Judaism that is eternal, why should we accept the principle of Torah from Heaven? It would be preferable for us to live by contemporary trends.

19 *Medicine and* Halachah

'We must respond to the woman who desires to eliminate the foetus that it is part of her body, that even her body is not her property.'

You mentioned that you are involved in questions of medicine and *halachah*. Could you elaborate?

In New York I was a synagogue rabbi, but I wanted to engage in additional activities: to write and lecture, for which I had the time. I was very interested in topics pertaining to medical ethics, on which I had written my doctorate thesis for London University. There is an organization that is part of the Jewish Federation active in the city that supports eight Jewish hospitals – Mount Sinai, Beth Israel, Maimonides, Montefiore and others – most of which took care of mainly non-Jewish patients. The Federation had a subcommittee for religious affairs, in which I was active *inter alia* on the subject of autopsies. I was informed of resistance by Jews to autopsies and I was asked to examine the subject, since by New York state law a hospital is licensed as a teaching hospital only if it performs autopsies on at least 30 per cent of the patients who die in it. I convened a number of rabbis and physicians to enquire into the matter and we found that, among the Jews, the number of relatives who agreed to autopsies was considerably lower than among the non-Jews, and did not reach 30 per cent. Many of them argued that the deceased had undergone enough suffering during his lifetime and this should not be compounded after his death. Moreover, the percentage of non-religious Jews opposing autopsies was similar to that of the religious; and even the physicians who generally supported autopsies and pressed for authorization to conduct an autopsy did not do so when their own next-of-kin were involved. This refusal is apparently based on a Jewish sentiment. The non-Jews, in contrast, are more receptive to the idea of autopsies. The law determines that an autopsy cannot be performed without the consent of relatives (except in an instance of a suspected criminal act or sudden death, when the cause of death is unknown).

To pursue my assignment I came to Mount Sinai Hospital and I asked to see how an autopsy is conducted. They brought in a corpse and they showed me the clinical report, in which it was written that the patient had died from a certain heart disease. When they opened up the body they established that he had indeed died from a heart disease, but from a different one, and if the attending physicians had known this they would have prescribed a different treatment and the patient may possibly have survived. 'It is clear from this', they told me, 'how essential are autopsies, so we do not repeat such mistakes.' This was a clear case of *piku'ah nefesh* [activity conducted to save life]. Nonetheless, it was my impression that the autopsy was not conducted in the necessary atmosphere. In order to preserve a sense of respect for the dead, I proposed lighting two candles during the autopsy. I also suggested hanging in the operating theatre verses from Jewish sources, such as. 'And God created man in His image' [Genesis 1:27], so that an atmosphere solely of research and laboratory would not reign there. My proposals were in fact accepted in a number of hospitals.

When does the *halachah* permit the performing of an autopsy?

Only if there is a real possibility of thereby saving the life of another patient. For example, if a new medication is used or in the case of a new operation that is still in the experimental stage, this is a case of 'a sick person before us [i.e. a concrete case]', and an autopsy is permissible. This procedure may be conducted in order to determine if the deceased died from his illness or from the new medication. The death of a child, possibly from a hereditary disease, may fall into this category so as to save others in the same family.

Today, everyone is presumed to have the status of 'a sick person before us'.

That is correct, and if there is a possibility that research in one place will find a solution for a patient in another place then performing such an autopsy is permissible, with which I fundamentally concur. Notwithstanding this, it happens many times that an autopsy is conducted for research for its own sake or for the needs of students.

As a rabbi, did you encounter questions pertaining to autopsies?

Yes, on occasion. Those who are apprehensive regarding autopsies ask their *yeshivah* heads, and I view this as a major obstacle. The *yeshivah* heads are generally stringent, because their world consists of their studies and students, and therefore they tend to be very strict. They do not relate well to the observant population at large. Relying on those who are not practising rabbis but rather are great scholars does not appear to be suitable to me.

If we do not restore to ourselves the status of rabbis who are involved in life and are present among their congregation, and are therefore responsible for the problems life raises, but rather rely solely upon those individuals for whom the *halachah* is their entire life, the *halachah* will not be able to develop. I say this even though I am very careful not to deliver a ruling, especially on a matter of life and death, without consulting with leading halachic authorities. In New York I relied upon the rulings of Rabbi Eliyahu Henkin, who was an outstanding *posek* [decider of Jewish law] and was regarded as the 'final' *posek* before Rabbi Moshe Feinstein assumed this premier status. In some matters Rabbi Feinstein was extremely lenient and in others he was very strict, at times apparently on the advice of his son-in-law Dr Moshe Tendler, who advised him especially towards the end of his life.

Can you give me an example?

Rabbi Feinstein was extremely stringent on questions pertaining to the beginning of life and lenient on issues relating to the end of life. Thus he ruled to stop treatments for a patient who was about to die if he suffered greatly, even if his life could be extended for some time. Regarding abortions, on the other hand, he was very strict, and ruled that the extraction of the foetus from the mother's womb before birth, by means of an abortion, is forbidden, even in order to prevent the birth of an infant suffering from Tay-Sachs disease. He maintained that even though the embryo has not yet been born, it is already alive, and he was very stringent on this issue. I wrote to Rabbi Tendler, who accepted this line of reasoning, that this prohibition was very surprising to me, because prior to birth there is no presumption of life, but I did not receive any response. In Israel, in contrast, Rabbi Eliezer Waldenberg permitted an abortion in a case of suspected Tay-Sachs, until the seventh month, because having such an embryo can be psychologically dangerous to the mother.

Regarding heart transplants, Rabbi Feinstein initially was very stringent and maintained that this procedure constituted two murders – of the donor and of the recipient. Afterwards, however, when the success rate of these operations rose sharply, he was more lenient, to the extent that – according to his son-in-law – he was willing to recognize brain death as the decisive sign of final death.

At present there are legal authorities who are lenient regarding the beginning of life and stringent regarding its end. When we deliberated on this in Israel, I was somewhat involved in the subject and I wrote to rabbis and newspapers on the topic. In 1972 I was invited by the Israel Medical Association to lecture on Jewish medical ethics. I mentioned the issue of abortions, after I was officially informed that the number of abortions in Israel at the time was 40,000 a year! And certainly not all of them were performed for medical reasons. Consequently, since the establishment of the State, more than half a million abortions had been conducted! A public controversy arose and the law permitting abortions was amended. According to the new law, at least two physicians must approve the abortion; in practice, however, this regulation is not strictly observed and the situation in this realm is still horrible. It is strange that, on the one hand, thousands of foetuses that were fit to live completely healthy lives are lost every year while, on the other hand, there are many young couples who seek children, are willing to adopt them but cannot find any!

I believe that I was the first to write, already in 1966, in *Judaism* magazine that the ultra-Orthodox and the religious are increasing at a much greater rate than other sectors of the Jewish population, and over the course of time they will become the majority. At the time, I was told that I was daydreaming but today this is being realized and is expressed, for example, in the election results in Jerusalem, as will be the case in other localities as well. The Matriarch Rachel said to Jacob: 'Give me children, or I shall die' [Genesis 30:1], and as a people we cannot exist today as well without births! In America, the number of Jews is decreasing, as throughout the world. Nonetheless, when there are medical reasons for an abortion because of circumstances that endanger the mother and her health, and even when the embryo's health is involved, there is room to permit an abortion.

What do you say to a woman who says that her body is hers alone?

No person has possession of his or her body. Man did not create his body nor does he own it. Maimonides calls the body 'the property of the Holy One, blessed be He'. A person is born against his will, lives against his will and against his will he dies. We must reply to the woman who argues that she wants to destroy the foetus because it is part of her body that even her own body is not her property. By Torah law, a person may not cause harm to himself. Added to this are moral considerations. We are regarded to be partners in the act of creation, and consequently man must assume responsibility. The approach that one can do with one's body whatever one pleases, that one can commit an abortion with no feeling of responsibility is unacceptable to me. In special circumstances, such as rape with a consequent pregnancy against the wishes of the woman, we may possibly consider an abortion but not for no reason. This is contrary to the spirit of Judaism. Pleasure and gratifying man's desires, without the taking of responsibility, constitute wantonness and ignorance.

Did you discuss this with Conservative and Reform rabbis?

Yes. The Conservatives had an expert named Isaac Klein from Buffalo who wrote about this. The leading halachic expert of the Reform was Rabbi Solomon Freehof, a learned individual who took into account the halachic sources and rules based on a sense of responsibility. Nonetheless, the Reform are very lenient and permit the performance of an abortion in instances in which we cannot be so permissive. I also discussed this with Catholics and with representatives of other Christian denominations. I lectured on this topic, upon their invitation, and I also conducted correspondence with them concerning it.

When I wrote my doctoral thesis in the 1950s, I sought a source for the information that appears in all the books on medical history that there was a medical school in Paris in the late eighteenth century where they began to perform blood transfusions. Most of those receiving transfusions died, because they did not yet know about blood types. Years later a Papal encyclical was published forbidding blood transfusions yet only a century later this procedure was begun once again. I wanted to learn the Vatican's reasons: were these medical, or religious considerations, about the taking of blood from a non-Christian to save a Christian? I searched for the document itself but I could not find it. I wrote to the Catholic University in St Louis in the United States where an expert in this field, Professor Kelly, taught, but he could not help me either. He referred me to the Royal Library in Copenhagen but I did not receive a clear answer from there either, so then I wrote to the Vatican library. They replied that they had searched but had not found such an encyclical. I suspect, although I have no proof of this, that there was such an encyclical but that the Church authorities were not interested in its publication.

On another occasion I read in a serious medical journal that since there are flights in outer space and it is necessary to reduce the weight of the space vehicle, by means of genetic engineering it would be possible to create small human beings, who would lessen the payload of the vehicle, thus saving a great deal of money. This proposal is repugnant to us from the Jewish point of view, since it challenges the Creator of the Universe. The making of a new, unnatural creature for the purposes of research or science is highly opposed to the spirit of

Judaism. A distinction must be drawn between correcting Nature in the case of disease – in which instance the physician is permitted to heal – and 'improving' Nature. For the latter we have not been granted permission, and this entire question requires much profound study.

And what about the attempts to create artificial life in the laboratory?

Generally speaking, when such experiments are conducted in order to cure some illness (even sterility), as this aids in resolving the cause of the disease, it is unquestionably permitted.

I am referring to scientists who proclaim, as it were, 'I can take the place of God' [based on Genesis 30:2] and attempt to create life *ex nihilo*.

As long as I utilize medicine for the good of the patient, I do not come in place of the Creator, the opposite is true. As a physician, I have been granted permission to use medical knowledge to be 'a partner in the act of Creation'. If, however, experiments are conducted for the sake of science itself or in order to improve God's creation, and they upset natural law, then this is prohibited. For this reason *kilayim* – the conjunction of plants, animals or people – is prohibited, and who knows what dangers in Nature will be caused by such experiments. The universe was created in its proper species, and I have no right to change it. Here too there are guidelines that may be found in the halachic literature, even if they need to be expanded. Today there are institutions that engage in this, and I try to make a contribution in this realm.

Are there medical realms in which you exerted an influence on halachic rulings?

First, interest in this subject has increased. Second, regarding abortions, although there is no fixed position that is universally accepted by rabbis, there is growing approval of my method – based on the Jewish sources – that a distinction is to be drawn between what pertains to medicine – and especially to the saving of life – and economic concerns. I always maintained that, regarding abortions, it is impossible to take into account reasons that are not purely medical, concerning either the mother or the foetus. Moreover, in new subjects, such as experiments on foetuses, for which there are no halachic rulings, the opinions that I expressed are taken into account. This is also the case regarding cosmetic surgery. I was the first to write about this, and most contemporary responsa are based on my statements. I am not a *posek*, and this was not my intention. I view myself as one who collects the sources in order to clarify the spirit of Jewish law that emerges from them. I wanted to indicate the differences of opinion in the methods of the various authorities, from which a decision emerges.

The issues today are serious and complex; for example, when a person is in a terminal condition and suffers tremendous pain, and if he is not given medication he will die. I concur with those who state that we are not obligated to prolong his life with medical interventions, but even in such a case there are restrictions. It is forbidden, for example, to starve the patient or to withhold blood or oxygen from him. On the other hand, we are not required to give him medication and prolong his life artificially.

But in the end, the scientific view will prevail!

Limitations must be established! Take an example of attuning the commandments of the Torah to the conditions of modern life. It is said that in antiquity there was a need for the Sabbath in order to rest from the labours of the six weekdays. Today, however, when so much is done by machinery, some ask why we should scrupulously observe the Sabbath and the 39 types of work forbidden on the Sabbath. I respond that, at present, there is an even greater need for halachically-mandated Sabbath rest because there is a tangible threat that the machine will become our master and we its slaves. Six days of the week man is the master, the ruler of the earth and the fullness thereof, who creates light and harnesses the forces of Nature to serve him. On the Sabbath, however, he is transformed from creator to created, and thus remembers once each week that there is a Master of all. Today man is a slave to the telephone and the television, to the car and to his concerns, and he has no rest, neither for the body nor for the soul. What kind of life will we have if we will be completely enslaved to our creations? Such a condition is contrary to Nature, and therefore the Sabbath comes and liberates man from his servitude.

Just as I find my freedom in not transgressing the prohibition of the 39 types of work on the Sabbath, so too does man have the possibility of thinking to what extent it is permissible and desirable to go on adventures for new discoveries. A great danger hovers over us, for if we do not take care in this, we are liable to bring down disaster on humankind and on the universe. Let us take, for example, atomic research: Einstein himself said that if he had known that as a result of his contribution to science, as the father of the Atomic Age, tens of thousands of human beings would be killed, he would not have engaged in this research. The same holds true for medical research. If no limitations are placed on research, the entire world will return to a state of chaos. This is also the meaning of the Sabbath. The Creator made something new on each of the six days of activity, but He did not continue to develop all of Creation by Himself, but rather left this for man to complete, as partners in the act of Creation. Otherwise, humans could not live in the world. Consequently, He ceased from His labours on the Sabbath day. In languages other that Hebrew, God is the 'Almighty' – an omnipotent hero – but the meaning of the Hebrew equivalent *Sha-dai*, according to the Rabbis, is the opposite. It is 'the One who said "Enough [*dai*]" to His world'; that is to say, He knew when to stop the Creation. We live on the threshold of a new world, possessing forces of which we did not dream, such as space and the atom, and the danger exists that we will become God without knowing how and when to stop and say, 'Enough'. This is what we are to learn from the legislation of the Torah, in the light of our times.

But new things have always been discovered, with religious leaders saying: 'This far!' Nonetheless, science advances from one generation to the next.

Until our time, there was no danger of universal destruction or a threat to the existence of all human life. This is a new phenomenon. Besides this, when man feels that he is not merely the work of the hands of the Holy One, blessed be He, but that he rules the entire world, he is liable to return to the Tower of Babel period. At present the significance of the Sabbath is more logical, and it is more essential than ever in our annals. The Jew must appreciate the importance of the Sabbath and within this, also show this to the entire world. If we do not bear the banner of the Sabbath, the danger to the continued life of all humanity will increase.

It is a fact that among religious technological experts – such as the staff of the Tzomet Institute [an Israeli institute producing technological solutions to problems caused by Sabbath observance] – ways are being sought to circumvent the observance of the Sabbath; I would almost say, to 'deceive' the Holy One, blessed be He, by means of special apparatuses such as a special telephone and even an automobile in which driving on the Sabbath is permissible.

All of this is being done in accordance with the *halachah*, to save human life, because this overrides all. Besides this consideration, these actions are done with a change, and in this way the Sabbath is remembered. This is what lies at the foundation of the concept of performing [usually prohibited] actions with a change on the Sabbath.

The same applies to the *eruv*. The very fact that I know that there is an *eruv* reminds me that today is the Sabbath.

What is your position regarding homosexuality?

A report was recently publicized throughout the world that homosexuality may possibly have its source in genetic tendencies; if so, then this is not the fault of the involved parties. In a letter to the *London Times* I argued against this, saying that it is not reasonable. Even, however, if this is the scientific truth, this does not constitute licence for single-sex relations. There are natural phenomena that do not intrinsically grant approval for their performance. I was later asked what is my opinion regarding abortions in order to prevent the birth of those with homosexual tendencies, and I replied that this was absolutely forbidden. On the other hand, if it were possible to find a treatment that would prevent the homosexual tendency (like treatment to prevent infertility) upon the parents' request, then this would be permitted by Judaism. My statements were distorted and it was said in my name as if I want to destroy those who are liable to be homosexuals, and to this day I am the target of demonstrations. The sanctity of human rights is fashionable today, and homosexual life is regarded as an 'alternative lifestyle'. Homosexuals have many supporters, even among those who are heterosexual. There are even many rabbis who do not want to enter this no-win situation and to swim against the current. I was almost the only one – together with Rabbi Fabian Schonfeld – to issue a public statement on this subject, and we received many protests as a result.

In your opinion, is homosexuality an illness?

I do not accept the theory that there is a human gene that predisposes to homosexuality; but as I noted, even if this hypothesis were correct, this still does not make such relations permissible. In the same way I am certain that there are men who want to live with married women out of their desire, and I cannot sanction this. Man was created in order to overcome his desires, and this is his moral obligation. There are also additional considerations. For example those who see nothing wrong with such relations know that they will not be able to produce offspring. They thereby also sin against Nature, morality and of course the Torah. The acceptance of this approach would lead to the destruction of human society because, 'He did not create it a waste, but formed it for habitation' [Isaiah 45:18]. The obligation to be fruitful and multiply is the first commandment of the 613 precepts in the Torah. They claim that this group includes 10 per cent of the population, but it appears that there are not more than 1 per cent who are homosexuals by nature from birth. Currently, however, there is a very powerful lobby throughout the world that supports them. For example about a million people demonstrated in Washington on their behalf. When I expressed my opinion against them, I was subject to harsh abuse in return. I received an honorary degree in Wales, and there was a demonstration against me. Since, however, the Prince of Wales also participated in the ceremony, strict security measures were in effect. They argue that discrimination against them constitutes a crime against human rights, but in all of history such a claim was never made, that a small minority will dictate conditions to the majority and force it to determine that there is no moral difference between heterosexuality and homosexuality.

They will tell you that Jews also are a small minority!

I do not speak as a minority, but in the name of the majority of humankind, that believes in marriage and in bringing children into the world. I do not impose the morality of Judaism on the entire human race. This, however, is a phenomenon that exceeds the bounds of human morality.

It is a fact that many countries have annulled the law prohibiting such relations.

If there are individuals who live in this manner, I do not bother them. But they cannot demand that I agree with the principle that there is no difference between those who believe in the sanctification of life by marriage and those who do not accept this. They do this by arguing that by my statements I attack human rights, and they forbid me to say that those people who maintain the sanctity of life on the basis of marriage live on a higher moral level. This is a new argument in the history of human morality! This would defy our biblical heritage, and make a mockery of family values cherished for thousands of years.

20 *Biblical Interpretations*

'In current-day ultra-Orthodox Jewry there is an appreciable movement that opposes innovations.'

Do you still discover new interpretations in your studies?

In my study of the Bible, the Talmud and the *halachah*, and also in my sermons, I usually attempt to find things which are new in some respect, even though in current-day ultra-Orthodox Jewry there is an appreciable movement that opposes all innovations. The greatest literary undertaking in all history in the sphere of faithful Judaism is that of ArtScroll in America. The prayerbook that they published has been sold in tens of thousands of copies, as well as the Passover *Haggadah* and other books. They are currently translating the Bible and the Talmud into English (and their project is more popular than the Talmud translation of Rabbi Steinsaltz). However their entire approach does not call for new interpretation but rather the citing of existing sources (anthological commentary). The Chatam Sofer employed this rule so as not to create new practices, but did not apply it to the realm of interpretation. This has become a fundamental principle for them, to the extent that even the views of Rabbi Soloveitchik, of blessed memory, are not mentioned in their writings. I have often stated, if excavations will be conducted in America in another 1,000 years, in order to examine the world of the ultra-Orthodox at the time, it will suffice to find just two pages – one from ArtScroll and the other from the *Jewish Press*. They do not accept the assumption that now, after the Holocaust, something should be innovated in Torah teachings, an approach that is accepted by hundreds of thousands of Jews.

And you are not pleased by this?

Once I was asked by the Memorial Foundation for Jewish Culture to speak about the state of Jewish culture after the Holocaust. In my speech I noted that despite the fact that since the Holocaust to the present, more new [Jewish] books have been published than since the invention of the printing press until the Holocaust, this entire literature contains nothing original, not even in secular literature or in Jewish studies. We have no great original works today like those that were composed before the Holocaust by the early Jewish scholars, such as Steinschneider and Graetz. There is a pronounced tendency in contemporary Jewish culture that is opposed to originality and perhaps we should regard this too as one of the consequences of the Holocaust. This trend does not deter me from endeavouring to find original interpretations and innovations in which I reveal a perspective unknown to me until now. I will provide a few examples:

Immediately following the agreement in Washington between Israel and the PLO [13 September 1993], I discovered in our prayers a new significance that had been concealed from me until then. At the end of the *Amidah* we say: 'Establish peace, goodness and blessing for us ... Bless us, our Father, all of us **as one**, in the light of Your countenance.' What is the meaning of the wording 'as one'? The answer, in my opinion, lies in the fact that there is no point in making peace with enemies if this will cause internal dissension within the Jewish people. We therefore request 'Bless us **as one**', that we will remain one people, specifically in the prayer for peace. This is not a homiletic interpretation but rather the simple meaning of the text.

Take another example. In the Blessing for the New Month something seemingly strange is recited: 'All Israel are fellows.' We may ask what the connection is between these words and the Blessing for the New Month? This phrase, that is known to all, does not appear in any other place in our prayers. I think that this may possibly be a reference to Jerusalem, based on the words of the Psalmist that Jerusalem is 'a city **knit [*chubrah*] together**' [Psalms 122:3]. The Jerusalem Talmud comments on this: 'A city in which all Israel become **fellows [*chaverim*]** to one another.' Jerusalem was not divided into tribal holdings and every Jew has a portion in it. The composers of the prayer most likely sought to mention Jerusalem in the Blessing for the New Month. From the time of Hillel II we follow the fixed calculation of the calendar. Before this, the proclamation of the new month was dependent upon a sighting and we pray that the time will come when once again we will be privileged to determine the new month on the basis of sighting. In order to attain this, we must renew the Great Court. According to Maimonides, this may be done only if all the rabbis of Eretz Israel agree that one of them will be formally ordained [*semichah* – not the present-day 'ordination' of rabbis], then he will ordain his fellows. There accordingly is a need for 'all Israel to be fellows', in order to renew the Sanhedrin. Here too this seems to me to be the literal interpretation.

I will bring yet another example. The three passages of the Reading of the *Shema* are parallel to the three fundamental principles of faith: the existence of God ('Hear ...'), reward and punishment ('If, then, you obey the commandments ...'), and Torah from Heaven ('... and recall all the commandments ...' that they are from Heaven, and therefore the *tzitzit* is a 'cord of blue', similar to the sky). Our Sages wanted these three basic tenets of faith to be expressed in the most important prayer in the prayerbook. The same thought invests the prayers preceding and following the Reading of the *Shema*. The blessing of 'the great lights', speaks of the manifestation of the Lord **in Nature**; the blessing of 'great love', refers to the subject of the manifestation of the Lord **in the Giving of the Torah**; and the blessing of Redemption reveals God **in the history** of the people of Israel. I find in this the significance of the order of the prayers, in accordance with the Rabbinic teaching: 'A person should always first relate the praise of the Omniscient, and then pray.' All of these and other ideas I included in the glosses I wrote for the prayerbook that I edited: the *Centenary Edition of the Authorized Daily Prayer-Book* (1991).

I give you yet another example. From the purchase of the Cave of Machpelah in the portion of *Chayyei Sarah* we learn: 'Taking, taking from the field of Ephron.' That is, a comparison is drawn between the taking of a wife ('A man marries – *yikach*, literally, **takes** – a wife' – Deuteronomy 22:13) and the purchase of the field of Ephron ('**Take** [*kach*] it from me' – Genesis 23:13). This is a strange comparison between the taking of a woman in marriage and the burial of a wife (by Abraham). Couldn't the rabbis have found something more appropriate for comparison? In my opinion, a profound secret is concealed here. Abraham desired to purchase a portion in Eretz Israel (Ibn Ezra already says this) and, by this purchase, he acquired the right of possession by means of which Eretz Israel was sanctified for all time. The Jerusalem Talmud states that this is the source of the first sanctification effected by the Patriarchs. The same principle is at work in the marriage of a man and woman. The taking of the woman is not solely a question of acquisition but also of sanctification. The acquisition leads to sanctification. The relationship between a man and his wife is similar to that between Israel and Eretz Israel. The rabbis sought to teach us this by their comparison between the purchase of the Cave of Machpelah and the 'purchasing' of a wife, and they therefore chose this example, specifically, of 'taking, taking from the field of Ephron'.

I will cite an example from the Talmud. The second *mishnah* in *Berakhot* (9b) asks: 'From when is the *Shema* read in the morning?' It replies: 'When one is able to distinguish between *techelet* and white' or 'between *techelet* and green.' A *baraita* in the Talmud adds: 'Rabbi Meir says: [It is read] from the time one can distinguish between a wolf and a dog. Rabbi Akiva says: Between an ass and a wild ass. Others say: From the time that he can see his fellow from a distance of four cubits and recognize him.' We may ask, what is the difference between the different opinions. Are these different times, and did the Sages really expect that before prayer we would go forth to the field in order to find a wolf or dog? And what do they add to the mishnah? In my opinion, they evidently wanted to tell us something else. The reading of the *Shema* is the only commandment that we are to observe twice each day ('when you lie down and when you get up' – Deuteronomy 6:7). The rabbis wanted to teach us that the reason for our having to read the *Shema* at night, when we are preparing for sleep, is to emphasize that even when man does not rule Nature, the Creator is above us; and during the day, when man controls Nature ('Man then goes out to his work, to his labour until the evening' – Psalms 104:23), and even has the capability of domesticating wild animals (a wolf to a dog, and a wild ass to an ass), and there is a danger that he may regard himself as the ruler of all the universe, then he must read the *Shema* a second time, so that he will acknowledge the existence of the Creator. The 'others say' that the outstanding mark of man's control over Nature is the moment when he 'can see his fellow from a distance of four cubits and recognize him'. Before this, the man is within his four cubits, which is his private domain, and only when he sees his fellow then he knows that he is not alone in the world but rather is part of society. This is the sign that distinguishes between day and night and, in my view, this interpretation too is the simple meaning, and not a homiletic understanding.

Do you regard yourself as more of a Talmudist or as more of a man of the Bible and commentary?

To use a phrase by Rabbi Soloveitchik, who spoke of the man of *halachah*, I consider myself to be a man of *halachah*, that represents not only Jewish thought but also defines the thought of the faithful Jew. The Bible is also accepted by the non-Jews, who have researchers and scholars who are engaged in the Bible, but as this was already formulated in the Tractate of Gittin: 'The Holy One, blessed be He, made a covenant with Israel only for the sake of the oral teachings.' The covenant between us and Him, and what distinguishes Israel from the non-Jewish peoples – who also hold the Bible in esteem – is the Oral Law, which is what characterizes the essence of Judaism.

If you were to sit down to write today, would you write novellae connected with the Bible or halachic novellae?

More Oral Law, which is 'wider than the sea', and in which I find many more topics that represent Judaism than in the Bible. But one should not put the Bible aside, and certainly not the Torah [Pentateuch].

Therefore, should greater emphasis be placed in the schools on the study of the Talmud than on Bible study?

I did not say that. According to a *mishnah* in *Avot*, there are different levels of study, based on age. I am angry with those who pay no attention to the Bible. They study the Bible from the citations in the Talmud, which is contrary to the teachings of the *mishnah*. I am strongly in favour of Bible study, and even more of *Rashi* who is the key to the entire Torah, both the written Torah and the Oral Law. Consequently, the *Chumash* [Pentateuch] with *Rashi* was the first [Jewish] book to be published, and until the nineteenth century was the most widely disseminated book, even more than the prayerbook and the Bible. I often say to my children and grandchildren that without the *Chumash* with *Rashi* it would be impossible to understand either the written Torah or the Oral Law.

It has already been said: 'The one who reviews 100 times is not comparable to the one who reviews 101 times.' I firmly believe in this and think that everyone must search in the sources and add something of his own to the treasures of humankind. One must say, 'the world was created for me', and he must exert himself to contribute something to the world. Without this, there is a lack in Jewish culture and also in the development of the *halachah* and exegesis. We must seek to penetrate the written texts, and then we oftentimes find new meanings.

21 *Last Conversations*

'I anticipate it, I wait for it and yearn for it every day, that we should speed the time when we are worthy to become the instrument of ultimate fulfilment.'

What are your views on the crisis and the horrible atrocities in former Yugoslavia? From a religious and from a moral point of view was the United Nations' decision to interfere a decision which should have been taken or was it not? Some people have had second thoughts about it.

When the decision was announced and executed I had my doubts and felt it was ill thought out. They were sort of stampeded into this situation for various reasons – political reasons in America and probably reasons here in Britain for supporting it. One could not quite understand why, frightful situation though it was, it excited them more to the point of intervention on such a scale than did other crises in Africa when they did not produce that kind of reaction although they cost millions of lives. I go much further: that is what upset me most about the whole situation. The UN certainly felt called upon to intervene on a colossal scale. I have not felt convinced that the action can be fully successful or was correct international behaviour

In the debate on war crimes there were big differences of opinion between the House of Commons, which three times voted in favour of legislation which was ultimately adopted, and the House of Lords, which – I am afraid – was strongly against it because the Law Lords – the legalists – didn't want retrospective legislation. So the Lords voted overwhelmingly against such legislation. But nevertheless I spoke on three occasions strongly in favour of it because I think until the world will put its house in order and say, 'we will not tolerate these kinds of crimes to be perpetrated', we are failing ourselves and all humankind. We must bring war criminals to justice, wherever they are in the world. In the case of Milosevic, here is a man who we well know is guilty but it wasn't a pursuit, or certainly it didn't start as a pursuit, of him.

Presumably there were many who were guilty! Moreover, as I said before, I was in doubt – am still in doubt – to what extent this action will succeed. But what bothered me much more than anything else in that conflict, and in many others, is that once again it was basically a religious conflict: the Muslims, the Christians and the Orthodox Church. All major conflicts in the world today are still religious conflicts. What happened very recently between India and Pakistan was of a religious nature, obviously what happens in the Middle East is still a religious matter. In Africa also most of the conflicts are basically religious. It bothers me a great deal that religion, which was meant to bring understanding, peace and goodwill to the world, is still not capable of creating an atmosphere of 'live and let live' and friendliness between all peoples and faiths. Accepting that we are different and therefore creating a form of tolerance will make it possible for different people to live together, at least not to the point of going to war with each other. Still we haven't succeeded! Therefore I see this as a tremendous challenge to religion, including Judaism. That is something that bothers me more than anything else in all these conflicts, including Israel; that somehow the influence that religion ought to have on us – to refine us, to make us more decent and tolerant, to teach us to treasure life more – has not occurred, not yet. I am sure it will come but we have to work towards it. This is where the point of contact between the situation in the Balkans and the situation in Israel and elsewhere weighs on me very heavily. I am not sure whether we have sufficiently reacted yet to the – I might almost call it – 'Jewish dimension' of this conflict as far as the factors should affect us.

One can argue and say that finally the UN troops reached a certain goal in the war and the atrocities came to an end, at least to a certain extent.

The situation is still fluid and there are still, every day, casualties, and there would have been many more. But I hope it will lead to a conclusion of that conflict – but it is a difficult birth.

Do you really think there is only political interest behind that decision or are there some moral arguments as well? If Clinton takes a decision like that, is there also a moral or maybe a religious consideration playing a certain role?

For Clinton himself perhaps it was in part a demonstration of personal power. But there may be all sorts of calculations here. Clinton had other preoccupations in America at the time and therefore he might have welcomed an opportunity to deflect public attention from himself. But the support he received was certainly morally motivated. I think the overwhelming support for Clinton was surprising. After all, everybody remembers the carnage of Vietnam. It so happens that there were hardly any American casualties but nevertheless the risks were enormous. It was the same here in Britain, I think; there was primarily a great strength of moral feeling on the matter. So the public opinion was that we can no longer tolerate this sort of situation.

You mentioned Clinton. Would you try to comment on his personal life and the Lewinsky affair – he was re-elected despite this – what would you say about it?

What upset me here more than the action itself – I mean nobody rated Clinton to be a saint or a moral crusader – was that ultimately what he did was accepted in America and, by and large, public opinion was not outraged. What outraged the American public was that he may have said an untruth, he may not have told the truth. Now who would tell the truth if he is caught red-handed misbehaving with a girl behind closed doors and so on – what do they expect of him? Therefore I thought that the reaction of the public was entirely misplaced. The strength of marriage was undermined here. Clinton did much damage to his wife and to **all** marriages. It is so wrong that the President of the United States behaving in this way didn't disturb public opinion. That impressed on me more, I think, than the immorality of it and the example that it set regarding the sanctity of marriage or the way in which marriages can be set aside for a fling, for a momentary pleasure.

So is it a certain indication about morality in America at large?

I think yes, and yet I find America is a morally very sensitive country. I find that to some extent morals matter more in America than they matter here, for a whole variety of reasons. Religion matters more, church-going is twice as high in America than it is in Britain, so there are aspects where spiritual considerations, religious considerations matter a great deal. However on this occasion I feel that it showed that the erosion of the moral conscience has already gone very far. We have to work very hard against this, strengthening the religious fibre, the spiritual fibre of the land to regain the reverence for life and above all the reverence for marriage, for the decencies of life. We must not allow these bad behaviours to become so common. Today the divorce rates have gone up by over 50 per cent, which leads to colossal price tags we have to pay for the erosion of the traditional family. The effect this has on children, the social damage, is enormous. Perhaps why our prisons are overflowing with criminals is in part because our children see no decent home life. What are we paying for this loosening of the marriage bonds? This escapade by the President has contributed further to undermining respect and reverence for marriage.

One can argue that it used to be like that in the past as well, just that it was done secretly.

Yes, but there is a big, big difference! I say that when the Prophet Jeremiah gave the ultimate censure, the ultimate criticism was when he said 'I am mortified and ashamed'. When you no longer have the feeling of shame then everything is gone, and therefore the last protection was that you feel a sense of shame. I once said what shame is to moral health is the same as pain is to physical health. If we couldn't feel pain we wouldn't go to a doctor and therefore pain, although it is painful, is a warning signal that we need to repair whatever is wrong. Similarly shame is a warning signal that you can't go beyond this. Today shame is largely under attack – we don't want to feel shame. We have psychiatrists who will tell us that shame is a bad thing to feel and that we must work against the guilt feelings. Jews are all in favour of guilt feelings; we have a whole day of Yom Kippur in order to produce guilt. Today if we have reached a stage where we don't feel that guilt, that is bad.

Now let us say something about the new regime in England – What about Tony Blair?

I have met him. I haven't got the same relationship with him as I had with Margaret Thatcher – I haven't had the opportunity. I have met him casually so far and he is certainly a very engaging personality. He has the right instincts – a great daring as he works for 'New Labour'. He was able to turn around nearly the whole Labour movement, which has deep roots and classic history in this country, and modernize it and create a new type of support from altogether new circles that have never thought of voting Labour before. That he has been able now to make major changes in the country is a tribute to his daring, his enormous skill in, above all, public relations. He is also very friendly towards our community and towards Israel. Some of his closest personal friends are Jews whom he has placed in high positions including in very delicate areas of Middle Eastern politics. He has given certain commissions, certain assignments to notable Jews. I find he is a man who is making his mark, quite remarkably so. He makes his miscalculations too I think; for instance on Europe, on the entry of Britain into Europe. I myself have my hesitations although, as I have once expressed it, there is no one here more European than I am. I was born in Germany, I married in France, I have five Irish-born children, I have lived in four different European countries and I speak several European languages. I am more European I think than most Englishmen. Moreover being Jewish in itself I think is an exposure to an outlook that is cosmopolitan. My faith, my religion, is cosmopolitan and therefore I ought to be inclined towards welcoming fusion of Europe. Nevertheless I have my doubts; I believe that nations are meant to be different up to a certain level and I think it is far too late here to introduce a United States of Europe in the way they have in America. That country, apart from the native Americans, is populated by immigrants, and they all came in as equals. Here it is too late. I don't think between the French, the Germans, the Greeks and so on you can create an underlying cohesion. This summer my wife and I went to Italy and saw the remnants of the Roman Empire, which was the last attempt to fuse Europe into a political unity and we know what the result was. A second attempt now made to reintroduce once more a political cohesion of this sort will, I think, expose us to causes for conflict that we want to be careful to avoid. Therefore I think a great deal of caution will be needed here not to plunge us into conflict situations that may be difficult to sort out.

Tony Blair could argue that you can't compare the situations of the Roman Empire and the present.

Yes.

But even you say the whole world today is a small village!

Yes, but nevertheless different countries still cherish national freedom, independence and sovereignty. In Europe we still have something like ten nations that have a monarchy and these monarchies are a source of great stability. Where we have great resources of national strength as well as international cohesion and stability, why change? The consequences could be the seeds of great conflict, as has happened in the past. We must not try to create unity for the sake of unity; it is only natural that people cherish their independence.

So the Tower of Babel should be a warning?

Yes. I think lessons are to be drawn here from history.

Let us turn to the Swiss bank accounts and the behaviour of the Swiss with regard to Jewish money and gold.

What I can say here is similar to what I said about war criminals. I said that however much time has elapsed since their crime, they still should be pursued and, as best we can, justice should be done. I feel the same here about the stolen monies. One should not allow monies illicitly obtained by the Swiss to stay with them. Very often this money was gained under the most gruesome circumstances, from people who invested their last savings in Swiss banks because they thought that one day they could recover them or, if not they, their heirs, their children, their descendants. To suppress the knowledge of who invested these monies, as the Swiss banks tried to do for 50 years, is wholly wrong. This secrecy has been broken largely as a result of Jewish pressure and activity which was quite remarkable. I can quite see that in Switzerland itself this has created a great deal of embarrassment to the Jews there, as I know from my sister who lives in Switzerland and has other relatives there. There is a cost, a price to be paid for even this exacting of justice; nevertheless when such justice is done, I rejoice. It is right they should now benefit from the wisdom of their parents, grandparents and great grandparents who made these deposits in the banks in Switzerland believing them to be safe. That is a reason for rejoicing.

Now that Sir Isaiah Berlin has left us would you like to say something more about his personality, his intellectual capacity?

He was widely rated as the most intelligent person in Britain, the greatest brain in Britain. I was proud to be good friends with him; we had him in our home several times, together with his wife. He wrote this extremely friendly foreword to my book [in Hebrew] under circumstances in which the majority in the community were not so supportive. He went out of his way to be supportive and to be seen to be supportive. This always gave me a great deal of gratification. While, strangely, he was not a great writer and did not leave momentous writings in the same way as other towering figures did, nevertheless as a thinker he was pre-eminent and brought the Jewish people a great deal of pride, an enormous pride which I shared. He had a peculiar and perhaps contradictory attitude to Judaism itself, even though he was nurtured in a very traditional home. He was very much aware of his roots and took great pride in his origins. He saw value in Jewish teachings and spirituality and in Jewish religious insights which fascinated him. So he was by no means a stranger to the inner dynamic of Jewish thought. He was a great historian, seeing things in depth through historical eyes. I admired his intellect, his contributions to knowledge and to the progress of the mind. We need personalities of this calibre to give another dimension to our existence.

Now let's come to Israel. Were you satisfied with the outcome of the elections of 17 May 1999?

Well, I was certainly hoping for this kind of outcome; I am glad to see that Ehud Barak was elected. I know very little about his personal background other than what is featured in the newspapers. The name itself had not been synonymous in my mind with the particular orientation and direction other than that he represented the Labour movement, that he regarded himself as a disciple of Rabin and wants to perpetuate his tradition – that was to me already a welcome sign because I think the death of Rabin created a vacuum in our world.

Incidentally, one of the things that pained me most after the Rabin assassination was that, in a way, the killers prevailed and were able to impose their political doctrine for a number of years. Not only for the first time in Jewish history for 2,000 years, or more than 2,000 years, do we have a Jew slain by fellow Jews for political reasons, but the killers get away with it, they even succeed. When Barak now succeeds at putting it right again, as it were, giving Rabin a posthumous victory over death, over assassination, that in itself gave me some comfort.

Apart from that I believe the only solution lies in the attitudes now being adopted. Peace can only be made at some cost; without retreating you cannot have peace. I cannot say how safe it is to give up the Golan, to give up, say, West Bank parts. I am not a politician but I **am** a religious leader, and from a religious point of view I am bound to say that we ought to spread the doctrine that for the sake of peace *Gadol Ha'shalom* ['Great is Peace'].

Peace is so great that eventually everything can be achieved only through peace. The religious political element is taking now a knock and may no longer be the arbiter of the policies that will be adopted. That to me is very satisfying. I want to see the religious element losing their political power which is not proportionate to their actual power in the country. I think it will do them good and will do the country good also. Certainly for the time being the new government's line is what I was hoping to see, until the religious element becomes a majority which will happen within 20 years or so.

Why, because of demographic reasons?

For demographic reasons solely; it is a matter of immigration versus emigration and the birth rate. It is bound to happen! When the religious element is in the majority, then the problems will start. This worries me. How will they run a state? How will they run an army? I think the religious element will adjust, just as they did in the past, but we have a long way to go. So I am glad that things are taking a turn towards a more rational form of Jewish statehood with the application of Jewish principles. Now we are not out to alienate both Jewish opinion and the rest of the world whereas the previous administration was very indifferent to public opinion both inside Israel and outside Israel. We need friends desperately, we are a tiny little people, a large number of us dispersed still among non-Jews. We need friends and we need understanding. Friends are more important than people who simply give in to Jewish pressures. We need genuine friends and, above all, we need people whom eventually we can influence so we can make a mark on progress in the world.

For what do we need our independent State today – and I am speaking from a religious point of view? As you said, on the one hand the prospects are that religious people will become the majority; on the other hand you are one of the very few to argue that, basically, the religious Jews or religious authorities don't cope with the modern State. That is the truth today, isn't it?

I will say only that we need our independent State for the great majority.

There is no serious attempt to cope with these problems?

No, not any more than with the Holocaust.

The Holocaust is the past. Maybe it is impossible, but when speaking of practical issues in the present you simply withdraw and go back to your ghetto, you don't touch the real basic issues. Maybe it's not necessary; you see people here in London living a good religious life and they are not confronted with these issues. Maybe we should wait until *yemot ja'm'shiach* ('Coming of the Messiah').

Yes, well, I do not share that view.

Would you explain?

I welcome the opportunity for a return to a restoration of Jewish statehood, I acclaim the State as a divine manifestation, as one of the biggest events in post-destruction Jewish history. I count myself in among the supporters of the Jewish State but I seek to use the State as an instrument to advance Jewish commitments, Jewish insights, Jewish hopes and aspirations for the future. I hope that the State will eventually, especially once the religious element becomes a majority, become a tool for the realization of Jewish aspirations, not on a personal basis, not on an individual basis, but collectively. Individually we are now able to live among the non-Jews and be Sabbath observant, keep *Kashrut*, have Jewish schools and Jewish education, but collectively we cannot live a Jewish life. We cannot show what a society, *chevra*, would look like that is dominated by specifically Jewish commitments. Now with the State we will have that chance and that time will come. Our minds will be free from today's preoccupations, of the cajoling for political influence or even of rabbinic arguments for position.

The time will come when we will be able to turn to the prophetic dimension of Judaism. This is just as essential and just as integral a part of Jewish thought and the Jewish hope for the future as anything else which we associate with the hope of the ultimate realization of our Jewish aspirations. After all Messiah in the *Tenach* and for the Sages is associated not just with kosher butcher shops and with observing the Sabbath, but above all with inter-human relations, international relations and with the influence that we can bring to bear first on ourselves and then on wider society. Therefore a Jewish State gives us the first opportunity that we have to live collectively as a national society, to order our lives accordingly and to show what life would look like if we allowed Jewish insights, commitments and persuasion to govern our national visions and aspirations.

Therefore, yes, I do see a purpose in the return; nevertheless *Bechol Yom Ani Mechakeh*, I anticipate it, I wait for it and yearn for it *every day*, that we should speed the time when we are worthy to become the instrument of ultimate fulfilment. This world cannot exist merely to perpetuate itself, that life will remain with all its problems and its agonies for ever. That *Tziyon* (Zion) will become *Tziyun* – a signpost – showing the correct direction. We can live as Jews here, but not as full Jews in the sense of realizing our ultimate destiny, our ultimate purpose. After all, the prophetic dimension is a very major part of the teachings of Judaism. Take the *Tenach*. A very major part of it is how we envisioned the long-term future for the Jewish people, the influence that we would have on the world at large. That opportunity I think can only be created by the foundation of the Jewish State in the land of Israel. The fact that the State is in Zion, centred in Jerusalem, is itself of significance, because we believe in a link here between the earliest origins of our people. Abraham was told *lech lecha*, you go to Zion and there, in that land of Israel, you will find the opportunity for the promise made by the Almighty to Abraham: 'through you [Abraham] will be blessed all the families of the earth'. This will serve as inspiration to the rest of humankind.

The return to Zion and the establishment of a Jewish independent State has, I think, positive value. I certainly don't believe that the State ought to consist of a considerable proportion of non-Jews living under Jewish domination; that was never envisaged by our prophets or by our history. In a way I am glad about the way things are gradually taking shape and developing. We ought to become more realistic, I think, in our aspirations and not think that every little conquest that allows for Jewish domination fulfils the Jewish purpose. I think some of it is doing the opposite. I want to show as much support as I can for the wide ideals of the Jewish purpose. We have survived all these thousands of years, the bitter past and the greatest destruction of all, the Holocaust, are behind us.

> **Yes, but would you admit that the attempt which was there in the first years of the creation of the State to try to incorporate halachic principles into the modern State has gone and that religious leaders or figures have given up?**

I see this and I regret it but I don't give up hope. All you need is a few outstanding people, and that time will come. Now even in more recent days you had Rabbi Herzog, I suppose, who was a different kind of Chief Rabbi. Rav Kook certainly was and I don't see why this can't be repeated. It's true today we don't train them especially, they are all *yeshiva* trained, they all get identical training, they all learn the same; we mass produce them and that's no good.

> **Not only that, but I have sometimes the feeling that their attitude towards the State is a negative one, even an indifferent one.**

Yes, that element is there, but still left is the *Mizrachi* element. I think that is still a very considerable element; although it is diminishing at the moment, but it will gather strength and momentum again, especially as sooner or later that world will come to terms with the modern world – they will have to. It is impossible today to live in permanent isolation. In Germany they had to find a way within Orthodoxy. It needed a Hirsch – a pioneer who dared – and finally he was supported, to some extent at least.

> **But that is exactly the point, you see it in England as well. These attempts are being rejected; there is a trend towards isolation.**

Don't forget that the Holocaust is still draining us of the concentrated resources that we had. Ninety per cent of the really concentrated forms of Judaism were destroyed and their aim is to make good these losses. To them the important thing is rebuilding a world that was left in ruins, and they have done remarkably well. To rebuild that world that was utterly shattered, utterly in ruins, could only be done by single-minded concentration on their part and that they have achieved with a vengeance, so at the moment they still live on the momentum of that success. They still dream of a world in which their power will spread to some extent beyond their own circles, beyond their own children. That is not a permanent feature; as I say in 20 years' time they will come to terms with the world in which we live, they will **have** to. They will have to produce their doctors, their engineers and their lawyers, they will have to produce their politicians and indeed their university professors and so on. Necessity is the mother of invention and the necessity will be there, they will be needed because they will become the majority and therefore they will have to fill these vacant positions. So I do not despair of the ultimate achievement of this goal that we will produce enough *B'nei Torah* who will at the same time acknowledge realistically the world in which they live and the idea of coming to terms with it – Jewishly and secularly, and integrate. Yes, under new conditions I don't think there will be another movement as Hirsch understood. By the way he would have been a big opponent of today's Zionism – he was a great anti-Zionist.

By the way, I have seen there is a pamphlet from Israel, an essay on the early origins of Zionism – on Herzl actually. Herzl had a remarkable vision: almost to the day he was correct when he said that in 50 years' time there will be a State. In some senses he had an uncanny knack of prophecy, he saw something that nobody else saw. On the other hand he was miles out; for example he thought that German would become **the** lingua franca! So, religious visionaries: some elements they do see and some elements they don't see! Reality will open their eyes so they respond as is needed. That time will come as it has come throughout the past; it has always been there.

So you are optimistic?

I am very optimistic that eventually the purpose will be fulfilled. The agonies may be great until then, but so long as we keep the visions right, we will reach our goal – that's why I don't think we will be judged so much by what we *have* achieved as by what we *want* to achieve, by setting our sights and saying, 'yes, that is where we have got to go' – and then the rest we have got to leave to God, to the Creator, to the Almighty. There is still something left for Him to attend to in the world.

Index of Names